Sport Management

Active Learning in Sport – titles in the series

Coaching Science	ISBN 978 1 84445 165 4
Personal Training	ISBN 978 1 84445 163 0
Sport Sociology	ISBN 978 1 84445 166 1
Sport and Exercise Science	ISBN 978 1 84445 1876
Sport Management	ISBN 978 1 84445 2637
Sport Studies	ISBN 978 1 84445 1869

To order, please contact our distributor: BEBC Distribution, Albion Close, Parkstone, Poole, BH12 3LL. Telephone: 0845 230 9000, email: **learningmatters@bebc.co.uk**. You can also find more information on each of these titles and our other learning resources at **www.learningmatters.co.uk**

Sport Management

Edited by
Karen Bill

LearningMatters

First published in 2009 by Learning Matters Ltd

British Library Cataloguing in Publication Data
A CIP record for this book is available from the British Library

ISBN: 978 1 84445 2637

Cover and text design by Toucan Design
Project Management by Swales & Willis Ltd, Exeter, Devon
Typeset by Kelly Gray
Printed and bound in Great Britain by TJ International Ltd, Padstow, Cornwall

Learning Matters Ltd
33 Southernhay East
Exeter EX1 1NX
Tel: 01392 215560
E-mail: info@learningmatters.co.uk
www.learningmatters.co.uk

Contents

Contributors

Karen Bill

Karen is an Associate Dean in the School of Sport, Performing Arts and Leisure at the University of Wolverhampton. She has responsibility for overseeing engagement with research and applied research. Karen has developed sport-specific enterprise education materials as part of her involvement on various national and regional educational projects as well as publishing in this area. She has recently completed an International Entrepreneurship Educators Programme and subsequently been admitted as an Entrepreneurship Education Fellow by the National Council for Graduate Entrepreneurship.

Richard Colman

Richard is Coaching Development Officer at Wesport (West of England Sport Trust). He has been involved in sports development for eight years, and has widespread knowledge of the area owing to his previous various roles as National Governing Body Officer and Local Authority Sports Development Officer, and working for two County Sports Partnerships. His Level 3 squash coaching qualification and voluntary roles on Club and County committees enable him to keep in touch with the sharp end of the delivery of sport.

Crispin Dale

Crispin is a Principal Lecturer in the School of Sport, Performing Arts and Leisure at the University of Wolverhampton. He has taught strategic management for tourism at undergraduate and postgraduate level for a number of years. Crispin has published widely in peer-reviewed journals on strategic management. His research has focused upon competitive structures and networks and strategic management for small businesses. Crispin has also written a resource guide on strategic management for the Hospitality, Leisure, Sport and Tourism subject network of the Higher Education Academy.

Will Foster

Will is an Associate Dean with the School of Sport, Performing Arts and Leisure at the University of Wolverhampton. He spent his initial career in the commercial sector working in a variety of businesses in senior leadership/management and director roles.

He spent nine years of his career in the recruitment and selection sector and has research interests in leadership, organisation development, coaching and mentoring.

Simon Gardiner

Simon is a Reader in Sports Law at Leeds Metropolitan University and Senior Research Fellow at the Asser International Sports Law Centre. He has published widely in a number of areas of sports law. He is lead author of Gardiner et al, *Sports law* 3rd edition (Oxford: Routledge Cavendish, 2006), author of 'UK Sports Law' in R. Blanpain and F. Hendrickx (eds) *International encyclopaedia of sports law* (The Hague: Kluwer, 2008), and co-editor of *Professional sport in the European Union: regulation and re-regulation*, 2nd edition (Cambridge University Press, 2009) (with R. Parrish and R. Siekmann). He is editor of *Sport and the Law Journal* and is on the editorial board of the *International Sports Law Journal*.

Sue Minten

Sue is a Senior Lecturer in Sports Management at the University of Central Lancashire and course leader for the MA Sport Management. She started her career in the public sector, spending five years in sports facilities management before moving into academia 15 years ago.

Fiona Phoenix

Fiona is a Senior Lecturer in Sport Business Management at Sheffield Hallam University (SHU). Fiona teaches in the areas of marketing, sponsorship and event management, both at SHU and international partner universities abroad. She also undertakes consultancy work with SHU in the field of marketing. Before working at SHU, Fiona worked in both the private and public sector, delivering sponsorship programmes and managing events.

Mark Piekarz

Mark is an experienced Senior Lecturer in the fields of sport and adventure management at the University of Worcester. Previously he worked for many years as a sports facility manager and community sports development officer. He has taught and researched risk management for many years.

Andrew Pitchford

Andrew is Deputy Head of Department of Sport and Exercise at the University of Gloucestershire. He has taught and researched in the field of Sports Development for over 15 years and is a former Sports Development Officer.

Peter Robinson

Peter is a Senior Lecturer and Course Leader for Work-based Learning in the School of Sport, Performing Arts and Leisure at the University of Wolverhampton. Peter has previous senior management experience in the public, private and voluntary sectors, including that of Visitor Services Manager. He specialises in employability, sustainability and management.

Debra Wale

Debra is a Senior Lecturer in the School of Sport, Performing Arts and Leisure at the University of Wolverhampton. She teaches on the Sports Management programme in Singapore, and Marketing on undergraduate and postgraduate programmes. Her industry experience includes Brand Management, Event Management and Sports Management, which have given her experience across the private, public and not-for-profit sectors.

Rob Wilson

Rob is a Principal Lecturer and Teaching Fellow in Sport Business Management in the Faculty of Health and Wellbeing at Sheffield Hallam University. His subject specialisms are financial reporting and management accounting, and his main research interest is the economics and finance of sport events. He is the author of *Finance for sport and leisure managers; an introduction* and is a recognised expert in learning, teaching and assessment in higher education.

Caroline Wiscombe

Caroline is a Principal Lecturer and Head of Department in Leisure Industries at the University of Wolverhampton, having spent many years working in industry. The department's most recent development has been a BA (Hons) Sport Management, delivered transnationally. Caroline is an expert in applied financial management for SMEs and charitable trusts and specialises in performance measurement and financial strategy.

Acronyms

ACORN	a classification of residential neighbourhoods
AGCAS	Association of Graduate Careers Advisory Services
AGM	Ansoff's Growth Matrix
AIDA	attention, interest, desire and action
AIG	American International Group
ALETC	All England Tennis Club
BGM	Boston Growth Matrix
BOA	British Olympic Association
BOGOF	buy one get one free
BREEAM	Building Research Establishment Environmental Assessment Methodology
CASC	community amateur sport clubs
CBI	Confederation of British Industry
CCDP	community club development programme
CEEQUAL	Civil Engineering Environmental Quality Assessment and Award Scheme
CIHE	Council for Industry and Higher Education
CIPD	Chartered Institute of Personnel and Development
CCT	compulsory competitive tendering
CREST	Coastal and Rural Extreme Taskforce
CSN	community sport networks
CSP	county sport partnership
CSR	corporate social responsibility
DCMS	Department for Culture, Media and Sport
DIUS	Department for Innovation, Universities and Skills
ECJ	European Court of Justice
EEC	European Economic Community
EIS	English Institute of Sport
EPL	English Premier League
EU	European Union
EU EMAS	EU Eco-Management and Audit Scheme
FA	Football Association
FAPL	Football Association Premier League

FIA	Fédération Internationale de l'Automobile
GAAP	Generally Accepted Accounting Principles
GP	General Practitioner
GLL	Greenwich Leisure
HE	Higher Education
HESA	Higher Education Statistics Agency
HMRC	HM Revenue and Customs
HR	human resources
HRA	Human Rights Act
HRM	human resource management
IAAF	International Association of Athletics Federations
IBRM	Institute of Baths and Recreation Management
IP	intellectual property
IPR	intellectual property rights
ISO4001	International Standards Organisation.
ISRM	Institute of Sport and Recreation Management
ISPAL	Institute for Sport, Parks and Leisure
IT	information technology
ITC	Independent Television Commission
KPI	key performance indicator
LA21	Local Agenda 21
LTA	Lawn Tennis Association
Ltd	Limited Liability Company
MEP	Member of European Parliament
MESG	major events support group
MoR	management of risks
MOSAIC	a global network of segmentation tools
NESTA	National Endowment for Science, Technology and the Arts
NDFG	New Designs for Growth
NDPB	non-departmental public body
NGB	National Governing Body
NRS	National Readership Survey
ODA	Olympic Delivery Authority
ODPM	Office of the Deputy Prime Minister
OFLOT	National Lottery Commission and the Office of the National Lottery
PDM	partnership development manager
PDP	personal development planning
PE	physical education
PESTEL	Political, Economic, Social, Technological, Environmental and Legislative factors
PLC	product life cycle
plc	public limited company
RBV	resource based view
RMS	risk management systems
ROE	return on equity
RTCP	Restrictive Trade Practices Court
RTPA	Restrictive Trade Practices Act 1976

SDO	sport development officer
SEU	Sheffield Sports Events Unit
SHU	Sheffield Hallam University
SSA	sector skills agreement
SSCo	school sport co-ordinator
SSP	school sport partnerships
SSSI	Site of Specific Scientific Interest
SWOT	strategic tool (identifies Strengths, Weaknesses, Opportunities and Threats)
T,P&L	Trading, profit and loss accounts
TH	TAG Heuer
UEFA	Union of European Football Associations
USP	unique selling point

Acknowledgements

First, I offer thanks to Anthony Haynes, for suggesting that I write this book and providing the opportunity in the first place. It certainly wasn't on my to do list but I have grown to really appreciate the prospect!

I would like to extend my heartfelt thanks to all the contributors. The writing of this book was truly a collective effort, involving many individuals from a range of different institutions. The professionalism and expediency with which this book was put together was both remarkable and enjoyable, so thank you.

Last, but certainly not least, to all the boys in my life! My husband, Tony and four sons, Simon, Dominic, Aidan and Anton and my Dad. Throughout all my endeavours, your love, support, guidance, and endless patience have always been there. Thank you Simon for drawing the football boot on my mind map. Truly a family affair!

Karen Bill
April 2009

Chapter 1

Introduction

Karen Bill

Context

> As the world changes, so does the workplace. Managers of the 21st Century operate in environments quite unlike those they first entered, and must regularly update their skills to meet the challenges of a dynamic global market and a more diverse workforce. (Innovation and Business Skills Australia [ISBA], 2006)

This claim by the IBSA, whilst applied to management in general, is particularly relevant for sport management in the UK. The sport and recreation industry is very dynamic and in constant change, and consequently a number of different forces drive performance and business competitiveness, which SkillsActive summarised as:

- customer trends and increasing health awareness;
- increase in older customers with more leisure time, requiring low-impact activities;
- globalisation and technology, limited to management of bookings;
- government policy increasing participation in sport innovation in provision. (SkillsActive, 2005, p6)

The Department for Innovation, Universities and Skills (DIUS) acknowledges this theme of a dynamic world placing new demands on future managers:

> Britain can only succeed in a rapidly changing world if we develop the skills of our people to the fullest possible extent, carry out world class research and scholarship, and apply both knowledge and skills to create an innovative and competitive economy. (DIUS, 2008)

Sport managers of the future will therefore have to have 20/20 vision to ensure the appropriate sport enterprises they work for have a viable future, whether this is producing goods and services which sell and make a profit, or offering non-profit services which deliver personal and social benefits. It is in this context that this book is grounded, whereby it will explain to students on sport management or sport studies programmes both the traditional areas of studies and the new areas which must be understood. This book has the following five key aims.

1. To develop a business approach to sport that demonstrates that sport is much more than a game.
2. Through a detailed analysis of sporting examples to develop awareness and critical understanding of the complex and dynamic relationship between sport, business and management.
3. To engage readers with a critical introduction to a series of business and management themes that are fundamental to an understanding of the sport sector.
4. To develop a critical understanding of the various business elements and concepts, both traditional and contemporary, that can be applied to sport and through the use of current learning materials embed the theory in practice.
5. To develop awareness of how the different branches of management relate to each other and are constantly affected by forces emerging from the external environment.

Structure

To help organise your introduction to sport business management the book is organised into three sections.

The first section focuses on the context of sport business and provides an overview of the traditional core business elements. It also focuses on introducing the new core functional areas of management, for instance, entrepreneurship and risk management, as well as depicting the sport labour market and sector-specific skills. The first section includes Chapters 1–3.

Chapter 2 gives an overview of the sport industry, highlighting the breadth of management opportunities that are available. Particular attention is given to illustrating how sporting activities act as a hub for numerous other business activities, which on first inspection may seem unrelated to sport. These management opportunities are then explored in relation to the provision sector in which they may operate, illustrating the key tension between profit-making sport activities, and non-profit sport activities which are designed to achieve particular social objectives. The chapter then develops a sport management system to highlight how the different business branches, such as marketing and financial management, are modified by the nature of the organisation, which shapes the type of activities or outcomes generated, all of which must be done within the existing legal framework, and which is constantly affected by internal and external forces which generate change

Chapter 3 explores the sport labour market with particular regard to the place of graduates within the sport industry. It examines the skill needs of the industry and the range of initiatives that have been introduced to upgrade employees' skills. It also analyses the nature of careers within sport, again with particular reference to graduates.

The second section has two distinct themes. The first of these is the more traditional business branches (Chapters 4–8), while the second comprises the more innovative, emergent, non-traditional areas of business management which the contemporary sport manager will need (Chapters 9–13).

Chapter 4 examines the effects of the application of marketing principles and methods to the contemporary sports environment from a strategic perspective. It evaluates marketing strategies as well as exploring the sports marketing process.

Chapter 5 introduces the sports manager to sports organisation structures. It considers accountability of those organisations to different stakeholders. This can be both financial and non-financial depending on the focus of those stakeholders. However, financial accountability for most sports organisations is mandatory and therefore cannot be ignored.

In Chapter 6 the process of strategic management is explained as it applies to organisations operating in the sport management industry. This includes an analysis of the external sport management environment, the strategic choices that sports organisations can adopt and how these strategies can then be implemented effectively.

The systems and processes of human resource management are explained in Chapter 7 in relation to the sport industry. This includes human resource planning, recruitment and selection, performance management, the psychological contract and training development. Specific issues relating to sport are also covered such as the management of volunteers.

Chapter 8 considers the minimum analysis needed to ensure that plans can be implemented, budgetary control is monitored and quantitative performance is evaluated. The chapter uses a management accounts case study to illustrate points made.

In Chapter 9 the concept of entrepreneurship is uncovered in the context of the sports world. The chapter focuses upon the processes of creating entrepreneurial mindsets and developing the behaviour, attributes and skills associated with being entrepreneurial in order to equip the sports graduate for the life world of work. It introduces the notion of setting up a business venture by facilitating opportunity recognition, creation and the harvesting of sport business ideas and opportunities.

A short overview is presented in Chapter 10 as to why risk management has become more important in relation to sport management. The chapter then goes on to identify the key elements involved with risk management, making a clear distinction between the idea of risk cultures (how risk is defined and understood) and practical risk processes (how risk management is actually conducted). It also shows how risk management can be utilised at a practical operational level, which deals with day-to-day management, and at a strategic level, which deals with more long-term risk opportunities and threats.

Chapter 11 considers, from very much a practitioner focus, how sports are currently managed by major organisations in order to help participants develop lifelong participation. It explores the various ways, for instance, in which agencies such as Sport England, the National Governing Bodies of sport and County Sports Partnerships operate and advocate practical policy and new ways of working through partnerships.

In Chapter 12 a short overview of the scale of the sport event management market is provided. It makes a distinction between planning for different types of events, which range from the large, strategic macro sporting events, to small, low-key events run by a small club. It pays primary attention to the basic project management process overviews, illustrating how the range of tasks needs to be adapted according to the scale of the event.

Chapter 13 faces head on the task managers face in finding funding, investment and sponsorship for sports against a background which has seen diminishing financial resources supplied by government and a strain on the availability of voluntary assistance to support many clubs and sports organisations. Dealing with the financial constraints on providing sports activity is, in many instances, about adding value and this chapter, while considering profit for some organisations, begins a discussion about the funding of sport to provide wider social benefits.

Finally, the last section covers the more environmental aspects of the sports business industry in a legal and sustainability context. Chapter 14 provides an exposition of current sports law. It examines the legal framework within which sport operates. It also explores civil and criminal liabilities, including the law of negligence and contractual rights, as well as contemporary law and legal developments relating to the sports industry.

Chapter 15 considers contemporary issues in sports management in the 21st century and discusses principles of good practice in sustainable business management, business planning and development. It addresses the range of positive and negative impacts the sports industry can have on local, regional and national economies, natural and built environments, and societies and culture. The concept of sustainability and its application to sports management is considered in the context of environmental, economic, political and socio-cultural aspects of sustainable development.

The book is delivered through a series of Learning Outcomes: that is, statements of what the learner is expected to know, understand and/or be able to do at the end of each chapter, based upon the development of particular information, knowledge and skills.

The sports industry is dynamic and changing. We hope that this text will stimulate you to develop your managerial knowledge in ways that will help you understand more deeply what it means to be an innovative sports manager of the future.

Chapter 2

An overview of sport management

Mark Piekarz

The sport industry offers numerous management opportunities, which can range from entrepreneurial, profit-making activities, to the more familiar sport centre manager, who is involved in delivering non-profit community sport programmes. The management activity can range from focusing on a particular branch of business management, such as marketing or financial management, to having to operate as a 'generalist' manager, where all the different business management branches and functions need to be used in the day-to-day operation of a facility or organisation. This chapter explores the sport management industry, how it can be categorised and the many areas of the sport industry which need to be managed. To help illustrate the breadth and diversity of management opportunities and careers available, a sport management system model is developed at the end of this chapter, which can also be used to further explain how the different chapters in this book relate to each other.

Learning outcomes

This chapter is designed to enable you to:

- gain an insight into the scale of the sport industry;
- recognise that sport is delivered by three broad sectors (private, public and voluntary);
- identify the traditional business branches and functions of sport management;
- identify the new sport business branches and functions which the sport manager of the future needs to be aware of;
- explain how all these concepts relate to each other in terms of a sport management system.

The importance of the sport industry

It can be surprising how many people fail to appreciate how significant the sport industry has become in the modern world. Part of this ignorance is based on the simplistic view that because sport is seen as a leisure activity, which is associated with having fun and enjoyment, this somehow makes it less important, or less serious. In reality, sport is a significant business sector, which employs millions of people, generates huge amounts of economic activity (see Learning activity 2.1), is often used as a political tool, and has become an important measure of the quality of life for many people. The following points elaborate on the important role sport plays in the modern world.

In terms of its *economic significance*:

- the UK sport market was estimated to be worth £19.5 billion in 2006 (Sport England, 2007);
- by 2011 it has been forecast that the value will increase to £24 billion (Sport England, 2007);
- sport clothing and footwear is one of the most dynamic sectors of the sport market, totalling £4 billion in 2006 (Sport England, 2007).

Learning activity 2.1

Choose a specific English football premiership game and try to identify as many different jobs created via this event. Where possible, try to find out the number of people involved with each job area, such as policing or catering. Also, where appropriate, try to find out the average price people would pay for the services and products consumed, such as the tickets for the game (primary spend) and the many other elements, such as programmes, refreshments and transport (secondary spend). Try to represent the jobs and money involved as a scatter gram. The point of this activity is to illustrate how the game played by the 22 players represents an incredibly small fraction of the resources (such as time and people) needed to stage a single game. The game you see really does represent the tip of the iceberg, which hides the huge amount of business and economic activity which is generated and which needs to be managed.

In terms of its *social significance*:

- Sport can be seen as an important part of welfare programmes, particularly those related to using sport to improve people's physical, mental and social health. For example, over the years there has been a growth in GP referral schemes, whereby doctors may prescribe a course of physical activity rather than the more traditional prescription of medicine, which may be delivered at local sport centre.
- Sport has been used as a tool to help nurture and strengthen a sense of belonging and pride to communities, particularly if they have suffered from many years of deprivation. For example, one of the key aims of the London 2012 Olympics is to regenerate the Lower Lea valley in east London, which is a relative poor area, with the land that will be used for the sporting venues being largely derelict or abandoned. The idea is to use the Olympic event and the new sport facilities which are developed, as a catalyst or spark to help revitalise the area, by improving transport links, creating new housing and shopping developments, while also seeing many improvements in the natural environment as the area is cleaned up.

- Sport can be used as a means to try to reduce crime, particularly among youths, giving them a legitimate outlet for their energies. For example, through Sport England's Communities Investment Fund, a number of collaborative projects have been set up around the UK which focus on diversionary activities for young people.

In terms of its *political significance*:

- Despite some notions that sport should remain aloof or separate from politics, its use as a political tool has a long history, going back to the ancient Greeks and Romans. For example, the ancient Roman idea of *bread and circuses* referred to the idea that the citizens of Rome would give up certain political rights and support the Emperor, in exchange for being fed (the bread) and entertained (the circuses – epitomised by the huge gladiatorial contests which took place in the Coliseum, in Rome). The idea of using sport as a means of social control still has resonance today, particularly in relation to crime prevention.
- It has been used in the process of nation building. For example, the former president of South Africa, Nelson Mandela, used the rugby and cricket world cups staged in the country as a means to strengthen a single South African identity, rather than one divided on racial lines.
- It has been used as a means of political leverage to try to encourage political change. South Africa again illustrates this, when it was banned from international sporting events for decades, while it operated a political system of apartheid, which meant that the black majority were denied political rights (such as voting for the government in an election), and unable to mix in designated white areas, which ranged from buses, beaches and schools.

In terms of *personal significance*:

- It can be a vital source of stimulating experiences which are necessary in maintaining our sense of well-being. The mistake people make is to believe we simply progress through a hierarchy of needs, such as those outlined by Maslow, where we have to satisfy one need, such as needing to eat, before we can progress on to the next need. In fact, many needs can operate at the same time, and the need for stimulating, challenging experiences is a vital component for a healthy existence.
- Sport is increasingly becoming a source of identity, ranging from the classic football fan of a club, to the growth in adventure sport lifestyles, such as surfing or climbing. Here, people can define themselves not necessarily through the jobs that they do, but the sports and lifestyles that they participate in.
- Sport is often represented as key means where people are socialised into positive forms of behaviour, such as team building, obeying rules and leadership.

Although sport provides numerous positive benefits, it should be appreciated that sport can also have a number of negative aspects. Understanding the problems with sport is important as it allows for a more balanced perspective to be taken, together with developing more robust arguments in defence of sport. This is considered in Learning activity 2.2.

Learning activity 2.2

For as many of the positive benefits of sport identified earlier, outline counter-arguments to show how sport can be problematic or generate negative effects. Try to provide examples to illustrate your answers.

Sport is clearly a serious business, which needs to be managed like any other business. It will therefore need to utilise a number of key management branches, which range from managing financial resources, to managing people. These many different functional areas are discussed later, under the heading 'Key sport management operational elements and functions' with Chapter 3 exploring in more detail the many careers in sport management which are available.

The three sectors of sport provision

The delivery of *sport goods* and *services* (used here as distinct concepts rather than interchangeably as many textbooks do) can be understood as being supplied through three key sectors: the *private*, *public* and the *voluntary* sectors (which can also be termed the not-for-profit sector). Each of these sectors is briefly elaborated on in terms of what they are and why they exist below.

The *commercial*, or *private sector* is a huge part of the sport industry whose prime focus is profit. This sector includes football clubs, TV channels, fitness centres, stadium operators and the growing number of tour operators, who are tapping into a vibrant sport tourism sector. If the early development of sport in the UK was often led by the voluntary sector, in the past 20 years it has been the commercial sport sector, often dominated by large global businesses such as Nike, which have perhaps been one of the most dynamic parts of the sport industry.

The *public sector* relates to government involvement in sport. In the UK, government is essentially divided between the central government, based in London, and local government, based at city, town and county levels. The devolution of power to the Welsh and Scottish Assemblies has created another layer of government. Governments are primarily involved with sport:

- via *regulation*, such as laws passed governing stadium regulation, or outdoor activity centres;
- as a *facilitator*, such as giving money to agencies, such as UK Sports, which in turn give it to various sporting projects;
- or as a *direct provider* of sport services, which is done by local government providing a variety of leisure facilities. Central government does not directly provide sport services, while those provided by local government have become more complex because of the impact of Compulsory Competitive Tendering (CCT), which is discussed later in this chapter.

One of the reasons that governments intervene in the sport market place is *market failure*, a concept which is drawn from the discipline of economics. While commercial organisations can provide sport services profitably for some of the people, it is not financially attractive for them to provide them for everyone, so the market is said to fail. Yet, as has already been discussed, sport has many benefits and so can be deemed as a *merit good* or *service*: the more people who participate in it, the greater the benefits for the society as a whole. Services offered often operate at a loss, but because they achieve social objectives (see the section on 'Recent trends' in this chapter for more details) they are subsidised by government.

The *voluntary sector* is a vital component in the sport industry, ranging from small groups of people coming together to organise their own sport club, to large organisations, which employ paid staff to run the organisation, such as the International Olympic Committee (IOC). The idea of a voluntary organisation employing paid people can be confusing; it may be tempting to place such an organisation in the commercial sector. Simply put, what differentiates such organisations from commercial ones is the focus of their work, which may relate to programmes which have a social objective, rather being run for profit; also, the governing trustees or governors give their time to help run the organisation on a voluntary basis, rather than because they are paid. This sector is sometimes also classified as the not-for-profit sector, or the third sector, but as this can overlap with many government-related organisations and activities, the preference here is to use the term 'voluntary sector' as this helps to maintain a sharper difference between the sectors.

One of the reasons why the voluntary sector emerges is that, just as governments are forced to intervene because of market failures, so too can governments fail to deliver key services. These *market* and *government* failures leave a gap that is often filled by the voluntary sector, such as the numerous charities which develop to help meet different needs and funding gaps.

If you want to find out more about why the three sectors emerge, Gratton and Taylor (2000) give a particularly clear and useful discussion about the three sectors, which is approached via the discipline of economics.

Recent trends in the three sectors

This three-sector model of the UK sport industry supply of sport goods and services is becoming more complex because the distinctions between the sectors are becoming more blurred; a development which can be described as the *collapsing of the sectors*. The factors which have driven this collapse can be summarised as:

- the sectors operating in similar ways;
- the growth in the three sector partnerships;
- contracting out and partnerships;
- new notions of viability.

Each of these areas is elaborated on further below.

The sectors operating in similar ways

The public and voluntary sectors, in order to justify or secure funding, have to run themselves in a more business-like manner. While they may not be concerned with profit, they still need to appear professional and ensure that they are as *efficient* (ensuring the maximum *output*, such as sport programmes or products, in relation to a given *input*, such as staffing) and *effective* with resources (this primarily focuses just on the quality of outputs, which Torkildsen (1994, p85) defined as 'the right opportunities, at the right time, in the right place'). The private sector is not immune to this trend; they are increasingly having to adopt many social objectives and consider issues of ethics, such as sustainability (discussed in Chapter 15).

The growth in the three sector partnerships

For both large- and small-scale projects, partnerships are often a key factor in their success. This can range from sponsorship deals, to fundraising activities, to capital project developments. The London 2012 Olympics is an interesting example illustrating the importance of partnerships. While central government has been a key catalyst and facilitator in the initial bidding and staging of the games, it also needs to secure millions of pounds of private money, much of it through sponsorship. In addition, in terms of staging the Olympics, thousands of volunteers will be needed, with the recruitment process needing to comply with proper employment practices and offering job training, which will begin two years before the actual event.

Contracting out and privatisation

The 1979 election of the Conservative Party, led by Mrs Thatcher, marked the beginning of radical change for the provision of sport and leisure services. Simply put, the Conservatives wanted to bring the *disciplines of the market place* to the public sector, which was part of a wider strategy of reducing central government expenditure in order to try to control inflation. One of the ways of doing this was to *contract out public services* to commercial operators, in a process known as compulsory competitive tendering (CCT), which is not the same as *privatisation*, as this involves selling off the actual physical assets, such as the sport centre. Instead, while the local authority would still own the physical sport facilities, the management and day-to-day running of the centre would be managed by an outside agency or organisation. This contracting-out process initially began with cleaning, catering and refuse collection services, but was extended to local authority leisure services in 1989.

The immediate question which may be raised is why would a private company want to manage a leisure facility which would operate at a loss? The key is to understand that what companies bid on was the size of the subsidy they would ask for from the local government. With this subsidy, plus the revenue the company generated and any additional savings made, they could then calculate whether they would make a profit or loss. The hope was that this process would make services more efficient and reduce costs, as companies would be more concerned about offering services that people wanted and cut down on any unnecessary waste. In fact many argued that it just made services more *economic* (reducing the cost of the inputs, such as staffing, but which meant there was a decline in the quality of the outputs, such as sport programmes), with many social objectives sacrificed.The election of a Labour government in 1997 saw the contracting process adapted with their policy of Best Value. This has given more impetus for sport facilities to be managed by *charitable trusts* rather than private companies, and, in theory, allows for greater focus on non-profit social objectives.

The notion of viability

These trends mean that it is useful to utilise a concept of organisational viability which goes beyond a simple notion of profit. While for the commercial sector the idea of the *bottom line* is vital for their future viability as an enterprise (this refers to the bottom of the balance sheet where the overall profit or loss is shown, as discussed in Chapter 5), for many other sport organisations what ensures viability is more complex. It should be appreciated that many of the benefits of sport highlighted earlier are not necessarily profitable activities and can cost a great deal of money. An economist would call many of these spin-off effects *externalities*, which can be both good (such as improvements in health), or bad (a sport injury). Many of these benefits can be defined in terms of *social objectives*, such as reducing crime or improving health, and provide a key rationale for many sport organisations' existence. For sport organisations operating in the public and voluntary sector, what ensures their viability relates to providing evidence that they are achieving some of the less tangible social objectives, which can help secure their future funding.

The key sport management operational elements and functions

What should be emerging now is that sport is a complex and diverse industry which needs to be managed like any other business. One can add a number of further elements to try to convey the breadth of sport management activities that people can be involved with. In addition to the different sectors that a manager may operate in, they can also be distinguished in the following ways:

- Sport *service*-related management is management in relation to *service provision*, which primarily involves the design, implementation and monitoring of sport programmes. For example, a manager of a sport facility may have responsibility for the many different programmes which operate in the centre, which can range from being *structured* and directed, such as swimming lessons, or a keep-fit class, or offered on a casual *pay-as-you-play* basis, which means that people themselves decide how they want to fill their time doing the activities, such as a casual swim or using gym equipment. Sport services are offered by all three sectors.
- Sport *product*-related management is management in relation to *product provision*, which relates to coordinating manufacturing processes and distributing these products to different retail outlets, such as shops. An example is a production line manager of a sport shoe company, who is involved with ensuring that the shoes are put together to the required quality on the production line, packaged and then distributed to various retail outlets. Management of physical goods is predominantly provided by the private sector.

Sport management can also be considered in terms of physical location, distinguishing between:

- Facility/production management. This simply relates to whether the manager is primarily involved with managing directly the physical resources of a sport facility or factory – the traditional focus in terms of sport management; and
- Non-facility based management. Increasingly there are job opportunities whereby services are created by external agencies which utilise a variety of facilities and organisations to help deliver the services. For example there has been a growth in sport development officers (SDOs), who may utilise a variety of sport venues, ranging from schools to public leisure centres, in order to provide for a variety of sport services .This area has become very important and often needs many management skills, which is why it is discussed in more detail in Chapter 11.

Sport management can also be considered in relation to the level at which it operates. Various terms can be used to describe the different levels, such as the line manager, middle managers and senior managers. In this book, two key levels are given more detailed discussion.

- Operational management. This is characterised by the more limited timescales and resources that need to be managed and is focused on the day-to-day processes involved in getting goods and services (the *outputs* as seen in Figure 2.1) to customers and clients. It is about the management of resources, such as staffing (the *inputs* as seen in Figure 2.1), in order to ensure that operations run smoothly and safely. Although this area of sport management is not dealt with in a separate chapter, it should be appreciated that many of the operational functions are dealt with in each of the chapters. A simple way of representing operational based management is to think of a manager who is involved in the day-to-day management of a small to medium size facility, whose activities can range from designing new programmes, organising staff rotas, recruitment and controlling the centre budget.
- Strategic management. This is characterised by the longer timescales (usually over a year, often focusing on three-, five- and ten-year periods) and the scale of the resources that need to be planned for and managed in order to achieve the organisational goals or objectives. Strategic management is discussed in detail in Chapter 6. A key element is the illustration of how a plan which sets the future direction of an organisation needs to consider how external forces, such as the economy, can create opportunities or threats which must be managed. This is represented as the lightning bolt in Figure 2.1, which shows how external factors can affect the organisation's operations. A simple way of representing sport strategic management relates to a senior manager responsible for a large sport facility, or coordinating the operations of a number of sport facilities, whose job activities can range from controlling budgets to strategically coordinating programmes.

It should be recognised that, realistically, when students enter the job market, they often enter as a line worker, or at a supervisory level, progressing into operational management, then later in their careers entering into management at a more strategic level. Although some of the knowledge and skills which relate to strategic sport management may not be needed in the short term, it is vital that you have an awareness of the strategic management level, as this helps with seeing the 'bigger picture' in which you operate. The key is not necessarily remembering all the knowledge necessary to develop strategic plans, but remembering where to access information.

Sport management can also be considered in relation to the many different business elements or branches that have developed. The classic division of branches is sometimes presented as: operational, strategic, human resource, marketing, financial and information technology. The preference here is to separate the operational and strategic from the other branches, as they will overlap with them so much. In relation to this book, these other branches are identified as follows:

- Marketing. This is not about advertising – a common misconception held by students – but about understanding customers and clients, and designing services to meet their *needs* and *wants*. It can be regarded as a general mindset, whereby to be *market-orientated* is always to place the customer at the heart of the service. It is also a practical process, which involves designing the product and service, then communicating it to existing and potential clients – with advertising just one aspect of this. In relation to sport marketing, the social objective dimension discussed earlier can make the marketing process more complex, because at times the clients' needs and wants may differ. For example, a coach of a children's football team may *need* them to develop their skills and enjoy the game; in contrast, the parents and children may simply *want* to win the game at all costs. Marketing is discussed in Chapter 4.
- Financial management. This is not a simplistic notion of how to make a profit, but how to monitor and control the flows of money in and out of the organisation. It is vital for students to refer back to the three-sector provision model and recognise that a large number of sport services are provided to achieve social objectives, which operate at a loss and need to receive a subsidy to operate. This does not mean, however, that proper financial controls are not important. It is vital that sport managers have an understanding of the costs of the products and services that they are involved with in order to operate as efficiently as possible, which is vital for both profits, or to ensure that public money is not being wasted. This is discussed in Chapter 5.
- Human resource management. People are at the heart of many sport services. Whether they are paid staff or club volunteers, they must be managed properly, ensuring that this is done within the law. This can range from adhering to legal guidelines (such as equal opportunities) in how people are recruited, to how they are motivated, integrated into a team and led, all of which occurs within a particular organisational culture or ethos. This is discussed in Chapter 7.

In addition to these more traditional business management branches, this book argues that there are a number of newer, additional business related strands which the sport manager needs to consider. These are as follows:

- Sport entrepreneurship. This primarily relates to the idea that the demands of sport, both in the profit and non-profit context, require entrepreneurial approaches in order to be successful. The competing demands on people's time means that programmes and goods need to stand out from those of competitors, and this requires innovation in terms of ideas and practices in response to a rapidly changing, complex business environment. This is discussed in Chapter 9.

- Risk management. The pressures of legal regulations, media attention and the attempt to deal with a complex world has encouraged the use of risk management practices to help frame many management processes. This is relevant at an operational level, such as with health and safety risk assessments, and at the strategic level in relation to business environment scanning processes. This is discussed in Chapter 10.
- Funding for sport. Traditionally, organisations in the public or voluntary sector have needed to secure funds in order to achieve their social objectives. A key source is obviously from government, and funds are usually distributed via local government or agencies such as UK Sport. But funds can also be sought from charities and commercial organisations, either donations or in the form of sponsorship. Securing funds has become a key factor in ensuring organisational viability, with the area of sponsorship being particularly important for elite sport organisations. Aspects of this are discussed in Chapter 13.

One of the business management areas which some business books may include Information Technology (IT). Clearly this is a vital area, but is not dealt with in a separate chapter, as it is embedded in all the areas discussed in this book. To illustrate the different management opportunities available, Learning activity 2.3 explores the more specific management job opportunities which are available.

Learning activity 2.3

Using a variety of online job websites, such as Leisure Opportunities (which can be found at: www.leisureopportunities.co.uk/), identify a variety of sport management related jobs, and map out where they may be placed on the following grid.

Grid 1

Job title	**Business branch e.g. marketing, finance, HRM**	**Level e.g. operational or strategic**	**Facility based?**	**Service or product**	**Descriptions e.g. salary, key skills, tasks, roles**

Both these old and new business management areas need to be considered, in turn, in relation to a number of key environmental external factors (see Chapter 6) which are helping to set the tone of many sport operations. In this book, just two key areas are explored. These are:

- Sport law. Students must appreciate that ignorance of the law is rarely admissible (i.e. accepted as evidence in court). It is therefore vital that sport managers are aware of a number of key regulations, court cases and legal principles. These are discussed in Chapter 14.

- Sustainable sport business. The idea of sustainability is perhaps not as tangible as many of the previous areas that are used for the basis of the book chapters. It is included here as it is an important illustrative example of how change in the external environment can profoundly alter the operating conditions for a sport organisation. In this instance, it relates to how organisations are under increasing pressure to adopt practices which are more environmentally friendly. This is discussed in Chapter 15.

It should be recognised that many other areas could be considered, particularly in relation to the last two chapters, which relate to wider legal, economic and social cultural changes that create both threats and opportunities for sport organisations. To try and further convey the wide number of issues, students are encouraged to do Learning activity 2.4.

Learning activity 2.4

Find out about the following concepts and highlight how they are relevant to the sport manager:

- leadership . . .
- quality management . . .
- managing volunteers . . .
- customer care. . .
- communications . . .
- organisational culture . . .
- globalisation . . .

Key definitions

This chapter has consciously kept back various definitions of sport, business and management until the end. Placing such definitions too early can sometimes be restrictive and distract from an appreciation of the vibrancy and scale of the sport industry and management opportunities. It is still nonetheless important to develop some conceptual clarity with regard to definitions, particularly when more detailed research is conducted, such as part of a final year research student project. What this section does is to help move from our intuitive understanding of these concepts to identifying the key themes of the concepts of *business*, *management* and *sport*.

The concept of management is perhaps the most important and complex of the terms to explore. When reading other textbooks on management, it is common to draw on the work of two of the early pioneers of management and organisational theory who were writing in the early twentieth century: Mary Parker Follet and Henri Fayol. Follett's succinct and often-used definition of management as 'the art of getting things done through people', although a little limited, is still useful in conveying an essential ingredient of what management is about. In terms of the more specific *management functions* which can be identified, Fayol's classic and frequently cited functional categories also offer another simple way to convey what management is. These management functions are as follows:

- Planning. This can relate to operational action plans, to the more strategic long-term planning of the organisational direction.
- Organising. This relates to the idea that work is broken down into its key components and the schedule of who does what and when is identified.
- Coordinating. This relates to the coordinating of actions and resources, with the idea of resources relating to such things as people and money.
- Staffing. This is to do with designing jobs and staff recruitment.
- Leading/Motivating. Once the organisation's direction has been set and the people recruited, they must be led and motivated. It is vital to appreciate that, in terms of motivation, people must first be energised to do the work, then this motivation must be sustained by the manager.
- Controlling. This involves checking progress against plans, which may need modification based on feedback. Developing appropriate controls and identifying relevant indicators of performance has been a key area which managers have had to deal with over the past 20 years, particularly in the public sector and with the advent of CCT.

These functional areas have been superseded by many other categories, definitions and ways of representing what management is about. For example, Mintzberg is another commonly cited writer who identified three roles of management, which are:

- Interpersonal. This relates to leading and acting as representative of an organisation or team.
- Informational. This relates to receiving and communication information across the organisation and team.
- Decision. This can range from allocating resources to acting as an arbitrator of disputes.

All these writers help to provide some of the key themes of management, while also highlighting that there is no definitive definition of what management is. Some of the themes of particular importance, relate to the manager clarifying the direction that people and the organisation need to move in, which is then reviewed, coordinated and sustained. It is also of interest how many of the definitions of management may add a qualitative element to it, such as stating that the managing is done as *effectively* or as *efficiently* as possible (see the earlier definitions). When one adds a qualitative element to management definitions, this can move management in the direction of *leadership*, which, while it is in many ways similar to management, is not necessarily the same concept. The area of leadership is one you are encouraged to explore further as it is beyond the scope of this book.

In relation to the concept of business, this involves the following key characteristics:

- provision of goods and services;
- exchange process of money or time;
- an investment of an *input*, such as staff or money.

All these elements, when combined, can go to form the sport industry. In the context of this book, the idea of a business management system is developed, which emphasises that the business activity can be for both profit and non-profit reasons.

In terms of definitions of sport, the definition adopted by the Council of Europe (1992) as part of the Charter for Sport is commonly cited in many textbooks on sport. They give the following definition:

> 'Sport' means all forms of physical activity which, through casual or organised participation, aim at expressing or improving physical fitness and mental well-being, forming social relationships or obtaining results in competition at all levels. (Council of Europe, 1992)

This definition is by no means perfect and one can always find areas of ambiguity, particularly in relation to sport management. A key theme in this chapter has been to stress how much sport stimulates large amounts of business and management activity, which at first glance may seem to have little direct involvement with sport activities, particularly as sport is defined by the Council of Europe. It is a mistake to believe that sport management is defined simply in relation to playing or participation in sporting activities. For example, there will be many different types of managers in a large sport clothing manufacturer, who will have relatively little direct involvement in 'challenging' sporting activities. The key is to see the actual sporting activities as a hub which spins off numerous types of businesses and jobs which are not necessarily sport specific. If one refers back to Learning activity 2.1 and the scatter grams which may have been produced, this will help convey the idea of a sporting hub of activities.

The sport management system

Using these different strands one can begin to develop a sport management system to illustrate how all the different elements relate to each other (this system is represented in Figure 2.1). There are five key elements to this model, with reference made, when appropriate, to where they are examined in more detail in this book. These key system elements relate to the following elements:

- Inputs. These relate to the idea that in order to produce goods or products, one must have resources, which in Figure 2.1 are represented as people (see Chapter 7), money (see Chapter 5) and ideas (see Chapter 9).
- Process. The input resources are then combined and shaped by the organisation's management processes. How the organisation is managed can be dependent on the sector in which it operates and the size of the organisation. In turn, in terms of actually generating the outputs, a number of key management elements need to be utilised, primarily based around designing the products and services as part of the marketing function (Chapter 4), utilising people to make or deliver the services as part of the human resource management (HRM) function (see Chapter 7), all of which must be properly scrutinised within proper financial controls, as part of the financial management function (Chapter 5). The added dynamics to these traditional areas are the need to use entrepreneurial

(Chapter 9) and risk management approaches (Chapter 10), along with project management skills (Chapter 12).

- Outputs. The outputs relate to the actual goods and services which are produced from the organisational system, which may be a sport facility, factory or enterprise. The types of services produced will again be modified by the extent to which they are designed to make a profit or are provided to achieve some wider social objective (Chapter 11).
- External factors. Change in business is a constant factor, with the generators of these drivers of change emerging from what is described as the external business environment (the area where businesses have little control), for example political, economic, social, technological, legal or environmental factors. Changes here can generate both threats and opportunities. The more practical aspects of how to deal with this are considered in Chapter 6 on strategy and Chapter 10 on risk, while the issues of sustainability (Chapter 15) is one of the more specific issues considered;
- Underpinning factors. Underlying all this is the legal framework, discussed in Chapter 14. In relation to the area of inputs, this means ensuring that funds come from legitimate sources. In relation to the process element, this means ensuring that staff are employed in proper working conditions. In relation to outputs, this means ensuring that the activities are provided in a way which does not endanger people's health or safety.

An example can be used to illustrate how all these elements come together. A manager of small publicly owned sport facility may have a clear remit to work closely with the local community in order to achieve various social objectives, many of which have a strong sport development context. The sport facility has a variety of *inputs* that can be utilised, ranging from its staff, sport facilities and the money which is obtained from the local government and a successful lottery bid. In addition, the manager can also utilise many partnerships, with, for example, voluntary community groups, regional sport development officers and a number of private businesses that are supportive of the healthy living campaigns. These resources are then *processed* via the organisation system, which, because it operates in the non-profit sector, will have a particular ethos and way of operating. These inputs are then coordinated and utilised to produce a variety of *outputs*, such as coaching programmes for youths, active recreation sessions for the elderly or keep-fit classes for all the community.

Review of learning outcomes

This chapter has shown how diverse sport management can be, whereby the management aspect may actually have little to do with the more obvious and visible sporting activities. Sport can be represented as a hub, which at its core demands management of numerous sport services and goods, which are primarily supplied by organisations which can be distinguished according to whether they are profit or non-profit orientated, or in a more refined way by referring to three key sectors. This three-sector provision is changing, or 'collapsing', in the sense that the different sectors

Figure 2.1: The sport management system

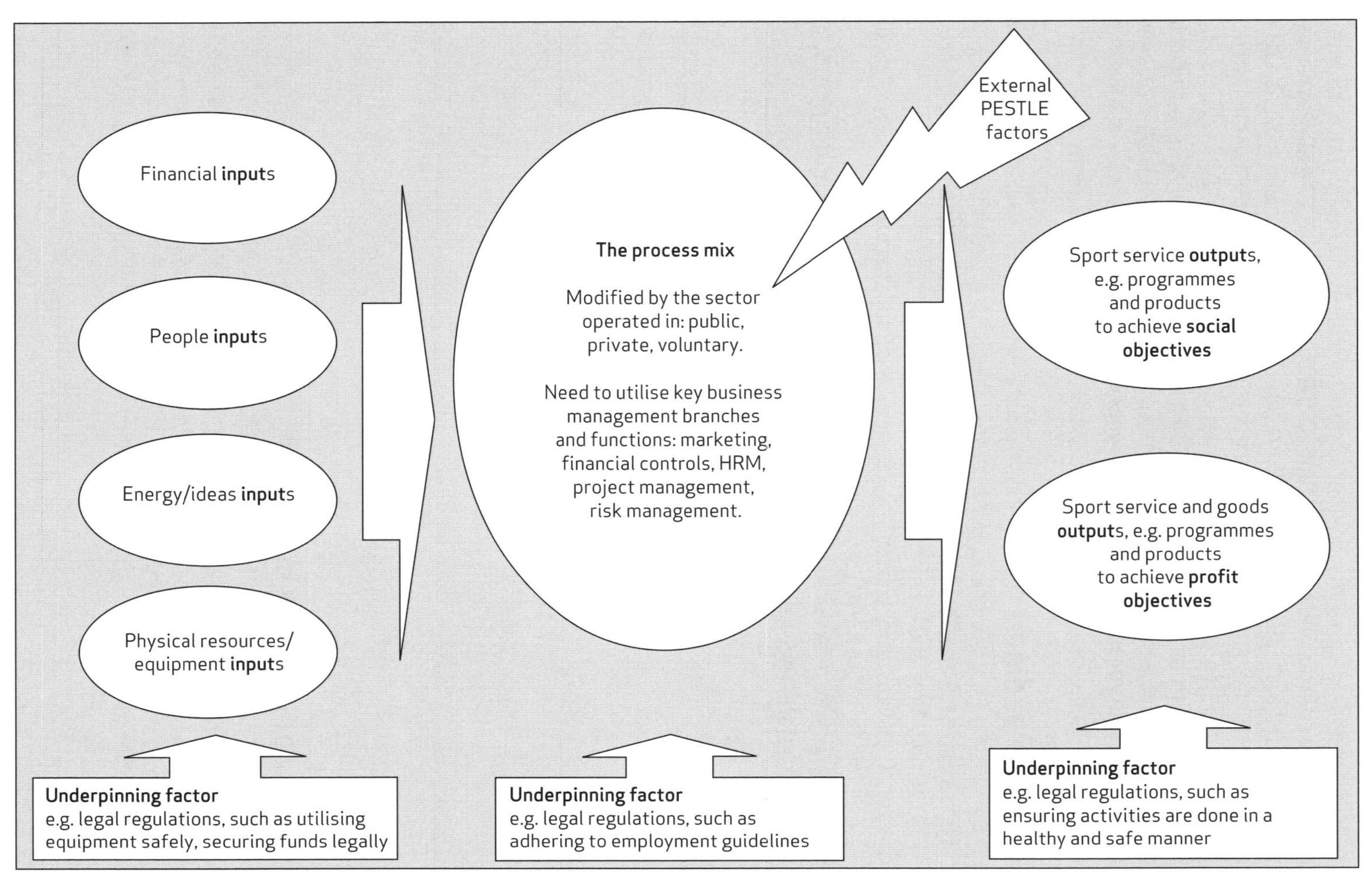

are having to operate and utilise similar management practices, while also needing each other more and more, which is reflected in the growth in partnerships between the three sectors. The sport hub also acts to generate numerous additional business activities, for which again there exist many management opportunities.

The breadth of sport management opportunities is further illustrated when one explores the core business management elements and functions. These can range from the traditional marketing, financial management and human resource management branches, whereby people can specialise in these different areas, or as is often the case in smaller facilities or organisations, managers can act as generalists and draw on knowledge and skills from all of these branches. In addition, changes in the external environment have encouraged the adoption of new functions and skills, in particular in the areas of entrepreneurship and risk management.

Further reading

Smith, A and Stewart, B (1999) *Sport management: a guide to professional practice.* Australia: Allen and Unwin,

Gratton, C and Taylor, P (2000) *The economics of sport and recreation.* 2nd edition. London: Taylor and Francis.

Hoye, R , Smith, A, Westerbeek, H, Steward, B and Nicholson, M (2006) *Sport management: principles and applications*. Oxford: Elsevier.

Chapter 3

Enhancing graduate employability in sport

Sue Minten and Will Foster

In order to enhance graduate employability most sports courses include modules and activities, such as personal development planning (PDP), that aim to develop personal skills and attributes. However, it may not always be immediately clear to students why this is so crucial. This chapter will explore the notion of employability and why it is important to enhance your employment-related attributes throughout your course. It will primarily focus on the sport industry, but as will be seen, high numbers of sports graduates choose to find employment in other industries, consequently it is also applicable to graduate employability in general.

The first part of the chapter focuses on graduate employability in relation to their transition into the sport industry. The second part will contain practical advice on how to enhance your employability, particularly in relation to your first job post graduation.

Learning outcomes

This chapter is designed to enable you to:

- develop an appreciation of employability in the context of the sport industry;
- take steps to enhance your own employability;
- consider how you will manage your career.

Introduction

Employability is a difficult term to define, at a basic level it is about obtaining a job, however this simple definition does not indicate the individual's capacity to function in a job. Most employability researchers recognise the complexity of the concept and that it can be interpreted in many ways (Harvey, 2001; McQuaid and Lindsay 2005; Yorke, 2006).

Essentially there are two approaches to employability: those that focus on the individual's characteristics and readiness for work, or those that are more holistic and suggest that employability occurs over a period of time. The holistic approach includes consideration of the range of factors that influence a person getting, performing in, moving between or improving their job (Yorke, 2006).

This chapter is based on the holistic approach but it also recognises the importance of understanding the needs of graduates in relation to employability, therefore the definition of employability that underpins the discussion is 'obtaining and retaining fulfilling work' (Hillage and Pollard, 1998, p12). In order to examine this in detail the chapter consists of the following sections.

The first section will provide an examination of the employment patterns and aspirations of sport graduates. The second section discusses the nature of the sport industry and how graduates fit into it. This leads into the third section, which focuses on the needs of sport employers and industry in general. Section four focuses on the graduate and explores how they can ensure that they develop appropriate attributes during their course to enhance their employability. Finally, section five examines the notion of the new career and how sports graduates can manage their future career.

Employment patterns of sports graduates

Graduate employability is usually reported using first-destination statistics that are collected six months after graduation. It is difficult to tease out the patterns of employment of sport-related graduates due to the way the data is categorised, both in terms of the graduate's subject area and the job areas that they undertake. However, the survey does identify the first destinations of sports science graduates and highlights some interesting patterns. Just under a fifth of them (19.6%) are employed in sport-specific jobs, with coaching and instructing jobs the most important in this area (Association of Graduate Careers Advisory Services [AGCAS], 2007). The other key areas of employment are:

- commercial, industrial and public sector managers (8.5%);
- education professionals (11.1%);
- clerical and secretarial occupations (10.2%);
- retail, catering, waiting and bar staff (11.0%);
- other occupations (20.7%).

(AGCAS, 2007)

The high number of clerical, secretarial, retail and catering posts reflect a fundamental flaw in first-destination statistics as many graduates undertake short-term work during this period that does not relate to their career aspirations. Many sport graduates go into these posts on a short-term basis to repay debts and then apply for 'proper' jobs the Christmas after they have graduated (Hansen at al., 1998).

The most detailed research into the recruitment and development of sport-related graduates was undertaken in the late 1990s with students and graduates from higher education (HE) institutions in England, Wales and Northern Ireland. Despite the length of time since this research was undertaken its findings were similar to the AGCAS survey: that high numbers of sport-related graduates do not go into sport related jobs (Hansen et al., 1998). Its findings on the employment areas of graduates who had been in the workplace for between one to three years is shown in Figure 3.1.

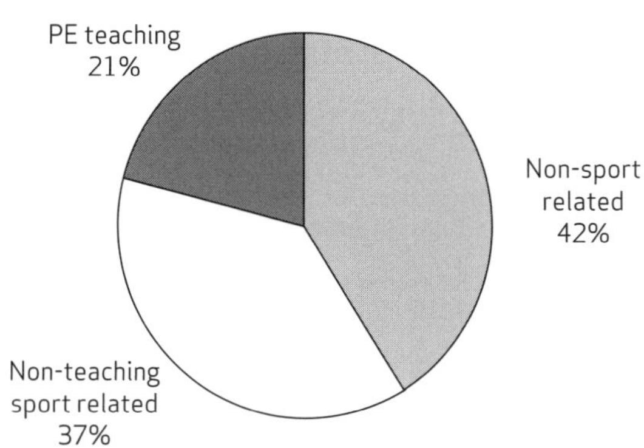

Figure 3.1: Areas of employment of sport graduates, Hansen et al. (1998)

A superficial evaluation of both these and the AGCAS results would suggest that there is a problem with the employability of sports graduates as large numbers are not entering into sport employment. Moreover SkillsActive (2006), the Sector Skills Council for Active Leisure in the UK, has interpreted such results in this way and identified this as a major issue for HE sports courses. The question is does it matter?

Further analysis of the AGCAS (2007) survey results shows that sports graduates are successful in gaining employment, sports science graduates actually have the highest employment rate among scientists, at 62.3 percent, and the lowest unemployment, at 4.9 percent. Furthermore, the report suggests that they have good transferable skills. Similar results were found by Hansen et al. (1998), who also found low numbers of sports-related graduates were unemployed.

A key reason for the employment patterns is that many sport graduates actually choose not to work in sport; Hansen et al. (1998) found that approximately half (48%) of those not employed in sport chose to work in other industries and had no intention of working in sport. In their survey of final year students they reported that 21 percent did not intend to work in sport. Moreover, in focus groups with final year students it was established that most students chose their course because they had an interest in sport and wanted to do a degree in an area that they enjoyed. There were few that had definite career options in mind and, with the exception of those who wanted to do Physical Education (PE) teaching, most had not undertaken the degree for vocational reasons.

Although these findings suggest that the issue is not necessarily about the numbers of sport graduates entering sport jobs, it does highlight the need to ensure that sport graduates develop transferable skills and attributes to enable them to enter into a wide range of occupational areas. Lack of clarity over career aspirations is an obstacle to obtaining a fulfilling job and studies have found that those who were most clear about careers from the outset tended to be the most satisfied with their early career progress (Minten, 2007; Nove et al., 1997). This issue will be returned to later in the chapter.

Learning activity 3.1

Undertake a survey of your year group to ascertain: their motivations to do the course; if they have thought about their future career; and if they have, which area of work they wish to enter.

If it is not possible to undertake a formal survey ask your friends about their motivations and career aspirations.

Compare your findings with those identified in this section

The nature of the sport industry and the place of sport graduates

Employability is based on a reciprocal relationship, consequently it is not only important to understand employers' needs in relation to graduates, but also to understand how employers' receive and manage those graduates to ensure utilisation of their attributes and job fulfilment. However, many commentaries and guides on employability in sport have tended to only focus on the skill needs of the sport industry and how sports graduates match up to these.

Identifying skill needs is important, but it is also crucial to understand the context of these needs. There is a danger that, while HE institutions develop graduates with all the appropriate attributes, these may stay dormant if the graduate obtains a job with an employer who does not enable their utilisation. This section will examine both sides of this relationship, beginning with the context of the industry and how this has impacted on the utilisation of graduate attributes and their job fulfilment. It will then examine the skill needs of the sport industry and industry in general.

A crucial feature of the sport industry is that it is not a traditional graduate employer and studies have shown that a degree has not been seen as a particularly relevant qualification for sport managers (Bacon, 1995; SkillsActive, 2006; Sports Council, 1969). There are two main reasons for this.

First, sport has developed out of a technical occupational area, as evidenced by the concentration of the early professional bodies, such as the Institute of Baths and Recreation Management (IBRM), on technical qualifications. However, since the 1960s there has been a call to improve the effectiveness of sport managers through education and training (Sports Council, 1969; Yates, 1984). Moreover, reorganisation of local authorities in 1974 enabled the expansion of sport in the public sector and consequently senior recreation managers were sometimes appointed without the appropriate higher-level education qualifications (Yates, 1984). This has created an industry where a minority of staff have a degree, for example the SPRITO skills foresight report (2000) found that only 10 percent of staff in sport organisations were graduates. More recently SkillsActive (2006) identified that only 26 percent of sports staff had a level 4/5 qualification (the level equivalent to a degree). Although, within the fitness sector, 39 percent of respondents to the annual UK Working in Fitness survey (SkillsActive, 2008) had a degree, suggesting that this is an area of work that graduates are beginning to colonise.

The second reason is that sport-related degrees are relatively new academic areas of study that mainly developed from PE courses in the 1970s and 1980s. The call to up-skill sport employees helped facilitate the development of sport-related courses and this has been further helped by the expansion of higher education since the 1990s – in 1994 there were 5,322 sport-related graduates, increasing to 14,239 by 2005 (Chapman, 2006; Higher Education Statistics Agency [HESA], 1996).

These two points mean that there has not been a clear entry point for graduates into the industry, consequently the culture has been for graduates to start at the bottom and work their way up, which means they are not using their graduate attributes (Hansen et al., 1998; Minten, 2007; SkillsActive, 2006; Yates, 1984). Exacerbating the problem is that graduates have had high expectations about their level of entry into the industry

(Hansen et al., 1998), which has meant that they become frustrated 'feeling over-qualified for low management but lacking the competence to operate at higher levels' (Yates, 1984: 87; see also Minten, 2007). As many sport managers do not have degrees themselves, this means that they may not have an understanding of the graduate's needs and how to exploit their attributes. This issue is reflected in the Leitch (2006, p67) review, which suggests that, as younger people within the workforce gain degrees, and if employers are not engaged with HE:

> it increases the likelihood of poor deployment of higher-level skills with relatively under-skilled owners, managers and leaders unable to find the best uses for new graduate recruits.

Most research into employability has been quantitatively based, using surveys of graduates' first destinations and obtaining lists of employers' needs. Johnston (2003, p419) argues that a key area of omission from the research into graduate employability has been the voices of the graduates, which are 'deafening in their silence'. There has been little published research on graduates' working conditions, job fulfilment and, crucially, an analysis of what employers say they want from graduates and what they actually want from them in practice. Research that has tried to address this issue in sport is discussed below.

CASE STUDY 3.1

Summary of research project: graduate employment in sport: the transition into the workplace (Minten, 2007)

Objective: To examine employability of sport graduates in sport through their transition into the workplace.

Employability was defined as 'gaining and retaining fulfilling work' (Hillage and Pollard, 1998, p12).

Method: Case study of four graduates' transition into sport organisations. The case studies were developed using '360-degree appraisal' techniques where the graduate, their manager, their colleagues and their staff were interviewed to build up a picture of the transition and performance of the graduate. During the interviews four other graduates were encountered, which enabled comparisons.

Findings: The graduates at the focus of the study were all perceived as being effective in their job. However, the graduates had differing levels of job fulfilment and two were actively exploring options in other industries. As the other four graduates were not the focus of the study, their performance cannot be evaluated, however three were unfulfilled in their job and were looking for other work, two in other industries.

Evaluation: The employability of the graduates was influenced by a combination of: the attributes that they developed during their degree course, their intrinsic personality/values, which enabled self-motivation and a proactive attitude to their job, the nature of their job and the effectiveness of their line manager –

CASE STUDY 3.1 continued

which influenced the opportunity for the graduates to utilise their attributes and further develop themselves.

Application: To achieve employability in terms of 'gaining and retaining fulfilling work' there is a need to ensure that graduates have the appropriate attributes to be effective in sport jobs; to retain graduates, however, employers need to understand graduate needs – which are for jobs and a management style that utilises the attributes they have developed and enables them to develop within the workplace. Moreover, graduates also need to take responsibility for their development by effectively undertaking the often low-level tasks required in initial jobs, but also proactively seeking out other tasks that can utilise their graduate skills that are of benefit to the employer.

The research does identify the responsibility on the part of the employer to enable the graduate to be fulfilled in their work and this relates to being an effective manager and understanding the needs of staff and managing them appropriately. However, the research also identifies the responsibility of the graduate to develop the appropriate attributes, which relates not only to their skills but also their values and attitudes to their work and career. This is reflected by Stephen Studd the CEO of SkillsActive:

> This step needs a partnership. It needs graduates with the right attitude and a willingness to continue to learn and develop themselves once they are in work; and employers who are willing to support them in their development, recognising that their graduate skills are often a long-term investment that will pay dividends over time as they gain practical experience. (in Benson, 2007)

In recent years concerns have been raised about the need for higher-level skills within the industry and the difficulties in recruiting and retaining appropriate staff (SkillsActive, 2005; Sport England, 2004a). Neil Jenkinson (2001), former Chair of the Nottingham Chief Leisure Officers group, noted that there was a shortage of young talented managers with the core skills that can be developed to meet the needs of sport and leisure organisations. There have also been encouraging comments about the sports industry's need for graduates; as Peter Johnson (2001, p52), former Chairman and Chief Executive of Circa Leisure stated:

> I think from the industry's point of view we do need a leisure degree, fitness, sports and recreation, call it what you like, it doesn't matter I'm not bothered about that, but we need some sort of degree for the industry. I think it says that the industry has arrived and I think it says something about the industry that's important.

Skills needs of industry

The discussion of employability has identified that it is more complex than the identification of the skills needs of employers and ensuring that graduates attain those skills. However, it is recognised that the development of vocationally relevant skills and attributes is a key part of this complex puzzle and a crucial part of the enhancement of graduates' employability. This is particularly pertinent to the recruitment and selection process examined in Chapter 7, where the use of person specifications mean that graduates must show evidence of the acquisition of the appropriate skills and attributes to be shortlisted and selected for jobs.

This next section will examine the skills and attributes that have been identified as being required by industry. It is crucial that students are aware of employers' needs in the early stages of their course to ensure that they make use of the activities provided by HE institutions that will enable them to enhance their employability. This is particularly important for those aspiring to careers in the sport industry because, as the discussion of the nature of the industry has shown, the culture is that graduates tend to start at the bottom and then work their way up. Consequently, there is a need to pick up practical, vocational skills to address the issue raised by SkillsActive (2000, p24) that employers 'think too many HE graduates lack the essential vocational elements, which would make them employable'. As a graduate's career progresses they are then able to make more utilisation of their graduate attributes, which will be complemented by their work experiences – HE could be said to be preparing graduates for their second or third job in relation to sport.

SkillsActive is the organisation that has responsibility for identifying the skills needs of the active leisure industry. Table 3.1 identifies the findings from research by SkillsActive into the skill needs of the industry in England.

Table 3.1: Current level of skill required: leisure and other personal service (England)

Skill level	Advanced %	High %	Intermediate %	Basic %	Not required %
Leisure and other personal service occupations					
Communication skills	30	44	13	13	1
Customer handling skills	29	39	29	2	1
Team working skills	22	46	21	9	1
Problem solving skills	18	27	31	14	11
Technical and practical skills	14	30	43	12	1
Management skills	9	19	31	15	26
Numeracy skills	6	12	26	46	11
IT professional skills	5	0	6	18	71
Literacy skills	2	20	34	43	1
General IT user skills	0	1	8	27	64
Foreign language skills	0	0	6	11	83

Source: SkillsActive and Spilsbury Research (2004).

The results indicate that social interaction such as communication, customer handling and team working are seen as vital across the levels. The need for these skills within the sport sector has also been reinforced by the regional Sector Skills Agreements (SSAs) developed by SkillsActive to identify regional skills needs of sports organisations (SSAs are covered in more detail in Chapter 7). Encouragingly, a study by Sleap and Reed (2006) found that interactive skills are perceived by sports science graduates as being developed during their HE course, as well as problem solving skills.

The SSAs also identified the need for sport staff to have more initiative. This relates to individuals being self-motivated and solving problems rather than simply finding problems, and fits with the findings of research by Minten (2007) that the successful graduates were those who were proactive. This is an area that graduates could excel in, through developing new ideas or evaluating how existing activities and processes could be improved. Consequently, it is a way that an employer could see the graduate as someone who will 'add value' to their business.

The need for the practical and technical skills identified in Table 3.1 relates to a range of vocation skills and qualifications, such as coaching, sports leadership awards, first aid, health and safety qualifications, lifeguard and pool plant qualifications. These are skills that are generally provided by HE sports courses as extra-curricular activities and it is crucial that students take advantage of the opportunities to obtain them throughout their course.

For those not wishing to obtain employment in sport, a survey for the Council for Industry and Higher Education (CIHE) identified the key attributes required by employers from a range of different industries. These are listed below and, as can be seen, there are a number of generic attributes that are similar to those identified for sport:

- communication skills
- team-working skills
- analysis and decision making (which could be related to problem solving)
- literacy
- numeracy
- planning and organisational skills
- intellectual ability
- integrity
- confidence
- character and personality

(Archer and Davison, 2008)

However, as with sport employers, concerns have been expressed by employers from a range of industries about the development of employment-related attributes in graduates in general. Almost a third of employers perceived that there were problems with graduates' skills in communication, team working and problem solving, a quarter were disappointed with graduates' attitude to work and a third were concerned about their ability to self-manage (Confederation of Business and Industry [CBI]/Pertemps, 2006). Reports such as these have led to the introduction of personal development modules and activities within degree courses, and if graduates wish to enhance their employability it is crucial that they value and take advantage of these opportunities.

Reflection 3.1

For the skills and attributes identified in this section reflect on those that are your strengths and those that are weaknesses.

For the weaknesses, make an action plan of how you will turn them into strengths during the rest of your course.

How to enhance your employability

The first part of this chapter has established the reciprocal nature of employability in terms of the importance of employers utilising graduates effectively, but also the necessity for graduates to manage themselves and ensure they meet employers' needs. It is crucial that students use their time in higher education to enhance their employability as much as possible and this next section will provide practical advice on how to do that.

As part of the design of most HE sport courses consideration will have been given to developing student's generic employability-related skills and these will be identified in course and module material. A key finding of the research by Hansen et al. (1998) was graduates' inability to articulate and provide evidence of the development of these attributes to employers. Many graduates saw their degree as 'just a piece of paper' rather than thinking about how they had developed during the course, this meant that they were unable to sell themselves to potential employers.

Learning activity 3.2

Using programme specifications, course and module handbooks identify the skills and attributes your course aims to develop.

How do the skills and attributes identified match up with the employer needs identified earlier in this chapter?

Reflect on the extent to which you feel you have developed these skills and attributes and write down your supporting evidence.

Work experience

Many HE sports courses also include work experience option to further enhance student employability as most employers see relevant work experience as a crucial graduate attribute (Archer and Davison, 2008). It enables the application in the workplace of the knowledge and skills that have been developed in the degree, and provides the opportunity for graduates to develop specific vocational skills that would be difficult to obtain during their degree. There are a wide variety of ways of gaining experience, some of which can be undertaken outside of the course.

Work placements are often available in sports courses as formally assessed modules. They enable you to apply theory in practice and sharpen your analytical and critical skills, which, when you return to your course, enables you to see the relevance of what you are studying and will hopefully increase your motivation towards your studies. Placements enable you to develop a range of personal and professional skills and attributes, as well as maturity, self-awareness and also an awareness of workplace culture. There is 'consistent evidence that students who reflect on learning derived from work experience, and can make good claims to valued achievements, have an edge in the job market' (Little and Harvey, 2006). Placements also help you to decide what you want (or do not want) to do after graduation, and may even lead to a future job with the placement provider.

Learning activity 3.3

Explore the opportunities for placements within your own institution.

Using the reflective activity 3.1, identify the weaknesses you could overcome by undertaking the type(s) of placement activities offered.

Part-time/casual/vacation work: many students have to obtain work in order to fund their way through HE, however this work is also crucial in developing appropriate work experience. If you have basic qualifications in first aid, lifeguarding or coaching, then you should be able to find work in your local leisure facility as many sport employers require casual staff who they can call on at short notice, and this can often lead to more regular part-time work.

Activity camps abroad are also a good way of gaining experience, while also offering the opportunity to travel. If you undertake relevant, part-time work throughout your course, then you will build up enough experience to move up the career ladder after graduation rather than starting at the bottom.

Voluntary work: while this does not have the advantage of being paid, it does provide very real experience, developing practical, communication and problem solving skills. There are numerous opportunities for volunteering within sport, in fact research by the Leisure Industries Research Centre (2003) calculated that the number of hours of volunteers was equivalent to 720,000 additional, full-time equivalent workers in sport.

Sport is dependent on volunteers and it has been recognised that there is a need to develop their skills, this means there may be access to funding to help you undertake qualifications in return for undertaking a specific number of hours of voluntary work. Hansen et al. (1998) found that many students have a level 1 coaching qualification, but they had not gained the experience in coaching to support it, which puts them at a disadvantage – volunteering would address this issue. Many employees view volunteering very positively and it tells them something extra about you. Your HE institution may have a specific officer that will help you find voluntary work or you could access the following websites: **www.volunteering.org.uk**; **www.timebank.org.uk**; **www.vinspired.com**.

Other ways of engaging with employers

If you are not able to gain work experience, or if you wish to develop your links with employers further, then there are other ways of engaging with employers through your coursework. Many HE courses include project/research-based modules or assessments, such as dissertations or consultancy projects. A way of developing a relationship with an employer and showing the types of skills you have is to undertake a piece of research on their behalf, for example doing research on a new market/product or evaluating a service. This also increases your motivation as you are externally accountable and it helps you relate the theories you are studying to the 'real world'.

Learning activity 3.4

Look through the modules for the rest of your course and identify those that may provide you with opportunities to engage with employers/external organisations.

Managing your career

In the past, career management was perceived as something that was shared between employer and employee; however the onus is now on the individual as people no longer move up the corporate ladder but hop from job to job to further their career (Sturges et al., 2000). This is the notion of the 'new career', which maintains that careers are the responsibility of individuals not organisations (Cohen and El-Sawab, 2006; Sturges et al., 2000). Cohen and El-Sawab (2006) question whether 'a job for life' was ever really available to the majority of workers. This doubt can certainly be applied to sport, as studies have found that there has always been a lack of career structure within the industry (Henry, 2001; Houlihan and White, 2002; Yates, 1984). Consequently, it is essential to understand that your career is your responsibility; however, there are a lot of places to get help.

One of the findings of Minten (2007) and Hansen et al. (1998) was that graduates felt they had not received enough career guidance. Most HE institutions now include careers activities as part of their sport courses and students also have access to HE careers services. Unfortunately, the activities and services are often undervalued and underused by students, and it is often not until they graduate that they realise their importance. It is crucial that you begin to think about possible career options from the start of your course; as highlighted earlier in this chapter, a lack of clarity of career aims could impact on job fulfilment later on. Additionally, having broad career aims will help you navigate through the course and choose appropriate modules.

Arnold et al. (2005) have identified several steps relevant to a person making effective career decisions.

- *Self-awareness*: it is important to have an accurate appraisal of your own strengths and weaknesses, values, likes and dislikes. Your careers unit will have activities and tools to enable you to do this, however a starting point is Cottrell (2003). Chapter 2 of her book 'Skills for success' enables you to undertake an in-depth self-reflection and a simple careers questionnaire is provided in Chapter 8.
- *Knowledge of occupations*: it is important to find out about the area of work that you wish to enter. This chapter has only provided a starting point – two websites

that provide much more detailed information are SkillsActive (**www.skillsactive.com/resources/careers**) for sport-related jobs and Prospects (**www.prospects.ac.uk**), which provides information on a wide range of occupations, including sport.

Learning activity 3.5

A good way of finding out about careers is to talk to someone in that occupation. Carry out an interview with a person who is undertaking a career that you would like to do.

- *Putting self-knowledge and occupational knowledge together to identify career areas*: this is often difficult and it may be that there are still several occupations that may suit. This leads to career exploration, which is a long, progressive process of choosing education, training and jobs that fit your interests and skills. To some extent, you have already started the exploration by choosing your course and you should use the opportunities provided by your course to continue this.
- *Job searching* is the final step and is the short-term pursuit of a position that matches your financial and career goals.

Despite the emphasis on the importance of planning ahead and developing career aims, it must also be remembered that career development is inherently dynamic and factors such as chance, unpredictability of the job environment, the limits of knowledge at the point of decision making and the non-linearity of change will all affect career paths (Bright and Pryor, 2005). Therefore there is a need to continually review and adapt career plans to the world around us.

Review

This chapter has examined graduate employability in the sport industry and established that it is a complex phenomenon. It has identified that the non-graduate traditions of the sport industry mean that graduates' attributes are not always fully utilised and that there is a culture of working up from the bottom. In order for graduates to succeed in the industry it has been established that they require the vocational skills and attributes that meet the needs of employers to gain their initial job in order to build up experience. These can be developed by taking advantage of the opportunities to enhance employability provided within sport courses and undertaking extra-curricular activities. Graduates also need to identify their broad career aims from an early stage in their course, and be proactive and self-motivated in managing their career pathway.

Review of learning outcomes

What are the key factors that may affect the employability of graduates within the sport industry?

Outline the key steps you are going to undertake during the rest of the course to enhance your employability.

Outline how you intend to manage your career during the remainder of your course and during the first two years post graduation.

Further reading

Cottrell, S (2003) *The study skills handbook*. London: Palgrave Macmillan.
This workbook enables you to read and reflect on your personal skills many of which relate to employability.

Littleford, D, Halstead, J and Mulraine, C (2004) *Career skills: opening doors into the job market*. London: Palgrave Macmillan.
This book provides a practical guide to applying for jobs.

Useful resources

The following websites provide graduate jobs and also careers advice.

www.prospects.ac.uk
www.monster.co.uk
www.get.hobsons.co.uk
www.skillsactive.com/resources/careers
www.ukgraduatecareers.net

Chapter 4

Sports marketing

Debra Wale and Fiona Phoenix

Many people think that marketing consists only of selling and advertising. Those components, however, form only the tip of the iceberg. Marketing should be conceived as a process for satisfying customer needs. This chapter will introduce the reader to the principles and concepts of the marketing process and provide a set of practical tools.

Learning outcomes

This chapter is designed to enable you to:

- understand how (what is known as) the marketing mix may be used to plan tactical marketing campaigns to communicate products and services to new and existing customers;
- understand how contemporary marketing communications can be applied to sports businesses to help them gain competitive advantage;
- consider brand management, and its importance in the marketing process;
- understand the process of marketing planning;
- consider and evaluate the marketing environment to develop marketing choices;
- understand how consumer behaviour, segmentation, targeting and positioning help a business or organisation to focus marketing activity.

What is marketing?

The process of marketing has been developed around the idea that the customer is the most important person to the company or organisation. In order to do well, or indeed continue to exist, every company must work hard to retain its existing customers and to secure new ones. For an organisation to be competitive in today's society, it must start with the needs and wants of the market by undertaking customer research, rather than being led by internal perceptions of what products or services should be sold. Marketing is concerned with the entire business, as seen from the customers' point of view Drucker (1999).

Within the sports industry, marketing is used to communicate and sell the benefits of products and services to potential and existing customers. This might be in the form of a service (e.g. a forthcoming sports event) or a new sports product. An example would be a new design of performance shoes, where the aim is to make customers aware of features such as lightweight material which differentiates the product from that of a competitor.

Marketing does not take place only within private sector organisations. Marketing tools are also now employed in the public and not-for-profit sectors. This is especially so in the light of a blurring of boundaries between sectors caused by the need for sports organisations to account for themselves financially, the trend towards broader accountability, and the growth of privatisation and competition in the market place.

Sports organisations must utilise a toolkit of marketing concepts and theories which must be adapted to match the sports consumer, customer, participant or fans. The marketing environment in which the sports organisation wishes to communicate its product or service to in order to achieve the desired purchase behaviour should be analysed. Marketing tools are needed to maximise the sale of subscriptions such as memberships, or season tickets; to increase awareness of a growing sport or to differentiate a product from its competitors.

In order to succeed an organisation must attract and retain a growing base of satisfied customers. Marketing programmes are aimed at convincing people to try out or keep using particular products and services in order to maintain a strong position in the market place. Marketing is the activity of creating, communicating, delivering and exchanging offerings that have value for customers, clients, partners and society at large (Kotler and Armstrong, 2008).

Learning activity 4.1

Think about the following within the sport, leisure and physical activity industry:

- products
- facilities
- services.

Draw up a list of good/bad marketing campaigns – why do they stand out?

The marketing mix

The marketing mix is a concept made up of a group of factors widely known as the seven Ps, namely: (1) product, (2) price, (3) promotion (communication), (4) place (distribution), (5) people, (6) process and (7) physical evidence (when marketing services). Organisations need to blend these effectively in order to get the required response from the target customers. An effective organisation will strategically utilise elements of the marketing mix in the most appropriate way to communicate products and services to consumers.

Product

Figure 4.1: Diagram of a product
Source: Kotler et al. (2008).

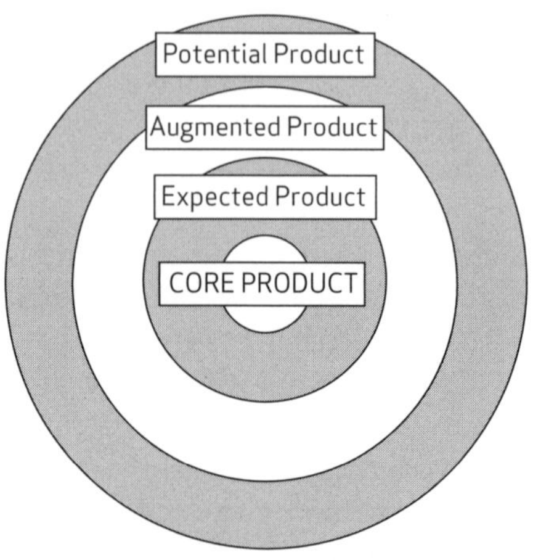

A product is made up of four facets (see Figure 4.1): core product, expected/real/ actual product, augmented product and potential product. These are explained in Table 4.1.

Features and benefits

When a customer purchases a product or service they are buying a solution to a problem. For example a gym membership may be purchased to aid weight loss: in other words, it is purchased as a solution to the problem of being overweight. Consumers buy the benefits that accrue from a product or service, rather than merely the features of products and services themselves. Marketers need to ensure that features and benefits satisfy consumers' needs, wants and desires and so stimulate purchase behaviour.

Unique Selling Point

The unique selling point (USP) is what differentiates a product from competitors. For example, the USP of Samsung's F110 Adidas phone (see case study 4.1) consists of its features (heartbeat monitor, step counter and MP3 player) and their associated benefits (notably that they enable consumers to assess their performance).

Table 4.1: Explanation of product facets

Facet	Explanation
Core product	The core product is the essential benefit or service the product provides for the customer; e.g. a pair of running shoes will provide comfort, speed and ultimately self-actualisation in achieving a lifetime goal such as completing the London Marathon.
Expected (real/ actual) product	The tangible elements of a product or service make up the expected product. They include: design, features, packaging, brand name, quality level (Kotler and Armstrong, 2008).
Augmented product	Service and intangible elements make up the augmented product, such as technical sales advice, delivery, credit, warranty, after sales service (Kotler and Armstrong, 2008). The augmented product is the experience of purchasing and wearing a particular brands sports performance wear and the associated service experience should the product be faulty.
Potential product	The potential product includes future product development, diversification into other product lines and updated ranges.

CASE STUDY 4.1

USP; positioning the F110 Adidas phone

Samsung launched an integrated marketing campaign in 2008 to back the UK launch of its F110 Adidas phone. The F110 system, targeted at fitness fanatics, features a heartbeat monitor, step counter and MP3 player. This was positioned as a rival to the Nike+ training system, which includes a computer chip that runners put in their trainers to send data about speed and distance to their iPod (Jones, 2008).

Product life cycle (PLC)

The product life cycle refers to the succession of stages a product or service goes through. Product life cycle management is the succession of strategies used by management as a product goes through its life cycle.

New product development stage

This first stage can be very expensive and risky. No sales revenue has yet been generated. Expenditure may not be recovered for a long time. Indeed, some products do not progress beyond the product development stage. It is essential at this stage to research target customers' perceptions of the product or service to ensure that it fits with their wants and needs.

Introduction

Costs are still high due to low sales volume. If it is a new product or service coming into the market this can mean that there is little or no competition. It is vital at this stage to watch for acceptance from customers. New products are heavily discounted and advertising is used to push the product to the customer. Growth is slow at this stage of the PLC.

Growth

The aim at growth stage is to build consumer preference by putting the product/service in the customer's mind. At this point costs are reduced by economies of scale, meaning that if larger quantities of products are produced, the cost per item is lower. At this stage the sales volume increases significantly leading to profitability, greater public awareness and hopefully loyalty to the product or service. If the product or service is popular, competition is likely to increase. For example, when the iPod became a market leader, Sony introduced their own version of the MP3 player in order to compete with Apple.

Maturity

A product reaches maturity when sales stabilise. Often other companies enter the same market with similar products or services. Marketing activities such as discounting or promotions are used to improve sales of these products. It may be necessary to diversify the product or bring a new updated version into the market place as each competitor seeks to gain market share. Costs can be very low as the product is well established in the market at this point. Sales volume peaks and an increase in competitive offerings will lead to prices dropping due to proliferation of competitors. It is essential to differentiate from competition and to focus on developing brand loyalty.

Decline

At this point in the product life cycle sales and profits fall. As sales decline it is necessary to decide whether to extend, rebrand or remove the product or service.

Boston Growth Matrix (BGM)

The Boston matrix is a chart created by Bruce Henderson for the Boston Consulting Group in 1970 to help organisations analyse their business units or product lines. The BGM is used to categorise a company's portfolio of products into market growth and market share. High growth rate may be defined as 10 percent or higher. High market share is defined as equal to, or greater than, that of competitors with category leadership.

The BGM comprises four categories of products: stars, problem children, cash cows and dogs.

- A STAR product has high market share and high market growth. These tend to be relatively new, fast-growing products. High market share and high growth means that it will be a top selling product. However, there is also increased threat from both current and potential competitors.
- A PROBLEM CHILD is a product that is performing badly at present, but has potential to grow considerably in the future, as indicated by the high market growth. The product's future can be uncertain if the correct marketing tactics are not utilised to gain more of the market share. An organisation should either invest heavily in the product or get out of the market altogether before losses are incurred.
- A CASH COW is a breadwinner, at least in the short term. The market growth is low, so the product may typically be in the last stages of the product life cycle. This at least means that potential competitors will be unlikely to enter the market. However, because it has high market share it will maintain a high income.
- A DOG product has a low market share. Market growth is low, so the situation is unlikely to improve. The organisation should discontinue such lines.

It is important to remember that stars and problem children products or services are in the growth stage of the product life-cycle. As a particular industry matures and growth slows, products or services tend to become either *cash cows* or *dogs*.

Price

There are a number of approaches to pricing. One or many of these methods may be used depending on the stage of the product life cycle, external market factors, and the rest of the marketing mix.

Prices may be determined by buyers, for example when choice is abundant and prices similar, buyers can force companies to discount. Alternatively, when there is limited product choice or competition, price premiums can be applied. They might, however, discourage repeat custom if the price is set too high.

Promotion/marketing communications

Promotion is the part of the marketing mix, which uses marketing communication methods to sell products and services to targeted consumers. The promotions mix includes advertising, merchandising, sales, public relations, direct mail and sponsorship. E-communications incorporates the promotions mix in a variety of electronic formats. Objectives of promotion could be to grow the organisation through increased sales or to create greater brand awareness. Alternatively, the objective could be to differentiate the product from those of competitors or to educate the market.

It must be remembered that it is not enough for a business to have good products sold at attractive prices. To ensure sales and interest in the product or service, the features and benefits have to be communicated to customers. Different types of marketing communication are described below.

Advertising

Advertising involves communicating a message to a target market through the most suitable channel that motivates purchase behaviour. Advertising techniques include e-tools and print methods. Advertising channels include media; cinema, television, internet, radio, print, information kiosks (touch screen), billboards: static and digital (see case study 4.2). Advertising communicates the brand image and personality to the consumer. Memorable adverts have used characters, typology, colours, personalities and music all of which reflect brand attributes.

CASE STUDY 4.2

Digital billboard advertising

TAG Heuer (TH) ran a four-day campaign on digital outdoor billboards in London. The advert consisted of six images of Lewis Hamilton wearing his racing kit and a TH watch. For this campaign the strapline was extended to: 'What are you made of? It's time to deliver.' The digital technology allowed time-sensitive messages to be displayed on the digital screens based on Lewis Hamilton's performance at the British Grand Prix 4–6 July 2008 (Anon, 2008, p13).

Relationship marketing

Loyalty schemes are ways in which companies build 'clubs' of consumers with similar traits and buying behaviour. Customers are rewarded with priority points, offers, early notification of exclusive deals, member-only promotional events, freebies and discounts. These personalised perks are designed to keep the customer loyal.

Public relations

Public relations (PR) is the practice of managing the flow of information between an organisation and its public. The practice of PR is planned around the core business activities of an organisation (in line with its mission, vision and values). In practice the PR role is a balancing act of providing 'good image' information and managing 'bad news' stories. It involves making sure that all activities carried out by the organisation, its intermediaries and stakeholders maintain the reputation of the business. External PR interaction may consist of putting out the right message about the organisation through communication channels such as the media, television or conferences. The London 2012 team used the handover of the Olympic flag as a PR exercise (see case study 4.3).

CASE STUDY 4.3

PR – London 2012

Team GB's success in Beijing has raised expectations for 2012. London was quick to build on the nation's 'feelgood factor' engendered through PR from the unexpected medal haul. It staged a heroes' parade and a free concert and celebration on the Mall (to mark the handing over of the Olympic flag to London) on 24 August 2008.

Sponsorship

Sponsorship is big business in sport. Sports personalities, sports teams and events provide opportunities for business relationships between sporting and non-sports related businesses (Chapter 13 covers sponsorship in detail).

Merchandising

Merchandising is selling a brand through producing and selling (or distributing free of charge) related products, which appeal to consumers' cognitive processes and induce buying behaviour.

E-marketing communications

The noughties (the term given to the years 2000–09) have seen an explosion of e-marketing spurred by a rapid revolution in the development of communications technology. The economic downturn in 2008 resulted in marketing departments scaling down and consolidating their marketing activity. When marketing budgets are tight, companies will use the cheapest most effective forms of communications to reach consumers. E-marketing can be very cost effective as packaging and distribution costs may be avoided.

Portable devices and WiFi

Portable devices such as the iPhone and access to WiFi have provided another form of communication. The marketing opportunity here is for companies to make sure that they are the search choice for consumers. In a sports tourism example, a customer decides to book tickets for a sports event as part of their holiday experience. They can use a portable device to plan, organise, book (including seat selection), route plan and find and reach the venue (door-to-door maps).

Search (engine) marketing

Search (engine) marketing is a technique used by brands looking to help customers find their products and services online faster and with less effort. The Internet is used by businesses to motivate customers and maintain consumer interest in their brands. The aim is to be top of the list when a user searches. Companies will pay a premium for this service, as it relates to increased sales and the ability to analyse consumer behaviour data (Fernandez, 2008). Another benefit for companies is the immediacy of availability; being in front of the customer just as the idea enters their head, and the element of gaining chance buyer behaviour, by being hit on randomly through the search engine. According to Fernandez the 'challenge is to provide interactive, well-designed, clever; engaging and preferably downloadable content' (2008, p37).

As mentioned at the start of the marketing mix section, the remaining elements of the marketing mix – people, process and physical evidence – focus heavily around the service sector, where customers are purchasing an intangible offering, therefore it is important to take other aspects of marketing into consideration.

Place (distribution)

The place component of the marketing mix covers not only the physical location of where a firm might choose to sell its goods, but also how it gets its goods to the final customer and what distribution channels it makes use of. The place part of the marketing mix involves getting the product or service to the target market, via the right distribution channels, in the right amount of time, at profit.

Distribution channels are the routes by which companies deliver their products or services to customers. Channels can be direct (i.e. straight to customer) or indirect, via a channel intermediary. The more intermediaries involved the more the potential for complications to arise in the supply chain. Intermediaries may be: wholesalers, ticket agents, retailers, distribution companies or the Internet.

From a marketing perspective, control of place (distribution) involves management of relationships within the supply chain. Many companies seek to control this by owning all the processes within the distribution chain.

People

The people component of the marketing mix relates to all stakeholders involved in the product or service during its life cycle. People are responsible for every element of sales, marketing strategy and activities. The ability to select, recruit, hire and retain people with the skills and abilities to do the job you need to have done is crucial. In the service industry, operations staff are the face of the brand, whether in person or voice, and need to be trained in customer service techniques relating to quality excellence.

Process (brand management/quality assurance)

This is concerned with the procedures and mechanisms by which a service is provided and managed: stages in the lifecycle of a product or service from conception to after sales. Brand management and quality assurance involve setting down standardised operational procedures for all processes in the lifecycle of a product or service and audits to ensure their management. Audits can be internal or external. Internal audits include operational checklists. External audits are usually performed by an external body and result in external accreditation of quality assurance standards achieved for individual facilities. Sports related examples include ISO 9001:2000, Green Flag, Charter Mark and Quest (www.sportengland.org). Quest is the UK quality scheme for sport and leisure designed for the management of leisure facilities; it defines industry standards and delivery (www. Quest-uk.org). Quality standards enable organisations to design, develop and manage processes in line with industry standards.

Physical evidence

This comprises the environment in which the service is delivered and any tangible goods that facilitate service performance. Customers look at the tangible evidence to make predictions of what the service quality might be like. This includes premises, vehicles, company websites, and appearance and behaviour of staff.

Learning activity 4.2

Choose a brand of sportswear and plot the products from their portfolio in BGM.

- Who is the target consumer for each product in the portfolio?
- What would be the best marketing communication method for each of the products you have plotted as stars in the BGM?
- What marketing activity could you consider for the products you have plotted as cash cows?

Branding

The following definition of branding may be taken as a standard:

> A name, term, sign, symbol, design or a combination of these, which is used to identify the goods or services of one seller or group of sellers and to differentiate them from those of competitors. (Kotler and Armstrong, 2008, p229)

Below we discuss a number of key concepts involved in brand management. Underpinning all such management lie brand values. An organisation needs to understand and articulate the values of its brand.

Reflection 4.1

London 2012 – the Olympic and Paralympic values

The Olympic and Paralympic Games are about much more than sporting excellence. Underpinning the Games is the philosophy of Pierre de Coubertin, the founder of the modern Olympic movement. These values are:

Reflection 4.1 continued

- Respect: fair play; knowing one's own limits; and taking care of one's health and the environment.
- Excellence: how to give the best of oneself, on the field of play or in life; taking part and progressing according to one's own objectives.
- Friendship: how, through sport, to understand each other despite any differences.

The Paralympics values are based on the history of the Paralympic Games and the tradition of fair play and honourable sports competition. They are: courage, determination, inspiration and equality.

(**www.getset.london2012.com**)

Brand identity

The basis of brand identity is achieving the same visual and consumer experience wherever the brand appears. It covers every aspect of the brand: signage, vehicles, architecture, uniforms, stationery and communications. Brand values underpin this corporate identity.

Brands often identify themselves visually through a logo; a graphic device that distinguishes a product or service. Colour and typography are used to increase visual impact and provide greater recognition. The Nike swoosh is a good example of a distinct typography that works alone. The London 2012 logo caused controversy at its launch in 2007 (see the case study 4.4).

CASE STUDY 4.4

London 2012 Olympics logo

The Wolff Olins designed logo was unveiled in June 2007 as the 'new brand identity, based on the principle of London 2012 being Everyone's Games' (Gorman, 2007a, p5). The emblem was heavily criticised:

> . . . commentators have been vying with each other to find unflattering comparisons for the 2012 logo, from copulating characters from the Simpsons, to a deformed swastika or unhappy echo of the MTV logo. An online petition quickly gathered 50,000 signatures before being closed . . . and the promotional video's flashing lights triggered epileptic attacks and was quickly pulled. (Stones, 2007, p22)

The emblem consists of four sections representing: access, participation, stimulation and inspiration. They culminate in the brand vision of Everyone's Games (Smith, 2007), the design incorporating London and the Olympic rings. It is the first time that the logo has incorporated the Olympics and the Paralympics in

CASE STUDY 4.4 continued

one identity, in an attempt to signal the message of social inclusion that London 2012 seeks in its legacy. Positive commentary on the logo has praised its 'contemporary' nature. A spokeswoman from Lloyds TSB, which is believed to have paid £80 million to become the first domestic sponsor, commented: 'The new brand identity captures the spirit of the Games perfectly. It is young, vibrant, innovative and really brings the values and the excitement of the games to life' (Stones, 2007, p23).

Brand personality (characteristics)

Brand personality refers to the mix of human traits attributed to a brand. This is often achieved through sponsorship of sports personalities whose personality offers their brand the human traits-characteristics that they aspire to portray (see case study 4.5).

CASE STUDY 4.5

Lewis Hamilton

In October 2008, Lewis Hamilton (LH) became the youngest Formula One World Champion. Tag Heuer (TH) who have sponsored Lewis since 2003, will reap the rewards in sales of watches (Gorman, 2007b). In a press conference held by TH halfway through the British Grand Prix in July 2008, the director said, 'there's no better story than a rookie who wins big'. LH portrays the brand characteristics – stylish, cool and daring – attributed to their watches and this helps to reinforce this sleek, expensive brand. Lewis is one of a portfolio of brand ambassadors (mostly sports stars) used to endorse different TH watches. Lewis is used to help the brand sell the Formula One watch to a young audience seeking similar aspirations.

Brand essence

A brand encapsulates the very essence of a business. It conveys the core values of the company, its ethics, its heritage and its people.

Brand attribute

Consumers have a choice when purchasing sports clothing. Brand attributes may cause consumers to select a product and, in some cases, pay a premium. For example, a branded football shirt may be 90 percent more expensive than a supermarket's own brand shirt.

Learning activity 4.3

Nike and Adidas

You will need to access the Nike website at: **www.nikebiz.com** and the Adidas website at **www.adidas-group.com** to complete this activity.

- What are the companies' brand values? How do they differ?
- What do the two companies do to reflect their brand values?
- What is the vision of each company (this might be their aim or goal)?
- Both companies chart their history in decades. How does each brand build on their heritage? How is heritage reflected in brand values?
- What categories does each of the brands have in their portfolios and how do they differentiate these in the market place (see section on segmentation)?
- Choose a product from each of the companies' portfolios which you would buy. What are the characteristics (features and benefits) of the product that appeal to you?
- How do the two companies market your chosen product? Are their communication channels the right ones to reach you? If not, how could they get you to buy their products (see the section on promotion in this chapter)?

Marketing environment

In order to successfully utilise the marketing mix it is essential for an organisation to be comprehensively familiar with the environment in which it operates. It is therefore necessary to know as much as possible about the organisation's competitors, target market, potential future market growth and the market in which it operates. This can be broken down into three components: internal, micro and macro environments.

The internal environment relates to what is happening inside the organisation (for example staffing, equipment, finance). The micro environment influences the organisation directly. It includes suppliers, shareholders, consumers and customers, employees and other local stakeholders. The macro environment includes all factors that can influence an organisation, but that are out of their direct control (see the discussion of PESTLE factors in Chapter 6).

In order to analyse the market environment research can be carried out. Tools such as PESTLE (see Chapter 6), SWOT (see Table 4.2) and Porter's five forces (see Chapter 6) are used to understand the factors influencing the marketing environment both internally and externally. A SWOT analysis can help a business to design a strategy that helps distinguish a business/organisation from its competitors. It helps to uncover internal factors (strengths and weaknesses). Strengths are the characteristics of the company and its products/services; weaknesses can be uncovered and eliminated by assessing what the organisation does badly in comparison to the competition.

Case study 4.6 on West Ham United Football Club illustrates how changes in the external environment can impact on a marketing plan, which may need to be revised to respond to change in environmental factors.

Table 4.2: SWOT analysis – examples from football clubs

Strengths	Weaknesses
• Sponsorship deals with market leading companies, e.g. Arsenal's partnership with Emirates Airlines. • High-capacity stadium allows record attendance figures: Manchester United's Old Trafford Stadium expanded to 76,000 seats in 2006. • 'Top 3' Premier League position for last decade, has strengthened the club financially. • Loyal customer base: season ticket holders. • Catchy advertising for a product endorsed by a player has raised profile of the football club overseas. • Long-term contracts with loyal 'star' players.	• Internal disputes between manager and the club's board members. • Late adopter of e-communication sales methods has disadvantaged company in relation to competitors. • Club finances tied up in poor performing players near the end of a five-year contract (dogs). • High staff turnover: manager and/or players changing constantly creates lack of team cohesion. • Club's striker has injury leaving him on the bench for most of the season. • Club has recently been relegated to Championship and reduced income threatens clubs survival.
Opportunities	**Threats**
• Potential of new products: high demand for latest product in range (this season's replica kit). • Manchester City's home ground 'Eastlands', the venue is a legacy of Commonwealth Games 2002 (stadium for the games which was converted to a football ground). • Increasing the market base: signing of a new international player opens up a market in the player's home country. • Celebrity wife's (WAG) high profile creates interest in club: e.g. Chelsea FC player Ashley Cole's wife Cheryl Cole as *X Factor* mentor. • Increased finance from Sky due to promotion to Premier League and coverage of games.	• Negative press for players' bad behaviour off the pitch may tarnish the brand. • Competition for the 'premier league' title. • Price wars forcing discounting and distribution of free tickets to fill stadium. • Exclusive TV rights to show games may reduce attendance at football matches. • Downturn in economy, 'credit crunch' reduces consumer spend on luxury items. • Competitors have superior access to channels of distribution: club's own TV channel e.g. Chelsea TV. • Players' international duties may reduce availability for home side's fixtures.

CASE STUDY 4.6

West Ham United Football Club

When XL airlines folded in September 2008 it left West Ham United with a difficult decision regarding its merchandising. Having just launched its 2008 season strip, it would be a relationship disaster to make its fans buy a newly branded kit at this stage in the season. West Ham took the decision to suspend all sales of replica shirts and removed all XL branding from West Ham United platforms, and players sported an unbranded kit while a new sponsorship deal was negotiated (Austin, 2008). In December 2008 West Ham found a new sponsor SBOBET and a new kit was launched. West Ham United rewarded its supporters with a replacement for the XL branded kit free of charge

Marketing planning

When an organisation has undertaken an analysis of the market, it is then possible to set marketing objectives to work towards and provide the first steps in the development of a marketing plan. An organisation's marketing objectives will be based around one or more of the options below:

- existing products in existing markets;
- new products for existing markets;
- existing products for new markets;
- new products for new markets.

All objectives set should be SMART (Specific, Measurable, Achievable, Realistic, Timed). An organisation's marketing plan should be based on a market analysis that will provide a strategic direction for the organisation, as explained in Chapter 6. Marketing planning involves analysis of the market, the choice of marketing activity, and its implementation through marketing campaigns in order to communicate products and services to target customers

Understanding customers and consumer behaviour

Part of the market analysis is to carry out research to gain an understanding of the desired target market or customers' wants, needs, likes and dislikes. A marketing orientated organisation will aim to provide customer satisfaction as a way of attaining its business objectives. In a rapidly changing marketing environment, marketing and sales strategies must change frequently. Consumer needs and demands evolve; new means of communicating messages and information are influenced by the business environment, including economic changes (such as the credit crunch in 2008) and rapid developments in technological advances.

It is essential that an organisation can communicate its products or services in a format that will stimulate the intrinsic motivators (needs, wants and desires) within the targeted customer in order to induce buying behaviour. Intrinsic motivators such as emotional stimuli may be targeted by communicating messages that appeal to consumers' senses and evoke a purchasing response because consumers are motivated to buy in order to reap the associated benefits (see case study 4.7).

CASE STUDY 4.7

Emporio Armani SS08 underwear campaign

Emporio Armani produced a marketing campaign for their SS08 underwear using David Beckham in a sexy pose that plays on his 'golden balls' nickname . When the advertisement was unveiled in Times Square, New York in 2008, traffic came to a standstill. The emotional marketing message of this communication is that consumers will reap the same successful benefits (sex appeal and high performance) as Beckham if they wear Armani underwear. His success and his ability to appeal to both sexes have helped him become the most profitable brand in sport (Gorman, 2007b). In 2007, Beckham is believed to have earned between £24m and £31m from playing football, sponsorship and advertising deals (Bold, 2008).

It is important to be aware that the customer (in the sense of purchaser) is not always the consumer (in the sense of user); therefore the marketing strategy may need to reflect different people's wants and needs from the product. For example, a children's football training session will need to take into consideration not only the children's wants of the training (e.g. to have fun, win prizes and learn new skills) but also the needs of the parent (e.g. the desire for a safe environment, qualified coaches, suitable timing of the session and reasonable price). Organisations have to measure not only how many people *want* their product, but how many people are *willing* and *able* to buy it. Marketers aim to influence demand by seeking to ensure that the product is suitable, attractive, reasonably priced and easily obtainable to target customers.

Marketing segmentation, targeting and positioning

Marketing segmentation, targeting and positioning are the key to a successful marketing campaign. They are explained below.

Segmentation

Market segmentation is the process of dividing various groups of buyers or potential buyers into more specific groups with relatively similar product needs. Undifferentiated or mass marketing techniques are becoming increasingly rare. It is essential to segment the market in order to better serve customers, compete more effectively in the sporting market place and achieve organisational goals

Organisations usually have limited resources to spend on marketing. Concentrating their efforts on one or a few market segments and targeting them gets the best return from small investments. Segmentation involves identifying those people most likely to buy the product or use the service by considering a number of variables.

These may consist of a number of types of variables: demographic, sociological, cultural, behavioural, psychological, and geographical.

The selection of segmentation variables involves looking at the attributes of consumers in order to match products and services to their needs. By understanding consumers, the right product can be produced and marketed through the appropriate marketing channel.

Segmentation methods

There are many methods of segmenting customers and the choice depends on which attributes match customers to the product or service which is to be targeted. Well used segmentation methods include NRS (see below), Acorn (see below) and MOSAIC: a global network of segmentation tools that classify a billion people worldwide (see www.business-strategies.co.uk). Sport England has developed sport specific segmentation classifications (see case study 4.8).

National Readership Survey (NRS)

The NRS method of segmentation uses the socio-cultural variables social class and income.

A Higher managerial, administrative or professional
B Intermediate managerial, administrative and professional
C1 Supervisory, clerical, junior administrative or professional
C2 Skilled manual workers
D Semi-skilled and unskilled manual workers
E State pensioners, widows, lowest-grade workers.

A Classification of Residential Neighbourhoods (ACORN)

ACORN utilises geographical and demographic variables (geodemographic) for segmentation. ACORN uses statistics from the UK national census to determine characteristics of people in their habitat. It allows marketers to target geographical areas, for example by direct mail.

Access ACORN classifications at: **www.caci.co.uk/acorn**.

CASE STUDY 4.8

Sport England market segmentation

In relation to sport specific segmentation Sport England has developed 19 sporting segments to help understand the nations' attitudes and motivations – why they play sport and why they don't. The segments provide organisations with the knowledge to influence people to take part. This work is part of a drive to get 2 million people doing more sport by 2012. Each segment can be explored at differing geographic levels. It is possible to find out what people's sporting habits

CASE STUDY 4.8 continued

are in a particular street, community, local authority or region. The market segmentation provides those working in community sport with insight into the sporting behaviours, and the barriers and motivations to taking part, among existing participants and those we wish to engage in a more active lifestyle. From this it is possible to infer which sporting interventions are more or less likely to be successful. Information on why people participate and what would make them participate more is also available. The segments identify the tone and type of message that different segments are more likely to be receptive to. This can be applied to the style of programme offered.

The profiles include information on the type of media different segments respond to. This is particularly useful if an organisation is starting a new marketing campaign. It also includes information on local radio and newspaper consumption. All of this information is summarised in the pen portraits which highlight the essence of each of the 19 segments. These are available from: **www.sportengland.org/index/get_resources/research/se_market_segmentation.htm**

Targeting

Having segmented the market, the next step is to determine how many and which segments to approach. Questions to consider include: What is the size and growth potential of the segment? Is there potential for good results, i.e. how likely are the segments to purchase the product or service? And what are the organisational objectives and resources (competences), in other words, is there the ability within the organisation to deliver? Therefore, targeting involves selecting the most appropriate marketing communication channels to reach consumers in specific segments. There are various different types of targeting techniques.

Undifferentiated targeting

In order to gain competitive advantage, a product or service is mass marketed at a lower cost than the competition. The product is usually a low-end, no frills product which is cheap to produce, has low overheads and can be distributed to a mass market at a cheaper price than competitors. Marketing tends to focus on promoting low-cost benefits e.g. supermarket own brand sportswear.

Differentiated targeting

Marketing based on differentiation focuses on matching features and benefits of a range (categories) of a brand's products and services to attract a range of customers to the brand. For instance, a company producing sportswear will produce a range of products for different sports, and these will be available for different age groups, sexes. Marketing spend is distributed between the different market segments on a cyclical basis. This might follow a seasonal approach, e.g. club football strips marketed at the beginning of the football season in August.

Niche (focus) targeting

Companies with a number of brands or product lines focus marketing spend on products capable of category leadership, e.g. Nintendo's Wii Fitness which is a new product within a heavily populated market. The Wii USP of encouraging people to engage in exercise while playing on the third-generation computer gaming system has enabled Nintendo to focus marketing efforts on the Wii Fitness range due to heavy attention being given to health and fitness issues both in the UK and globally at this present time. Promotion for this specific product is aimed at encouraging a niche target market of females who have not previously been the core market of users within this market to engage with their products and brand.

Learning activity 4.4

Go the Sport England web address (in case study 4.8), and refer to the segments 'Paula' and 'Ralph/Phyllis'.

- Compile a marketing plan to get the two segments participating in sport/physical activity.
- What 'issues' are there with each segment that would need to be taken into consideration?
- What products/services would you provide?
- Where would the activities take place?
- How would you promote them to these 'target' groups?

Positioning

Products and services may be positioned against competitors' offerings in order to establish a competitive advantage. A positioning strategy determines how companies want customers to think and feel about (features and benefits) of a product or service. Researching the target market is an important part of determining how to position a product. The opinions and perceptions that target customers hold regarding a brand must be explored to ensure that the right image is being portrayed in order to position the product or service effectively. Successful positioning puts you at the forefront of the minds of prospective customers.

When positioning a product, it is essential to take into consideration the product's USP, which differentiates it from its competitors. Once the company has developed a clear positioning strategy, it can communicate that positioning efficiently through the marketing mix.

Sometimes it is necessary for an organisation to reposition itself when the market develops, for example when competitors enter or exit the market, or when customer expectations and needs change. For example, Lucozade used to be sold as a product that people consumed when they were ill to help give them energy to feel better. When sales started to decline, it was repositioned into the new market of sports drinks by utilising elite athletes to endorse the product. Lucozade has since diversified by bringing new products: a range of sports energy supplements, such as gels, into this range.

Perceptual positioning mapping

Perceptual positioning mapping is a technique used by marketers that visually displays the perceptions of customers or potential customers. The position of a product, product line, brand or company is displayed on the map in comparison to the competition. When

Figure 4.2: Positioning map speed and distance monitors
***Source*: *Runner's World*, January 2009.**

plotting a perceptual map, two dimensions are chosen for the axis; the selection of these will relate to the perceived or actual strengths of the product or service. Figure 4.2 shows a perceptual positioning map based on Speed and Distance Monitors.

The data is from a *Runner's World* (2009) test of a range of monitors, which were rated in five categories: set-up, functionality, accuracy, value for money, and added features. On the positioning map, five monitors have been compared by the variables price and performance (based on the *Runner's World* poll). It is interesting to look at three monitors at the same price (Garmin, Adidas and Nike+). Garmin (the best rated of these three) could use the results of the *Runner's World* poll to get competitive advantage over its immediate competitors.

Learning activity 4.5

Draw your own positioning map for a product of your choice in the sports and leisure wear market. Plot different brands on the map to see where there are gaps in the market.

For this activity, search the Internet for sportswear comparison websites which rate products, or look at specialist magazines such as *Which?* magazine or specialist sports magazines like *Runner's World*.

Further reading

Important periodicals include *Marketing Week* and *Marketing*. The Mintel database is a good resource for market intelligence.

Chapter 5

Financial accountability in sports organisations

Caroline A. Wiscombe

This chapter introduces the sports manager to financial accountability through the exploration of sports organisation structures. It acknowledges that success for sports organisations is often not financially driven but stresses that the mandatory reporting of financial transactions is essential. The chapter also examines the issue of liquidity and cash flow as a vital part of the sports managers remit.

Learning outcomes

This chapter is designed to enable you to:

- define the business structures that underpin sports organisations;
- understand the role of financial accounting in a sporting context;
- explain the unique nature of accounting for sports organisational performance.

Introduction

Sport in the UK is a vital part of the culture and fabric of society. The organisation of sport can be profit making or non-profit making. Profit making organisations have a number of structures: sole traders, partnerships, limited liability companies (Ltd) or public limited companies (plc). These structures are based on both investment and risk. Accountability for sports managers in profit making companies is to investors and there is mandatory or compulsory record keeping in order to pay tax, but this is complicated by the nature of sport which demands 'success' for its teams and competitors. Accountability therefore may also be to 'fans,' participants, employees and other stakeholders.

Non-profit making organisations pervade sport. They are funded from a number of sources and sports managers are accountable for ensuring funding is spent wisely and produces effective results. For charitable trusts and voluntary organisations mandatory accounting may also be necessary in order to ensure compliance with legislation. Small voluntary organisations comply with a code of accountability which allows for the reporting of an annual position to their members.

All organisations report on a minimum of an annual basis, but for profit making organisations financial information may be given quarterly, biennially or annually on a non-mandatory basis to keep investors abreast of developments.

All organisations need to produce financial reports as part of their annual review and these can be analysed against key performance indicators (KPI) as measurements of organisational performance. They are not the only measures of performance and this is an anomaly of an industry where fans and spectators want to see wins, medals and titles that warrant expenditure while investors may be interested in increased revenues and profit. It is also an anomaly that where large companies exist in sports such as football, many large clubs do not make a profit.

CASE STUDY 5.1

Football, profit and the EPL

There are calls for prudence among the English Premier League (EPL) with demands that clubs are run on a sound financial base. Company directors have a fiduciary responsibility only to spend what they can afford and to protect shareholders' assets (the club). Some EPL teams, however, are looking at bankruptcy many financial accountants believe. For instance, Leeds United has debts of between £79 million and £103 million but still 'shops' for players who cost the club further millions of pounds. Accountability for EPL teams, however, is in winning games and climbing up the league to compete in lucrative European competitions. That cannot be accomplished without good players; they cost money and thus clubs go further into debt.

There is a mixed picture of industry needs in terms of financial accountability because of the differing focus between profit and non-profit making organisations. Financial accountability is not always the paramount reporting mechanism. Rather, the team performance, number of participants or spectators might be given more weight. Understanding sports organisations and industry structure clarifies some of the anomalies.

Sports organisations

Sport in the UK is organised through a network of relationships which affect even the smallest of clubs. This unique industry provides umbrella institutions such as the National Governing Body (NGB) for a sport, funded by memberships, government funding and other contributions, with a responsibility for both profit making and non-profit making organisations.

The industry encompasses private sector organisations, which may be very large public limited companies (plc), such as Manchester United Football Club, whose sport is governed by an NGB, but which is answerable to shareholders. In addition there are many non-profit making, often very small voluntary clubs and associations, more interested in just 'playing the game'. These smaller organisations sports are again governed by the same NGB. Voluntary managers are accountable to members, players, supporters and to the community in which they operate for team performances, spectators' and participants' enjoyment, or for their existence. However financial success may not be part of their remit.

The accountability of sports managers with regard to different targets (which can include financial targets, performance measurements, audience attendance or participation) will differ according to their place within the industry network and their funding and investment structure. The structure of the sports industry of private sector, public sector and voluntary organisations and their accountability is illustrated in Table 5.1.

Accountability

All organisations have to report on the financial viability of their operations. The structure and scope of the organisation will dictate the complexity of the financial information needed to manage the business both for external stakeholders (financial accounting) and for internal audiences (management accounting). Stakeholder theory suggests that the power each (internal or external) group holds will identify where

Table 5.1: Sports organisations – structures, funding and accountability

Sector	**Profit making sector of the economy**	**Not-for-profit sector of the economy**	
Structure	**Private sector organisations**	**Public sector organisations**	**Voluntary organisations**
Funding and investment	Funded by private investment, organisations vary in structure. They may be: • Sole trader • Partnership • Limited company • Public limited company	Largely funded by national or local government which for much UK sport now means allocation of lottery funding, e.g. Sport England	Largely funded by voluntary subscription, membership fees or donations, e.g. Walsall Ladies Hockey Club
Examples of accountability	To shareholders To 'fans' or consumers of the product To employees To government for taxation	To funding councils To the tax payer	To members To sponsors To patrons To spectators

sports managers focus their accountability structures but it is a fine balance (Lynch, 2003, p431). Newcastle United Football Club have suffered badly with stakeholder relationships with fans during the playing season 2008–09 from the release of Kevin Keegan as manager followed by poor team performance. While fans have a very vocal way of expressing distaste, their power is limited (Sky News, 2008).

Sports managers have a unique challenge in accounting for success to different groups of stakeholders. For example the management of Team GB Beijing 2008 were measured in the media, by spectators and participants, for the number of gold medals received. This is an extremely valid measurement and was taken into account when funding decisions were taken by UK Sport for the period 2009–12 *but* the media, spectators and participants did not check to see if those medals were gained through a well-managed financial budget. Despite the public view of accountability for non-profit making sports organisations, funding bodies will need to receive reports or accounts that show financial accountability. Most non-performance related accountability for sports organisations is linked to income or investment streams, which can come from members, consumers or spectators, government, shareholders, funding councils, patrons and sponsorship.

Learning activity 5.1

Choose a sporting organisation that interests you and find out where its income comes from.

- Can you categorise the income into the most important source of income to maintain the organisation?
- To whom is the organisation accountable?

CASE STUDY 5.2

National Governing Bodies – remit, responsibility and income

The National Governing Body for the playing of volleyball is Volleyball England. Expenses for NGBs are significant and for Volleyball England the largest proportion of its expenditure goes on the administration of the headquarters in which it is situated, improving performance, marketing the sport and organising and running competitions. As a body, it promotes volleyball and supports a host of, mainly voluntary, regional clubs.

In the year ending March 2007 the largest proportion of its income came from Sport England (66%). This had risen by 3 percent on the previous year and totalled £673,800. Other significant income streams are from competitions, performance and coaching operations, but, without the money from Sport England, a government-funded body, the organisation would struggle to cover its expenditure.

CASE STUDY 5.2 continued

By contrast the NGB for football, the Football Association (FA), is responsible for both large, private, profit making organisations, and a host of voluntary small local organisations. While the FA has some income from government funding it also has funds generated from broadcasting, the media and services.

As the governing body for the nation's most popular sport, the FA is responsible for promoting, regulating and organising the activities of 37,500 clubs (including 9,000 youth clubs), 7 million participants, 500,000 volunteers, 2,000 competitions and 45,000 pitches. This is in addition to the monitoring, training and regulation of 30,000 coaches, 45,000 referees and helping to develop programmes in 32,000 schools. The EPL is populated by some well known clubs such as Manchester United, Arsenal and Liverpool. Despite their size, the clubs are still subject to regulation by the FA.

In 2007 the FA's income was £237.8 million and the main source was the contract for broadcasting rights to televise games which is negotiated every four years. However, the FA is also made up of a group of companies which all contribute to income:

- the FA which seeks to promote the game of football;
- Wembley National Stadium Ltd which organises sporting and entertainment events;
- the National Football Centre Ltd.

Each of these companies contributes to the income of the whole association. Wembley stadium opened in March 2007 and, while 1.5 million people attended the 25 events held there in the year contributing to increased income for the association of £54 million, and £9 million in increased gate receipts, there are significant expenses which contribute to an overall loss in the period.

Payments to the game as a whole include prize monies, distribution of broadcasting rights income and tournament costs. This is in addition to funding provided for the Football Foundation, sport's largest UK charity.

The success of the FA provides continued support for 'grassroots' play in schools, youth groups and numerous small regional clubs that would otherwise be unable to remain viable. The FA receives some income from grant aid towards the major construction projects undertaken by the FA, which include Wembley Stadium and its surrounding areas. In 2007 Sport England gave funds totalling £78.2 million, the Department of Media, Culture and Sport (DCMS) £19.3 million and the London Development Agency £20.6 million. Further funds will be sought by the FA to continue to develop the National Football Centre, Burton upon Trent, which some may argue should be developed solely by the FA and its constituency, not through public funding.

These two NGBs could not be more different; one is very reliant on government funding for its existence while the other generates its biggest income from broadcasting.

Not-for-profit sector of the economy

The 'not-for-profit' sector of the economy includes public sector organisations and charitable or voluntary groups. Sport operations have a large presence in the UK not-for-profit sector and this makes them vulnerable to government policy and change.

Investment in sport during the 1970s and 1980s was not a government priority and many local authorities closed and sold off sports buildings and resources. However the DCMS, under Tessa Jowell, invested over £115 million in Sport England during 2007–08 in order to 'to improve the quality of life for all through cultural and sporting activities, to support the pursuit of excellence and to champion the tourism, creative and leisure industries' (DCMS, 2007, p2). Accountability to the DCMS on how funding is used focuses on participants, particularly among diverse groups, improvement to health, facilities created and spectator numbers. While financial records of funding are kept, the headline external accountability for projects is not financially driven.

Internally however the picture is very different. Not-for-profit sector organisations require a very detailed audit of the management of public money. Public sector organisations have often been termed 'bureaucratic' in their approach to maintaining financial records. In order to purchase a box of paper clips three forms may be needed to audit the chain of command that approved permission for the expenditure. It is difficult sometimes to accept this, but when dealing with public money the accounts must show that the purchase, no matter how small, is legitimately made.

Within non-profit making sports organisations, annual reporting and review often focuses on the results of the team, club or sport, looking at performance measurement against sport related targets. A good example to look at is the Annual review (2007) of the Badminton Association of England Ltd. The review includes team performances, tournament results and individual achievements – in total, a very detailed 53-pages accounting for the NGB's activity. Eight pages relate to finance and what is included has very little detail. That said, separate reporting processes will exist to provide funding authorities with a much more detailed financial review. But it is important to remember that funding bodies are not solely interested in financial indicators. A key part of accountability will include showing how many more participants have played the game or entered competitions compared to the previous period.

Voluntary organisations may have different accounting needs according to size and may be limited to an income and expenditure statement for the year, plus a statement of assets. Where organisations are part of a charity, however, accounting becomes very specialised. In requesting charitable status organisations have to undergo a rigorous applications process. They will need to satisfy the Charities Commission that they are *bona fide* and that all funds raised go to the charity they are supporting. Financial reporting of these activities is a specialist function and organisations will employ specialist auditors to monitor activity.

Private sector of the economy

Private sector business aims to make profits for the owners, who may be sole traders, partnerships or shareholders. Some sports organisations are so profitable they are bought and sold for their share value, such as Manchester United plc, taken over in 2005 by Red Football Ltd, a privately owned company, while other football clubs struggle to remain viable. It is interesting to note that while Manchester United fans were furious at the 'sell out' to an American based business empire, the contribution and investment made in the club saw positive football performances on the field. Fans of Liverpool were therefore not nearly as vociferous in their objections to a change of ownership when, in 2008, their club became the seventh EPL club to be owned by foreign investors.

To start up in any business an investment is needed. This investment is termed 'capital'. The capital purchases all the things the business needs to operate while leaving some cash in a dedicated bank account to help the organisation run on a day-to-day basis. This cash is termed 'working capital'. For a fitness business the capital invested might purchase the premises in which the business will operate, refurbish the premises by installing sprung floors, the gym equipment, showers, toilets, towels, drinks machines, food stocks for the cafe and so on; these we term the 'assets' of the business. The assets which are constant, such as the premises, are called 'fixed assets', those which are bought and sold, such as the food or drinks to stock the machine, the cash in the bank account and any money owed to the organisation are called 'current assets'.

In business terms, the capital invested becomes the worth of the business. The business is made up of all the 'tangible assets' that the capital bought, including 'cash left in the bank'. 'Tangible assets' refers to all the things the business owns which can be measured exactly in cash terms. The capital investment process is the same for large companies with multiple shareholders as it is for sole traders or partnerships. Thus the first principle for financial accountability is to show the equation that defines the business worth:

Capital Equals Assets, or Capital = Assets.

This is done through a 'balance sheet' and we will look at an example of this later in the chapter, but first we need to understand some other terminology.

The worth of the business is not the same as the 'value' of the business when it is sold. The value of the business includes 'tangible assets' and 'intangible assets'. Intangible assets can include an element of 'goodwill' plus other factors, such as skill, knowledge, reputation and future profits. 'Assets' are all the things the business owns.

The funding and investment to secure those assets puts private sector organisations into a number of different categories or structures (see Table 5.1). The different structures dictate the level of financial accountability. Sole traders and partnerships are accountable only to 'themselves' and their customers, as they are funded by their own capital. Their mandatory financial accountability is limited to the reporting of personal income to HM Revenue and Customs (HMRC) for tax purposes. Despite this the sole traders and partners produce annual accounts that follow key principles, the 'generally accepted accounting principles' (GAAP), in case of a review by the tax office.

Limited companies, which includes limited (Ltd) and public limited companies (plc) funded by shareholders, have different accounting responsibilities. Governed by the Companies Acts of 1976, 1985 and 2006, they are mandatorily required to submit annual financial reports to Companies House. Company Secretaries are usually employed whose responsibility includes compliance with the requirements of legislation, more details of which can be found on the Companies House website at

www.companieshouse.gov.uk. Organisational and operational size makes the production of legal documentation more complicated and therefore external auditors will be retained who affirm the accuracy of the information supplied.

Company (annual) accounts are limited in their value to external audiences as their very broad categories provide content distilled from the very detailed lines of sales, costs and expenses collected by the organisation's book-keeping system. For example 'income' listed in the audited reports for a sports organisation may include sponsorship, funding, ticket prices, donations, merchandise sales and so on. The inclusive category of 'income' would not provide the level of detail that managers need to plan, develop, control or evaluate. This is discussed further in Chapter 8.

Sole traders, partnerships, limited companies (Ltd) and public limited companies (plc) therefore differ in their requirements for mandatory financial accountability. There are also differences in the division of profits, taxation and the risks to the business entity. This is illustrated in Table 5.2 on page 61.

Learning activity 5.2

Your friend is thinking about starting up their own gym. They want to invest their savings and also borrow some money from the bank to ensure they have enough capital. They envisage that in ten years time there will be a minimum of 15 gyms, bearing their new logo. To do this they would have to have a number of shareholders investing in the growth plan.

- Use Table 5.2 to consider the risks to the friend. Which 'ownership' category would you suggest they start in?
- Why might that decision change in the future?

Financial accountability

'Financial accounting' is the branch of accounting that reports financial performance to external organisations. 'Financial accounts' is the term used to describe the sets of reports used which are developed using GAAP. Financial accounting is a historical record of the transactions of the business over a period of time, usually a year. For profit making organisations the accounts can comprise 'trading, profit and loss accounts' (or in some organisations the terminology has changed to an 'income and expenditure account') and a 'balance sheet'; for non-profit making organisations they comprise an 'income and expenditure account' and a 'balance sheet'.

The development of financial accounts is based on the collation of data that has been used to manage the accounts of the organisation. This process is called 'management accounting'. As opposed to the historical accountability produced in the financial accounts 'management accounting' is the branch of accounting which helps to plan the future of the business. The performance of the organisation is then controlled, monitored and evaluated against those plans. This is a key talent for all managers and is discussed more fully in Chapter 8. Management accountants will however use the historical records to help plan and forecast future performance.

Table 5.2: Differences in private sector organisations

Organisational structure	Sole trader	Partnership	Limited company	Public limited company
Type of ownership	One person; but does not preclude two people trading in this way.	Two people or more jointly raising capital.	Large groups of people coming together to invest in a company.	A company with limited liability that has over £50,000 of share capital and a wide spread of shareholders. The company can apply for those shares to be traded on the stock exchange
Management structure	Decided by owner.	Decided by partners; one person may manage the business and the other be a 'silent partner' according to skills and knowledge.	Board of control; elected directors who report performance to an annual general meeting (AGM).	Although boards of directors run public companies, shareholders own them. However, this can lead to a conflict of loyalties as managers pursue objectives that help their own careers. This has led economists to talk about a 'divorce of ownership and control' within public limited companies.
Investment	Capital from owner plus long-term loans.	Capital from owners plus long-term loans.	Investment is divided into 'ordinary' or 'preference' shares.	Investment is divided into 'ordinary' or 'preference' shares.
Payment	Drawings from business against original capital investment.	Drawings from business against original capital investment, by agreement between the partners.	Dividend on shares.	Dividend on shares.

Table 5.2: Continued

Organisational structure	Sole trader	Partnership	Limited company	Public limited company
Profit division	Equally among the owners, or reinvested into the company.	Equally among the owners, or reinvested into the company.	A dividend is paid to shareholders but, in addition, profits fund company growth.	A dividend is paid to shareholders but, in addition, profits fund company growth.
Financial reporting	Annually through self-assessment form.	Annually through owners' self assessment forms.	At least annually to shareholders; annually to HM Customs and Revenue.	At least annually to shareholders; Annually to HM Customs and Revenue.
To whom	HM Customs and Revenue.	HM Customs and Revenue.	(i) Shareholders (ii) Company accounts go to Companies House	(i) Shareholders (ii) Company accounts go to Companies House
Tax liability	Owner is taxed on their personal income.	Owners are taxed on their personal income.	Corporation tax	Corporation tax
Risk	No distinction between the business assets and private assets of the sole trader. If the business collapses the sole trader may have to sell part of their private assets so that the debt of the business can be paid.	No distinction between the partners' business assets and other private possessions. Collapse of the business may mean selling private assets, therefore if one partner invests more capital than another they may agree a higher share of any profit, so that they are repaid for the additional risk they have taken.	Owners are not asked to pay business debts from their private wealth. If the business collapses, the shareholders will be 'limited' in their liability, often to as little as a nominal £1; however, they may also lose their original capital investment, the share value and receive no return on assets.	Loss of control, and the share price fluctuations which accompany quotations on the Stock Exchange. Both Richard Branson of Virgin and Alan Sugar of Amstrad decided that having become plcs, they wished to revert to private limited company status.

Once the format is understood, the production of financial accounts is not onerous and sole traders may produce their own accounts, usually using a computer package, and submit, via their tax return, details of profit or loss. However accountants, who have a detailed knowledge of tax law, are usually employed to ensure that reclaims against tax payments are maximised.

Final accounts reduce the main headings of submission into broad categories; thus 'staff expenses' may include wages, pension payments, health insurance, training, staff conferences and so on. The detail which is absorbed in the broad category is vital to the management of the organisation but is of little interest to external audiences.

Larger organisations will employ book-keepers to collate the detail needed by financial managers to produce financial records. In addition, large private companies, charities and all public funded bodies will use external auditors to test the accuracy of the financial accounts that have been produced.

Accounting for 'income and expenditure' in non-profit making organisations

Non-profit making public sector organisations and voluntary groups exist to provide a service. They are not expected to collect large amounts of income which is not then used to promote the interests of the members, players, spectators and so on. However, it is expected that they do not make a 'loss' as this might make the organisation vulnerable. All income is listed and the expenses of the organisation subtracted to produce an 'income over expenditure' result. The document will be similar to that shown in Figure 5.1, which shows the format for a small sports club.

The format allows comparisons to be made across years 1, 2 and 3 on the performance of the club in achieving income that outweighs expenditure, showing where any differences or challenges appear to be causing difficulties and, importantly, encouraging discussion as to where future increases in expenditure or income downturns might cause problems. For a small organisation such as this, membership income will be vital to the operation. Often members will not want fees to rise, but increases in expenditure may mean this has to be considered. If small sports clubs can increase funding streams from sponsorship or fundraising they can prevent larger increases in membership fees.

Large public funded organisations will find it very useful to report on what would happen if income from National Governing Bodies, or other funding streams, were to fall in order to plan either to reduce expenditure or to find alternative sources of income. This is called 'accounts engineering'. It uses spreadsheets to produce scenarios based on past and future performance, or if funding or sponsorship streams were withdrawn.

Accounting for 'income and expenditure' in profit making organisations

Trading, profit and loss accounts (T,P&L) is the traditional accounting framework used in many profit making organisations. Some profit making organisations have simplified their accounts to and changed their terminology from T, P&L to 'income and expenditure'. The terminology does not change the core content of the reporting mechanism. Either term has an historical, mandatory reporting purpose in financial accounting and a future,

Figure 5.1: Income over expenditure account for a small sports club

	Year 1 £	Year 2 £	Year 3 £
Income			
Match fees			
Subscriptions			
Sponsorship			
Training fees			
Fundraising			
Insurance			
Equipment			
Interest received			
Annual dinner			
Total income			
Expenditure			
Insurance			
Pitch hire			
Training			
League fees			
Affiliation fees			
County membership fees			
Bank charges			
Fixture cards			
Trophies			
Equipment			
Coach fees			
Travel and transport			
Refreshments			
Referees' fees			
Tournament fees			
Total expenditure			
Income – Expenditure			

forecasting role in management and project accounting. In mandatory reporting the detail is reduced to summary headings and is prepared on an annual basis. In management accounting the record will be used to help forecast future performance and planning.

A limited company accounting record will broadly follow that illustrated in Figure 5.2 and is used to judge whether the company has made a profit, or a loss. There is some key terminology to explain before viewing the account in full.

Sales: this is the retail income less any sales tax (called VAT in the UK).

Cost of sales: this is the costs of the business which are directly related to the sale.

Gross profit: is the first measure of profitability and is calculated by sales minus cost of sales. In comparing gross profit from one year to another the gross profit margin is used. This is calculated by

$$\frac{\text{gross profit}}{\text{sales}} \times 100$$

and is expressed as a percentage.

Operating expenses: these are expenses used in managing the business to create the sale.

Operating profit: this is the profit of the sales of the business before any other expenses or income has been taken into account.

Interest income: this is created when a business may have investments, for instance in pensions or long-term savings plans that earn income. This cannot be included in sales figures otherwise calculations done to measure the performance of operating profit would be skewed.

Other costs: where costs and expenses cannot be allocated to the direct operation of the business they are included as other costs. If they were included in the operations figures they would skew the measurement of performance. For instance Sunderland Football Club's owners, Drumaville, changed the organisational structure of the club in 2008. A new chief executive was appointed, Steve Walton, and an international development manager. To make such high-level appointments costs money in recruitment and reorganisation and this is considered a 'one off' expense.

Profit before tax: the true performance of an organisation can only be seen after taxation has been taken into account. All Ltd and plc companies pay corporation tax and this is payable by the company. Sole traders and partnerships pay personal income tax on all combined earnings, which may be calculated on a number of business interests. Therefore sole trader and partner owned businesses do not show taxes on profits. Instead the total profit is allocated directly to the money owed to the sole trader or partnership.

'Profit' is the term used when the calculation 'sales less expenditure' gives a positive result. 'Loss' is the term used when expenditure exceeds sales. 'Break even' is the term used when neither a profit nor a loss is made. The layout of the income and expenditure account allows for accountability for both 'operations' through the determination of 'operating profit', as well as the company's overall performance, which may be affected by other income or costs not associated with the organisation's main business. This allows operations managers to understand whether the company's performance has resulted in its targets and objectives being met; this will be measured using 'ratio analysis'. The main ratio analysis, or financial accountability, applied to the profit and loss accounts concerns costs, expenses, profits and the return on equity.

Figure 5.2: An income and expenditure record for a limited company

	£	£	(Previous year) £
Sales Cost of sales Gross profit Operating expenses Operating profit Net interest income* Reorganisation costs** Profit before tax Tax on profit			
Profit for the financial year			

*Interest income is income made from the financial investments made by the business
** This company reorganised during the financial year and has included these costs as a separate item to show shareholders where monies outside the operational activity of the business have occurred.

Profit will be measured in terms of growth on the previous year, but also as a percentage of sales. Three key ratios are used to determine performance of profit against sales, cost against sales and expenses against sales.

(1) $\frac{\text{profit}}{\text{sales}} \times 100$

gives a percentage figure which can be used as a benchmark against competitor performance, no matter what the size of the organisation. (2) Costs and expenses will also be measured against sales using similar ratio techniques.

$\frac{\text{cost}}{\text{sales}} \times 100$

allows for effective accountability regarding the use of materials in producing sales.

(3) $\frac{\text{expenses}}{\text{sales}} \times 100$

shows how well expenses have been used to produce sales.

Learning activity 5.3

Look at an 'income and expenditure' account from a sports organisation of your choice.

Apply the three measures, or ratio analysis, described to see how well the organisation has done in producing sales from costs, sales using expenses and profit from sales.

Do this for more than one year and note any differences. Have percentages risen or fallen? Think about what this might mean for the organisation.

Further examples of ratio analysis for both trading profit and loss and balance sheet accounts is given in Chapter 8.

Balance sheets

The data set used to account for sales, costs, expenses and profit will not present the whole picture for any organisation in financial terms because it does not report on the assets, liabilities and capital held by the organisation. At any 'moment in time' an organisation, whether non-profit or profit making, will have a 'worth' that is equivalent to the investment of capital. Remember: capital = assets.

At first sports managers may not see the need to understand or know about the total worth of the company. As long as athletes win medals, or teams beat the competition, the operations of the organisation (training, coaching and equipment) may be seen as 'working effectively'. However, some aspects of the organisation's operational performance can only be truly judged if we know that the assets the business has purchased are being used as well as possible (especially where these were expensive to invest in). Another use for the balance sheet is to monitor the debtors position (those who owe money to the organisation) and whether the company is able to pay its creditors (called the 'liquidity').

For financial accounting purposes the balance sheet will declare a view of the company at a 'moment in time'. This means that everything the company owns at that moment is counted and given a value. Such counting of physical assets is called 'a stock take'. The company or organisation will also use the exact bank balance and lists of debtors and creditors at the moment in time to compile a true picture. In financial accounting this will be an exact science, in order to provide accurate and up-to-date information.

A balance sheet showing the worth of ABC Leisure, a sole trader owned business, is illustrated in Figure 5.3. Differences in balance sheets from sole trader accounts to those of limited companies will be in the make up of the 'capital' account. In limited company balance sheets this item it titled 'Shareholder funds' and will total up the shareholders' account, made up of share capital (ordinary or preference), dividend account and profit (or loss) account. This becomes the investment in the company (the capital) and thus balances with the assets (capital = assets).

ABC Leisure has a number of assets but also liabilities (liabilities is the term describing what a business owes). Assets minus liabilities will give net assets. ABC Leisure shows net assets calculated at £1.2 million in the year to 2007, a rise of £1.1 million on the previous year. While the company owes a lot of money, its trade creditors are listed as over £1 million, it owns a lot of stock and work in progress, listed as £835,900, which can be sold in order to pay those debts. How quickly it does so may mean the difference between 'solvency' and 'insolvency'. Finally the company is owed £675,900. Financial managers must collect this money as quickly as possible to help to create cash flow which allows it to pay its own debts. The speed at which this is done affects the ability the company has to pay its creditors, termed 'the liquidity' of the organisation.

Learning activity 5.4

Choose a plc sporting organisation that interest you and find their most recent annual review and accounts. Compare the profit and loss account, or income and expenditure account, and balance sheet for the organisation with the examples given here.

Learning activity 5.4 continued

- What are the names of the accounts being used?
- Is the organisation making a profit or a loss?
- Compare what the company owes (the creditors) with what the company is owed (the debtors). Is there any advice you would give the organisation about these figures?
- What is the organisation's worth? Is this less or more than last year at the same time?

Figure 5.3: Balance sheet for ABC Leisure as at 31 March 2007

	Notes	2007			2006		
		£00s	£00s	£00s	£00s	£00s	£00s
Fixed assets							
plant, machinery and motor vehicles	2		37,779			43,905	
Other fixed assets	3		8,696			8,696	
				46,475			52,601
Current assets							
Stock and work in progress		8,359			5,880		
Debtors and pre-payments		6,759			6,759		
Cash in hand		2,252			1,912		
			17,370			14,551	
Current liabilities							
Trade creditors/ accruals		11,322			7,533		
Loans and overdrawn bank accounts		25,629			45,647		
Other liabilities		14,830			12,916		
			51,781			66,096	
Net current liabilities				(34,411)			(51,545)
Net assets				12,064			1,056
Capital account							
Balance at start of the period				1,056			25,864
Net profit				70,176			23,697
Drawings				(59,168)			(48,505)
				12,064			1,056

Annual review, reports and analysis

Annual reviews and reports are provided for all sports organisations but the areas of detail will differ according to stakeholder needs. Reports for sports organisations will account for more than just financial results. Participants, team performances, competitions entered and won, spectator numbers and volunteers employed will all provide data that can become key performance indicators for sports organisations.

That aside, all organisations will report on their financial performance because accounting for the use of monies, particularly when these are supplied by external sources, is extremely important. Small voluntary organisations may provide summary financial data which covers one sheet of paper, while a large plc will report its financial data over many pages and provide in-depth analysis of performance.

Financial accounts contributing to annual reports are the 'income and expenditure account' or 'trading, profit and loss accounts' and the 'balance sheet'. In some organisations a collated cash flow will be provided that reports on how money has come in and out of the business. This would be particularly important if liquidity seems to be an issue. Shareholders or funding councils would need to know that the organisation is in a strong position to plan for cash moving in and out of its business.

For large organisations annual reviews contain full financial information with an executive summary providing key highlights. Those organisations that are funded by public money or are plcs will publish their annual review via their website or by issuing documentation to interested parties on request. Limited companies that are solely funded by private investment do not need to publish financial information; however, this is readily available to interested parties via the Companies House website for a very nominal fee. Sole traders and partnerships do not usually publish their financial information.

Return on investment (ROI)

Profit making organisations are expected to make fiscal returns to investors and these are reported within the annual review. How these are judged varies according to the investment. Some investors will measure the profit against their investment, this is termed 'return on equity' (ROE). As long as the ROE exceeds that which can be gained from leaving monies in a bank or other financial institution they are content. Other investors will be interested in the change in share price of the organisation on the stock market and their earnings from the stock holding. This is termed 'earnings per share'. Shareholders have an interest in the monies the company pays to them against what the ROE has been. This is termed the 'dividend'. Not all ROE is paid to shareholders in dividends in order to hold cash for future company investments.

However, many investors in sports organisations are much more sanguine and invest for the 'love of the sport'. This is particularly well illustrated by celebratory investment into the funding of English football clubs, with Delia Smith, a TV cook investing in Norwich City and Elton John, the pop star, investing in Watford.

Financial returns are not the raison d'être for non-profit making organisations, therefore substantial financial ROI will be incongruent. ROI analysis is illustrated in Table 5.3.

Table 5.3: Return on investment analysis

Area of investigation	Profit making organisation	Non-profit making organisation
Return on investment	Return on investment (ROI) Return on equity Return on common equity Earnings per share Dividend on yield equity Price/earnings ratio	Non-financial returns

Review

This chapter has examined structures of sports organisations and the differences that result in regard to accountability, particularly financial accountability. These differences can be mandatory and non-mandatory. Business structures have been defined, along with the type of investment needed and the risks associated with their liquidity. The final consideration is the reporting mechanisms used for annual review. Sports organisations will focus on a number of key performance indicators to do with the sport. However, any annual review will not be complete without both an 'income over expenditure statement' or 'trading, profit and loss account' and 'balance sheet'. Financial performance can be measured using the financial accounts supplied using a series of ratio analyses. The importance of such analysis varies in accordance with the company's mission however, some indicators are vital for the organisation. These include liquidity and cash flow. Ratio analysis is examined further in Chapter 8.

Review of learning outcomes

Investigate a sports organisation of your choice.

- Define the business structures underpinning the organisation. Is it a profit or non-profit organisation? Is it in the voluntary sector? If profit making, what is its structure; sole trader, partnership, limited company or plc?
- To whom must the organisation report on its financial situation? Is this a mandatory or non-mandatory requirement?
- What are the main factors reported on in the annual review of your chosen organisation? Are these mainly financial or mainly non-financial?

Further reading

To understand the sports and leisure industry in the UK read:

Torkildson, G (2005) *Leisure and recreation management*. 5th edition. Abingdon: Routledge.

To understand accounts and the accounting process read:

Dyson, JR (2004) *Accounting for non-accounting students*. 6th edition. London: Pitman.

McKenzie, W (2003) *The Financial Times guide to using and interpreting company accounts*. 3rd edition. London: FT Prentice Hall.

Millichamp, AH (2000) *Finance for non-financial managers*. 3rd edition. London: Continuum.

To understand how sports organisations are financed read:

Wilson, R and Joyce, J (2008) *Finance for sport and leisure managers: an introduction*. Abingdon: Routledge.

To enjoy more on accounts structures read:

Wiscombe, C. A. (2009) Financial awareness for travel operations management in Robinson, P. (ed.) *Travel operations management*. Oxford: CABI.

Chapter 6

Strategic management

Crispin Dale

This chapter explores the process of strategic management as it applies to organisations operating in the sport management industry. The chapter will introduce and discuss the individual elements of strategic management as a business function. Examples from the sports industry will be used to illustrate points made and the activities and case studies will assist you in understanding the application of the theoretical concepts and models.

Learning outcomes

This chapter is designed to enable you to:

- understand what is meant by strategy;
- explain the different elements of the strategic management process;
- evaluate the application of strategic management concepts and theories to sports organisations.

Introduction

'Strategy' is a diverse term that can mean a variety of different things depending upon the context in which it is applied. The term strategy originally emanated from the Greek word '*strategos*' which translates as army (*stratos*) and leading (*ego*). In this respect, strategy is used to consider how one army can defeat the opposition by displaying greater force and better military tactics on the battlefield. The term 'strategy' therefore has a number of military connotations and much of the language that is associated with the term has emerged from this broad interpretation. In an organisational context, strategy is often used to describe the process in which the enterprise will be engaged when it competes in a given industry or marketplace. There are many definitions of strategy and the extent to which these definitions are relevant in a sporting context should be examined.

Learning activity 6.1

Read the following definitions of strategy and answer the questions.

(A) Strategy is the direction and scope of an organisation over the long term which achieves advantage in a changing environment through its configuration of resources and competences with the aim of fulfilling stakeholder expectations (Johnson et al., 2008).
(B) Corporate strategy can be described as the identification of the purpose of the organisation, and the plans and actions to achieve this purpose (Lynch, 2005).
(C) Strategy is the means by which individuals or organisations achieve their objectives (Grant, 2008).

What do these definitions have in common? What words and expressions are similar in each of them?

How relevant are these definitions to sport organisations and enterprises? Write your own definition about what strategy is within a sporting context.

Strategy in sport

Though it has been acknowledged that a range of definitions on strategic management exist, for the purposes of this chapter a definition of strategy as it applies to sport is provided:

> Strategy is the focus of the sports organisation or enterprise towards a chosen direction based upon factors influencing the external environment, and the maximisation and implementation of the organisation's resources and capabilities so as to gain a competitive advantage or fulfil a service need.

Mintzberg and Walters (1985) distinguish between deliberate and emergent forms of strategy. Deliberate strategies are based upon a rational intention. An organisation may decide to pursue a particular direction and will proceed through a number of logical steps in the devising and implementation of the strategy. In comparison, the emergent strategy is based upon the organisation learning from external and internal factors and from the actions of those from within the business. The organisation, therefore, has to be flexible towards change, so as to enable it to adapt to strategies as they may emerge.

Reflection 6.1

If we consider Formula 1 (F1) motor racing, each team will develop a race strategy that enables one of their drivers to challenge for the F1 world championship. The race strategy will be based upon a number of factors. First, the team will need to understand the environmental conditions at the race that may impact upon driver

Reflection 6.1 continued

and car performance. This will include the type of circuit, the weather conditions, if the race is during the day or night and the total number of laps raced. Second, the opposing F1 teams' strengths and weaknesses need to be identified. What kind of skills and abilities do the other drivers have and are their cars equipped with superior technology or design? Third, the actual race strategy will be devised. This will be based upon what has emerged from the preceding analysis of the environment, the opposing race teams' strengths and weaknesses, and the respective grid positions of the drivers on the track. The strategy will include the type of tyres used and the amount of fuel in the car at the beginning of the race. Fourth, the F1 team needs to implement the strategy. In an emergent situation the F1 team would adapt its strategy so as to take advantage during the race. For example, if a crash occurred and the safety car was brought out this may influence the team's decisions on the timing of pit stops so as to capitalise on race positions. Finally, following the completion of the race, the strategy will be evaluated in preparation for future races.

What has been described is referred to as the strategic management process. This is a process that enables an organisation to develop a strategy and consists of a number of different stages as outlined in Figure 6.1. Each of these stages as they relate to different sports contexts will be discussed further.

Figure 6.1: The strategic management process (adapted from Henry, 2008)

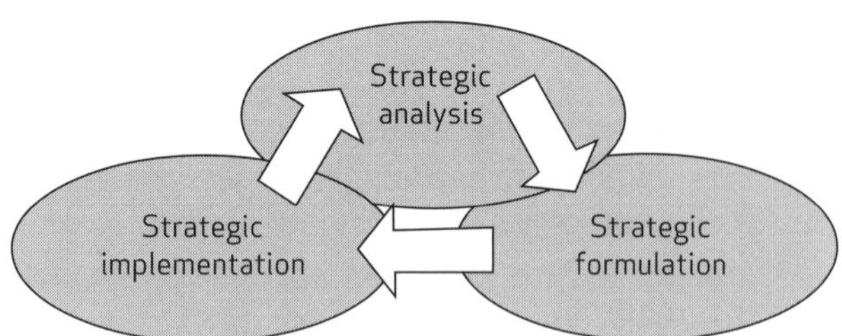

Strategic analysis

Definition: strategic analysis is the process by which sport enterprises survey the external environment so as to understand factors that may pose both opportunities and threats to the organisation.

The external environment can be analysed from two interrelated perspectives; the macro environment and the micro environment. The macro environment analyses the broad external environment and includes political, economic, social, technological, environmental and legal factors. This is often referred to as a PESTLE analysis and each of these factors will influence the strategic actions of the sports organisation. By analysing these factors the sports enterprise can take advantage of any opportunities and circumvent any threats.

Political factors can include governmental policies on sport participation. For example, the 'social inclusion' agenda, which aims to renew communities through sporting activity, has influenced governmental policy on sport for some time. Economic factors such as an individual's personal disposable income, which is affected by movements in interest rates and taxation, can impact upon expenditure on sports related activities and events. Social factors, including rising levels of obesity, particularly among those under 16 years of age, has meant an increased focus on providing sporting opportunities.

Technological factors such as new sport and fitness equipment innovations mean that gyms and fitness providers constantly have to keep their facilities up to date. The emergence of substitute sports related products such as the Nintendo Wii Fit and fitness related DVDs that have resulted from technological innovations also have an impact upon sports providers. Case study 6.1 outlines a health and fitness organisation that has exploited these social and technological factors as opportunities and positioned itself to target a growing market.

CASE STUDY 6.1

Shokk® Ltd

Shokk® is a youth health and fitness concept that targets 5–18-year-olds. It has representation in Europe, the Middle East, Asia and the Americas. Shokk® has developed equipment that appeals to a younger generation and is designed to meet their specific health and fitness needs. It states its aim as creating an exciting and stimulating environment to ensure young people are engaging in a positive physical activity experience. The concept of the brand, with a street based logo and black and orange colours which adorn their equipment and merchandise, appeals to a younger generation who may not participate in traditional fitness clubs and gyms. The gyms are equipped with advanced hi tech equipment including dance mats, running and weight training machines and are tailored specifically to the physical requirements of the target age group.

Source: www.shokk.co.uk

Environmental factors such as climate change have encouraged many sports enterprises to consider their energy policies as a means of reducing their carbon emissions in addition to offsetting costs. It is crucial for sports enterprises to comply with the relevant legislation, for example, health and safety legislation are, to ensure that participants and staff are protected against any possible risks to themselves. Employees are also protected by employment legislation and working time directives.

When analysing the macro environment it should be understood that not all factors will have the same significance for the organisation and impact upon it. It is therefore necessary to distinguish the extent to which they may impact upon the sports enterprise and thus what priority each factor should be given.

Learning activity 6.2

The PESTLE factors discussed are shown in Table 6.1. Select a sports organisation and identify further factors that are currently impacting upon it from the external macro environment. Information on the factors can be found from a variety of sources, including news based feeds, trade journals, market intelligence data and so on. When identifying the factors consider which of them may be opportunities and which may be threats. Identify the factors which should be of the highest priority for the sports organisation to consider.

Table 6.1: PESTLE factors

	Opportunities	**Threats**
Political	Social inclusion policies and sporting activity	
Economic		Recession
Social	Rising obesity levels	
Technological		Home-based fitness technologies (e.g. Wii Fit, fitness DVDs)
Legal		Health and safety legislation Working time directives
Environmental	Climate change	

The micro environment of the sport enterprise is made up of its industry sector(s), markets, competitors and industries. This is the immediate environment of the organisation and will impact upon its potential to compete alongside other sport related enterprises. In this respect, the sports manager needs to be aware of who the organisation's competitors are, where are they located, their strengths and weaknesses and, in terms of advantages, where the organisation is positioned relative to competitor offerings.

A model that can be used to further understand the micro environment is Porter's (1980) model of competitive structural analysis (which is alternatively known as the five forces model). The model provides an understanding of the competitive forces at play within an industry sector. According to Porter there are five competitive forces that influence competition within a sector. It is the collective strength of these forces which determines the profit potential of the sector. By determining the relative importance of each of the forces, the organisation can position itself to take advantage of opportunities and overcome any threats. The five forces are outlined below.

Threat of new entrants

A number of barriers can prevent new entrants from entering a sector. For example, if someone decides to open an athletics club they would need sufficient capital to acquire the facilities and operate the club. They would also need to be able to access channels of distribution to market their goods and services. The extent to which they could take advantage of economies of scale when purchasing equipment may also act as a barrier. Other factors, including the extent to which the athletics club would be able to differentiate its services from those of its competitors and the degree of government regulation in the industry, would also act as barriers.

Power of suppliers

Suppliers have power within an industry if other suppliers and substitutes are few, the costs of switching to alternative suppliers are high, there is the threat of forward integration from suppliers or the suppliers' products are differentiated. Sports product providers such as Nike can wield power over retailers due to the differentiated brand values that they have developed and the demand this generates from customers for their products.

Power of buyers

Buyers have power if they are concentrated in number, they are able to switch easily between alternative sellers, there is the threat of backward integration or products are undifferentiated. The buyer power of football fans is often perceived as being very low due to their loyalty towards a particular club and the high switching costs involved if they were to support another team. Football clubs can therefore charge prices for tickets and merchandise that will ultimately generate demand from the team's loyal fan base.

Threat of substitutes

The threat of substitutes occurs when an alternative good or service is provided that can satisfy the same need. Substitute goods and services are threatening when the switching costs for buyers are low and there is a high propensity for the buyer to purchase substitute products.

Reflection 6.2

The Wii Fit was released by Nintendo in 2008 and has sold over 5 million units worldwide since its release. The Wii Fit is a static balance board that acts as an attachment to the Nintendo Wii games console. It can be used for a number of sport related activities including yoga, strength training, aerobics and balance games. The Wii Fit tracks the user's performance and produces an activity log of their progress. The Wii Fit can be seen as a substitute for participation in the sporting activities that can be replicated on the device and which can be done in the comfort of one's own home.

Competitive rivalry

This is the central force of the model. The amount and intensity of competition is influenced by the amount, size and diversity of competitors, the rate of industry growth, and the relative exit and entry barriers to an industry. When a large number of competitors are competing within a market or industry, it is often referred to as being saturated. This means that the industry has peaked in terms of sales growth and there is no more scope for competitors to enter the marketplace. This can significantly influence the state of competition in an industry, where a shakeout of competitors may occur. This may take the form of withdrawals by competitors from the marketplace or the consolidation of the industry through mergers and acquisitions.

CASE STUDY 6.2

The sports fashion industry

From the mid to late 1990s the sports clothing and footwear market grew rapidly. Large fashion retailers such as Sports World (now known as Sports Direct) entered the market and expanded aggressively, growing from 100 to 300 stores. Sports World provided heavily discounted branded and replica sportswear which provided a major challenge to other sports fashion retailers. However, stagnating sales and falling prices led to a period of consolidation in the industry during 2005 and 2006. The competitive market place shrank from eight to three main sports fashion operators; Sports Direct, JJB Sports and John David Group. Competitive rivalry is further complicated by the Sports Direct group having strategic investments in Blacks Leisure Group and John David Group. In a fiercely competitive marketplace, which is compounded by falling consumer spending, sports fashion retailers have had to position themselves so as to more clearly differentiate their offerings to customers.

Learning activity 6.3

Choose a sport organisation or enterprise and analyse the five competitive forces in the industry or sector in which it competes.

To what extent is there the threat of new entrants? To what extent do suppliers and buyers have power? To what extent is there the threat of substitutes? What factors influence rivalry between competitors?

How well is the sports organisation positioned to take advantage of the competitive forces that are influencing the industry?

Strategic formulation

Definition: Strategic formulation is the decisions that sports organisations make when determining their overall strategic direction.

Once the sports enterprise has analysed the external environment it should know the priority of the factors which may have an impact upon the business and how well it is positioned to exploit any opportunities or counter any threats. From this analysis the sports enterprise can consider the various strategic choices that it can make in pursuit of a particular strategic direction. When ascertaining what the direction should be, the sports enterprise should develop an overall mission for the business. This often comes in the form of a statement which, according to the Ashridge mission model (Campbell and Tawady, 1990), should reflect what the overall purpose of the organisation is and why the company exists; the values of the firm and what it believes in; the behaviour standards and overall philosophy of the organisation; and the strategy and how the organisation positions itself relative to competitors. In addition, the mission of the organisation needs to consider the needs and expectations of the key stakeholders of the business, and also needs to clearly identify the organisation's source of competitive advantage. An example mission statement is illustrated in Reflection 6.3.

Reflection 6.3

Sports Coach UK is a charitable organisation and is the lead agency for sports coaching in the UK. The organisation is tasked with creating a world-leading coaching system by 2016. The Sports UK mission statement is as follows:

> Sports Coach UK is dedicated to guiding the development and implementation of a coaching system, recognised as a world leader, for all coaches at every level in the UK. We will work with our partners to achieve this by promoting:
>
> - professional and ethical values;
> - inclusive and equitable practice;
> - agreed national standards of competence as a benchmark at all levels;
> - a regulated and licensed structure;
> - recognition, value and appropriate funding and reward;
> - a culture and structure of innovation, constant renewal and continuous professional development.
> - The Sports Coach UK mission statement will be adjusted in line with the Group Strategy.

Source: **www.sportscoachuk.org**

Learning activity 6.4

Search the internet for mission statements of sports organisations. Compare and contrast the different mission statements.

- What are the strengths and weaknesses of the different mission statements?
- To what extent do the mission statements satisfy stakeholder needs and expectations?

Achieving competitive advantage

> Definition: Competitive advantage is the advantage one firm has over another in a given marketplace or industry.

When determining the strategic choice for the business and how it can obtain competitive advantage, it should be noted that there are different schools of thought. This includes the competitive positioning school of thought and the resource based view of strategy. The competitive positioning school of thought contends that the basis of strategy making should be derived from how the organisation positions itself relative to others in the competitive environment. Porter (1985) offers three generic strategies which provide the basis for an organisation gaining competitive advantage. These include cost, differentiation and focus. Porter argues that these strategies can either be broad or narrow in scope focusing either on the whole market or a particular sector of the market (see Figure 6.2).

First is cost leadership. An organisation is able to gain cost leadership when it becomes the lowest cost producer in the industry and thus gains higher profits. Cost leadership can be achieved through gaining economies of scale, reducing the costs of resource inputs or having more efficient distribution systems. Even though all competitors may attempt to attain an advantage through lower costs, it should be noted that there can only be one true cost leader.

Second is differentiation. This is based upon the sports enterprise offering something unique and selling it at a premium price. However, for the customer to pay a premium price, the product or service needs to offer added value which is perceived by customers as being superior to competitor's offerings. Sports organisations can achieve differentiation by providing, for example, better quality service, better design and brand reputation.

The sports organisation may decide that the strategies of cost and differentiation should be focused on a particular sector of the market; hence the strategy may focus on cost or on differentiation. The sector of the market may be based upon demographic variables such as age, gender or lifestyle status. Cost focus is when the sport enterprise

Figure 6.2: Generic competitive strategies (adapted from Porter, 1985)

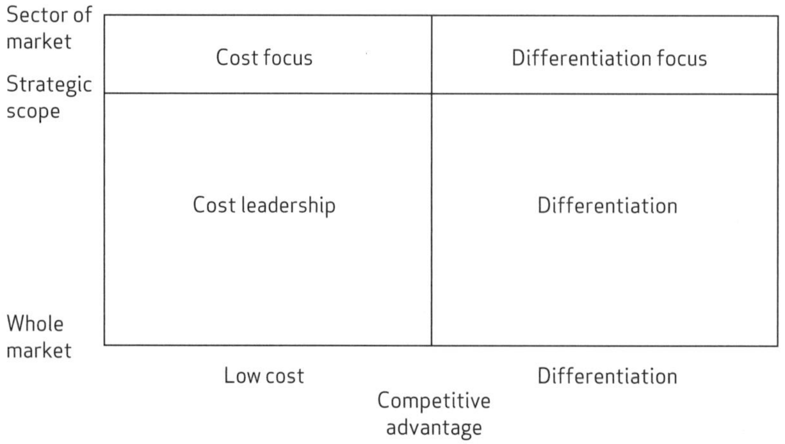

Strategic scope		
Sector of market	Cost focus	Differentiation focus
Whole market	Cost leadership	Differentiation
	Low cost	Differentiation
	Competitive advantage	

focuses on a sector of the market which may be price sensitive, whereas differentiation focus is when the sports enterprise differentiates the product to meet the needs of a niche market.

The sports enterprise needs to be clear about which strategy it is following otherwise, according to Porter, it will become 'stuck in the middle' and have no clear basis upon which to gain competitive advantage. However, further to Porter's generic strategy framework, Faulkner and Bowman (1995) note how organisations can have a 'hybrid' strategy, combining both low cost and differentiation, and a 'no frills' strategy, which targets price sensitive customers with the limited provision of any additional extras.

CASE STUDY 6.3

Competitive strategies at Fitness First

Fitness First is owned by the private equity group BC Partners Ltd and is currently the world's largest health club operator. Fitness First attempts to charge lower membership by pursuing a strategy of cost leadership and driving costs down to a minimum. In the majority of their clubs, Fitness First do not provide swimming pool facilities, which can be expensive to operate. They also use a mezzanine floor, which maximises capacity and enables the clubs to be built on a smaller area, thus driving costs down further.

Fitness First has begun to use a hybrid strategy combining both low cost and differentiation by targeting women only through their Fitness First for Women clubs. These clubs target women who are new to health clubs and want a non-intimidating atmosphere. Fitness First has also used a strategy of differentiation with the provision of their Fitness First Platinum brand, which includes a swimming pool and towel service. Also there is focused differentiation in its Kaizen clubs, which are targeted at 40–60-year-olds and are designed without mirrors in the gyms and no music to promote a more encouraging environment. The company also has a 'no frills' option in their Fitness First Express brand, which is based upon pay as you go fees and limited member benefits.

The sports enterprise will comprise tangible and intangible resources and the resource based view (RBV) contends that organisations can gain competitive advantage through the successful configuration of these resources and its competences. Tangible resources include human, financial and physical resources, whereas intangible resources include brand reputation and image. The resources can be further classified into threshold and strategic or unique resources.

Threshold resources are those that the business must have if it is to operate in the industry. For example, a lawn tennis club will need the physical premises and related equipment for the game to be played. It will also need personnel to maintain the club's lawns and facilities. Strategic resources are those which are over and above the industry standard and can enable the sports organisation to gain a competitive advantage. Strategic resources can be classified upon the basis of whether they are rare and difficult to obtain; whether the resource is valuable or becomes valuable over time; or whether the resource is difficult to acquire, copy or substitute. The All England Tennis and Croquet Club (ALETC) commands strategic resources as it operates, in collaboration with the Lawn Tennis Association, the world renowned Wimbledon tennis facilities and has on its committee key personnel who have established reputations and expertise in tennis and event management.

Competences are the attributes that a sports enterprise requires if it is to compete. Competences are derived from the organisation's bundle of resources and can encompass skills, knowledge and technology. So, for example, in order to operate as a leisure centre the organisation must possess a range of competences in distributing, marketing and selling the product; the maintenance of the club and related facilities; and the development and training of human resources. Core competences are those competences that are over and above the industry standard. Prahalad and Hamel (1990) note that core competences should satisfy the following criteria:

- the core competence should provide the company with access to a wide range of markets;
- the core competence should make a major contribution to the perceived customer benefits of the end product;
- the core competence should be difficult for competitors to copy.

Learning activity 6.5

Select a sports organisation and identify the strategic resources and core competences based upon the criteria outlined in Table 6.2.

Table 6.2: Strategic resources and core competences?*

Criteria	Strategic resources	Core competences
Rare		
Valuable		
Difficult to acquire		
Difficult to copy		
Difficult to substitute		

Once the sports organisation has reviewed the basis upon which it will develop its strategy, it then has to decide the method by which it will implement the strategy. A number of strategic methods are available to the sports enterprise. First is organic growth and the potential of the firm to utilise its existing resources to grow the business. This enables the sports organisation to reap all the benefits that may occur from the growth strategy. However, it also means that the organisation has to incur all of the risks involved.

Second is mergers and acquisitions. In a merger, two or more sports organisations will come together to form a single enterprise. When an acquisition occurs, one sports organisation will purchase another. Mergers and acquisitions can enable the sports enterprise to enter new markets and product areas more quickly than by pursuing the strategy independently. Acquisitions can sometimes be hostile in nature and the takeover of Manchester United Football Club by the Glazier family in June 2005 is an example, where fans (who owned shares in the club) were actively opposed to the acquisition.

Third is strategic alliances and joint ventures, where a formal agreement is created between two or more companies to co-operate with one another. The alliance partners can mutually benefit from one another through shared resources and access to untapped markets. In the case of mergers, acquisitions and alliances, it is hoped that a 'synergistic' effect will occur, where the resultant effect of the combined companies is greater then what can be achieved alone.

Finally, there is franchising, where a contractual arrangement exists between the franchisee who trades under the brand name of the franchisor. The franchisor obtains an initial fee and a percentage return from the franchisee once they are trading. Premier Sport (**www.premiersport.org**) is an example of a sports coaching organisation that uses a network of franchises to develop sporting activity among primary age school children.

Learning activity 2.4

Identify a sports organisation that has adopted one of the strategic methods.

- What has been the rationale for using this method by the sports organisation?
- What have been the advantages and disadvantages of using this strategic method for the sports organisation?

Strategic implementation

Definition: the process by which the organisation implements the chosen strategies to pursue a particular direction.

A number of factors have to be considered when implementing strategies, such as the degree of risk involved and the extent to which the culture of the organisation needs to change to enable the strategy to be implemented. In both these respects effective change management and strategic leadership will be crucial to the outcome of the chosen strategy. The remainder of this chapter will therefore focus on these two aspects of strategic implementation.

The implementation of the chosen strategy is likely to have an impact on the processes and structure of the sports organisation. The sports manager may, therefore, encounter resistance to change from personnel and this can be due to poor communication and consultation, opposition to the proposed strategy, internal politics, or lack of interest or incentive to change. Successful change management enables the organisation to move in the desired strategic direction. Lewin (1951) notes three stages in the change process. First is the 'unfreezing' of attitudes and behaviours which may be acting as a barrier to change. Second is 'moving to a new level', where the organisation needs to modify organisational behaviours, structures and culture so it can move forward. Third is 'refreezing' of the modified behaviours and culture. This can be achieved through positive reinforcement, where the change is articulated to personnel in terms of higher sales, increased customer satisfaction and so on. This needs to be backed up with an incentive structure so that individuals recognise the impact of the change process.

Strategic leadership is at the core of driving change forward within the organisation. Indeed, strategic leadership is a key factor in whether the strategy will ultimately succeed. Although everyone in the organisation will have a responsibility for implementing the strategy, it will often be the most senior staff within the sports enterprise who will have the greatest power and influence over the success of the strategy.

According to Johnson et al. (2008), strategic leaders can be classified into two categories: charismatic leaders and instrumental (or transactional) leaders. Charismatic leaders are inspirational and visionary in character. They instil a sense of drive and motivation in those around them and ensure that individuals are empowered to succeed in their efforts. Instrumental and transactional leaders are concerned with ensuring that the systems and structures of the organisation are sufficient for the strategy to be implemented. Their focus is upon control systems of reward and punishment that influence the behaviour of individuals in the organisation. Approaches to leadership will influence the type of organisational culture that is developed and will determine the success of the chosen strategy.

CASE STUDY 6.4

Duncan Bannatyne

Duncan Bannatyne was born in 1949 and grew up as one of seven children in a council house on Clydebank in Glasgow, Scotland. After leaving school at the age of 15 with no qualifications he spent four years in the Navy but was dishonourably discharged for threatening an officer. He then drifted from job to job when one day, at the age of 29 and based in Jersey, he decided to return to mainland England where he set up an ice cream business called 'Duncan's Super Ices'. He bought his first van for £450, built up the business and eventually sold it for £28,000. By capitalising on a government policy of subsiding elderly care, he then went into the nursing home business. His first care home was built in 1986. After developing a substantial portfolio of care homes he subsequently sold the business in 1996 for £46 million.

He then moved into the health and fitness market, launching Bannatyne Health Clubs. In 2006 he acquired the Living Well health and fitness chain from Hilton for £96 million. Bannatyne's health clubs is now the largest independent chain in the UK. He also has a range of other leisure businesses, including bars, spas and hotels. Duncan Bannatyne operates his businesses on the basis of delegation. While he concentrates on strategy and exploiting new opportunities, he empowers his management team to implement the business strategy. He is

CASE STUDY 6.4 continued

known for ruthless cost cutting and was renowned for banning the purchase of paperclips when he was running his care homes. In addition to becoming a media personality though the BBC programme *Dragons' Den*, he is also known for his charity work and in 2004 was awarded an OBE.

Learning activity 6.7

From reading case study 6.4, what change management issues would need to be considered when Bannatyne's acquired the Living Well chain of health clubs?

What type of strategic leadership style do you think Duncan Bannatyne has, and to what extent has this influenced the strategic growth of his business?

Review

This chapter has explored the concept of strategy as it applies to sports organisations and enterprises. The sport organisation needs to be aware of its current strategic situation and influences from the external macro and micro environment that may have an impact upon its future strategic direction. Sports organisations need to constantly survey the marketplace for opportunities and threats that may occur.

The sports organisation has to be receptive to factors that may emerge, and be flexible with regard to change in light of competitor reactions. By positioning the organisation relative to competitors' strategies, and by utilising the organisation's strategic resources and core competences, the sports enterprise can develop its business to gain a competitive advantage. However, strategies need to be effectively implemented and this will be dependent upon the change management process and the nature of the strategic leadership within the organisation.

Review of learning outcomes

Having read the chapter and undertaken the various learning activities you should be able to answer the following questions.

- To what extent is an understanding of strategy important within the context of sport?
- Select a sport organisation of your choice and determine what its current strategic situation is.
- What should be the future strategic direction of the organisation and how can it gain a competitive advantage?
- What key factors should the sports organisation consider when implementing the strategy?

Further reading

For a general introduction to strategic management concepts and theories read:

Capon, C (2008) *Understanding strategic management*. Harlow: FT/Prentice Hall.

Henry, A (2008) *Understanding strategic management*. Oxford: Oxford University Press.

For further critical application of the strategic management concepts read:

Grant, RM (2008) *Contemporary strategy analysis*. 6th edition. Oxford: Blackwell.

Johnson, G, Scholes, K and Whittington, R (2008) *Exploring corporate strategy*, 8th edition. London: Prentice Hall.

Chapter 7

Human resource management

Sue Minten and Will Foster

As a predominantly service based industry, effective sport organisations are reliant on having the appropriate staff in place to meet customer needs. The purpose of this chapter is to provide an overview of the key human resource (HR) processes that enable this to happen in the context of the sport industry.

Learning outcomes

This chapter is designed to enable you to:

- understand the key aspects of HR management that are applicable to the line manager within sport;
- contemplate your future journey through the HR process and consider how you may enhance your employability and prepare for your future career.

Introduction

Human resource management (HRM) is defined as,

> a series of activities which: first enables working people and the organisation which uses their skills to agree about the objectives and nature of their working relationship and secondly, ensures that agreement is fulfilled. (Torrington et al., 2002, p13)

This definition emphasises the reciprocal nature of HRM. To be successful an organisation needs to satisfy the needs of the individual; equally, by contributing to the success of the organisation, individuals satisfy their personal employment needs. The strategic and central importance of HRM is emphasised by Storey (1995, p5) who explains that it:

> . . . is a distinctive approach to employment management which seeks to achieve competitive advantage through the strategic deployment of a highly committed and capable work force, using an integrated array of cultural, structural and personnel techniques.

The fundamental importance of HRM is emphasised by the trend in many industries for the responsibility for staff resource management to be devolved to individual line managers. Therefore, most sport managers have, as part of their role, an HRM function. The reason for this is that individual managers are more directly aware of the strengths and weaknesses of their staff, since they work most closely with them.

Figure 7.1 shows the areas the chapter will cover in order to achieve the first objective – to provide a fundamental understanding of the key aspects of human resource management that are applicable to the line manager within sport. Moreover, students are encouraged to gain a deeper understanding of these processes through the reading and references that are included. In order to achieve the second aim tasks are included throughout the chapter to encourage students to contemplate their future journey through the HR process and enable them to think about how they may enhance their employability and prepare for their future career.

Figure 7.1: The structure of the chapter

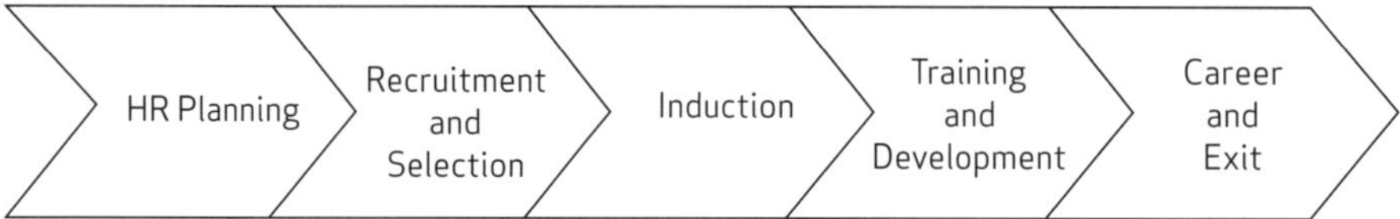

Human resource planning

The management of human resources needs to correspond to the strategic objectives of the organisation. Human resource planning is:

> . . . the process of systematically forecasting the future demand and supply for employees and the deployment of their skills within the strategic objectives of the organisation. (Bratton and Gold, 2003, p191)

Consequently, it is crucial for sports organisations to ensure they have an appropriate workforce to achieve their strategic objectives. In order to forecast future demand, organisations must have an understanding of the impact of the external environment on their HR strategies. A PESTLE analysis is commonly used to evaluate this under the headings: political, economic, sociological, technical, legal and environmental (Taylor et al., 2008). This was discussed in more detail in the previous chapter.

In order to determine the supply of human resources, an internal and external analysis of the labour force is undertaken. The internal analysis involves a skills audit of the workforce and an assessment of how the organisation's current workforce will change, such as how many employees will leave or retire and the number that will be internally promoted or transferred. This analysis is used to identify any gaps or surpluses in the capabilities in the workforce in relation to future HR demands and strategic objectives. The external supply analysis examines the extent to which the organisation will be able to find employees with the necessary skills to address any gaps through analysing labour force data.

General labour market trends that are likely to affect sport are the ageing workforce, immigration and economic conditions (Taylor et al., 2008). With regard to specific data on the composition of the sport workforce, a clearer picture is emerging through the workforce development research that has been overseen by SkillsActive, the sector skills council for active leisure. However, there have been difficulties in estimating the actual size of the sport work force due to the problems of defining the scope of the sport industry in the UK.

Research commissioned by Sport England estimate the numbers employed in sport related services in 2003 were in excess of 421,000, which accounted for 1.8 percent of all employment in England, an increase of 28 percent between 1985 and 2003 (Sport Industry Research Centre, 2007). Research commissioned by SkillsActive to identify numbers employed in sport, fitness and the outdoors estimated that there were 411,400 paid employees (Experian, 2005). Here again considerable growth in employment in sport was found which is reflected in all the regional Sector Skills Agreements (SSAs); for example the West Midlands predicts a 21 percent increase in sport employment between now and 2014 (SkillsActive, 2006b). An impact of this growth is the problem in filling vacancies, which was identified by all regional SSAs, and the difficulty in retaining staff. Consequently a key issue for HR planning in sport organisations is the difficulty in finding appropriate staff to fill posts. The regional SSAs are available on the SkillsActive website and are valuable resources for providing a snapshot of a range of issues within the sport related workforce.

Learning activity 7.1

Access the SkillsActive website and find the Sector Skills Agreement for your region: **www.skillsactive.com/resources/publications**.

Summarise the key workforce issues facing local organisations and reflect on how this may impact on your future employment.

Recruitment and selection

In order to address the difficulties in finding appropriate staff, sport organisations need to ensure they have effective recruitment processes, particularly as recruiting can be an expensive activity. However, the first part of the recruitment process is actually to determine whether or not there is a vacancy and whether it should be filled by a new recruit. There are several options that could be considered when a vacancy occurs:

- reorganise the work
- use overtime
- mechanise the work
- stagger the hours
- make the job part time
- subcontract the work
- use an agency.

(Torrington et al., 2005)

Thus an organisation needs to review its requirements, and if that leads to the decision to recruit then there is a need for a systematic review of the job requirements – a job analysis. This includes a description of duties that are to be performed, prioritised into the most important or responsible duties, the time spent on each duty, how often each duty is performed and the skills needed to perform each task. The process of job analysis then leads to the production of job descriptions and person specifications.

The job description identifies what the job involves and includes the following;

- the purpose of the job;
- the tasks that are to be undertaken;
- the duties and responsibilities;
- the performance standards;
- reporting relationships.

The job description provides the basis for describing the vacancy to others, thus underpinning the development of the job advert. It also facilitates the communication of expectations about performance to employees and managers to help ensure effective performance in the job. The person specification converts the job description to provide an outline of the kind of person required to do the job. The Chartered Institute of Personnel and Development (CIPD) (2008b) identify that, in general, specifications should include details of:

- skills, aptitude, knowledge and experience;
- qualifications (which should be only those necessary to do the job – unless candidates are recruited on the basis of future potential , for example graduates);
- personal qualities relevant to the job, such as ability to work as part of a team.

An example of a person specification for a local authority sports development post is shown in Table 7.1.

While it is important to ensure that the person specification covers all the necessary requirements for the post, it is equally important to ensure that indirect discrimination does not take place, for example by setting unjustifiable age limits or requesting qualifications which are not essential for the post.

Criteria are usually described as either 'essential' or 'desirable'. Essential requirements are those that the successful candidate needs to possess to carry out the job effectively. Desirable criteria are 'bonus' requirements that, while not essential, may enable the candidate to carry out the duties of the post more effectively.

Learning activity 7.2

From a recruitment website, such as Leisure Opportunities, find a job description and person specification for a job you would be interested in applying for in the future: **www.leisureopportunities.co.uk**. (You will need to look at a few as many sports organisations do not follow the good practice of using job descriptions and person specifications.)

From the person specification identify which of the essential and desirable attributes you have and how you would show evidence of them.

Table 7.1: Person specification: sports development officer

Essential requirements	Desirable requirements	How assessed
Qualifications A sports-related academic qualification (BTEC, National Diploma, GNVQ). A minimum of two Level 1 and one Level 2 National overning Body coaching qualifications. A current first aid qualification. A current child protection qualification	*Qualifications* A sports-related degree or equivalent.	Application form and interview.
Experience Proven experience of sports development work. Experience of working with children.	*Experience* Proven practical experience of working in or with the voluntary sport sector. Proven practical experience of supervising coaching colleagues.	Application form and interview.
Knowledge An understanding of sports development work, especially relating to target groups and young people's needs. Knowledge of health and safety.	*Knowledge* An understanding of partnership working. Working knowledge of Sport England and relevant Governing Body programmes.	Application form and interview.
Skills and abilities Good verbal and written communication skills. Good organisation skills. Ability to work alone or as part of a team. Computer literacy, i.e. Word, Excel, Outlook, Internet. Current full driving licence.	*Skills and abilities* Proven leadership skills.	
Other requirements of the job Ability to work unsocial hours. Willing to attend training and development events where required.		

Recruitment planning

Planning and project managing the recruitment process is essential in giving the best impression of the company in order to have the best chance of attracting the most suitable candidates from which to make a choice, and who would accept the job if offered it. Recruitment is a two-way process; it is as much about the candidate making their mind up about the vacancy as it is about the recruiter making their mind up about them. How the candidates feel about the organisation will be strongly influenced by the way they are treated, the information they are provided with and the level of professionalism evident during the recruitment process.

A key aspect of the recruitment process is the search and selection stage, particularly in sport, where organisations report that some vacancies are hard to fill. It is also one of the most important ongoing investments managers make as, simply in terms of costs, recruitment isn't cheap.

First, there are the direct costs. These could include advertising the vacancy (if you wished to advertise in a leading sport-specific magazine such as Leisure Opportunities, the advert would appear in their hard copy magazine, on their e-zine and on their on-line job board – and a one-eighth of a page mono advert would cost less than £500, whereas a full-page colour advert would be around £3,000 with various prices for different sizes between), using recruitment agencies (typically 15–30 percent of starting salary), 'bonuses' that may be paid to staff for recommending possible applicants, costs associated with any psychometric/personality profiling tests that may be carried out and travelling expenses that are paid to candidates who come for interviews.

Second, there is a 'hidden' cost in terms of time and resources that go into the recruitment process. Research has shown that the average hidden cost associated with recruiting a new employee is more than £5,000 (Berry, 2007). In total, taking the direct and hidden costs into account, the total cost of recruiting a new member of staff could be between £10,000 and £30,000, depending on the process used and the seniority of the role recruited, and that's before a salary has been paid.

Finally, there can be an additional consideration – that of legislation, which is continually changing when it comes to personnel, equal opportunities, discrimination and employer law. Therefore, when recruiting new staff it is essential to ensure that the organisation's processes are in compliance with latest guidelines and legislation.

While one of the greatest benefits to an organisation occurs when a suitable candidate is appointed, one of the greatest costs to a company happens when an unsuitable appointment is made. Depending on the role that the person is appointed to, a bad appointment can cost the company lost opportunities, damage to market image, the time spent by the line manager to 'performance manage' and take disciplinary action with that employee, in addition to severance costs and the poor morale that can be created amongst other staff members. Thus effective recruitment and selection procedures need to 'select the "right" individuals and reject the "wrong" ones' (Newell, 2005, p115).

The search

A number of routes are available to search for and generate candidates. These include:

- Advert. This could be in hard copy or electronic.
  Hard copy: local and national newspapers, specialist journals or trade magazines.
  Electronic: company website, jobs websites associated with the press/newspapers, generalist job site boards or specialist/industry-specific job boards such as Leisure Opportunities.
- Recruitment consultancy/agency
- Access to online candidates. Where there are a number of vacancies to fill an organisation can pay to access one of the online CV databases to conduct their own search for suitable candidates. This can be a time-consuming process but can also be valuable in deepening knowledge of the types of candidates available.
- Personal networks. This can be a much overlooked source of candidates, but within business contacts there could be an appropriate person for the vacancy and there is a certain degree of foreknowledge of the individual. Professional institutes such as the Institute of Sport and Recreation Management (ISRM) and the Institute for Sports, Parks and Leisure (ISPAL), local breakfast clubs or other networking events could prove useful.
- Job centres. Depending on the nature and level of the role, job centres can be a very useful and cost effective way of generating candidates.

The selection process

A major problem with the selection process is that it is ultimately 'artificial' and therefore fundamentally flawed. Even with the best selection process, errors can be made as judgements in the recruitment process are based on limited and incomplete information. Besides, as the process involves people, there will be subjective judgements. Foot and Hook (2005) describe this as perceptual selection where we select the stimuli to which we will pay attention, a selection which is determined by our own experiences, personality and motivation, thus creating subtle prejudices. Recognising the potential problems with selection will help an organisation design an effective selection process and avoid the pitfalls.

Shortlisting

The first stage of selection is usually carried out by reviewing the applications/CVs to create a shortlist of candidates for interview. There are many methods that can be utilised to screen candidates and the approach will depend on the volume of applications. If a recruitment consultancy has undertaken the initial screening process they may present between five and ten candidates, all of whom are suitable. After a careful reading of all the CVs and detailed discussions with the consultant, this may be reduced to four. Alternatively, an advertisement may have generated 200 CVs, and an initial screening will need to be done against the person specification, with one minute per CV being allowed (that's 3 hours 20 minutes!) to create three 'piles' of CVs 'definite yes", 'definite no' and 'maybe'. If a large number of candidates meet all the essential criteria then the desirable criteria can be used to screen further.

> ***Reflection 7.1***
>
> Using the person specification in Learning activity 7.2, reflect on how you can you ensure that you are in the 'yes' pile with your application. (Remember, the person looking at the CV may only take one minute to read it.)

As part of the planning process, the organisation will also need to decide how each criterion on the person specification will be assessed once the shortlist has been developed. A selection of assessment methods are provided below.

Telephone screening

A brief telephone interview is a useful method of quickly reducing the shortlist to a manageable number if there is a large number of candidates who look suitable on paper. However, it should be borne in mind that not every candidate will give their best performance on the telephone; but, in terms of clarifying queries with the CV and asking some preliminary questions, a lot can be learnt from a 10-minute telephone discussion. This may also be a useful approach if the person is required to use telephone skills in their job, such as posts as receptionists or in membership sales.

Interview/assessment

There is a range of selection techniques that can be used but a CIPD (2007a) survey found that interviews based on the contents of the curriculum vitae/application form are most frequently used. However, research has found that interviews are poor predictors of performance in a job (Makin and Robertson 1986). Moreover, Anderson and Shackleton (1993) have reviewed a number of studies in order to provide reasons for this finding. These include:

- *The self-fulfilling prophecy effect.* The questions asked are designed to confirm the initial impressions of candidates gained from before the interview or in its early stages.
- *The stereotyping effect.* Assumptions are made that particular characteristics are typical of members of a particular group. If decisions are made on the basis of sex, race, disability, marital status, sexuality, religion or ex-offenders, this may be illegal.
- *The halo and horns effect.* Interviewers may make a decision made on first impressions.
- *The contrast effect.* The experience of interviewing one candidate may affect the way others are interviewed later in the selection process.
- *The similar-to-me effect.* Preference is sometimes given to candidates perceived as having a similar background, career history, personality or attitudes to the interviewer.
- *The personal liking effect.* Decisions may be made on the basis of whether the interviewer personally likes or dislikes the candidate.

Organisations use a number of strategies to address these issues. Panel interviews involve three or four interviewers asking questions in turn, this enables a variety of perspectives and also enables observation of the candidate when not asking the questions. Another strategy is to undertake several interviews/meetings with the candidate over a period of time. People (interviewer and interviewee) can have 'off days' and 'good days', and seeing the candidate more than once (with time between meetings) provides the opportunity to reflect on what was said. If possible, the candidates could be in a variety of different settings to see how they perform; for example, some organisations provide lunch with staff, who are asked to provide feedback on the interviewees. Presentations may also be used where the applicant is set a specific topic.

To further overcome the issues of weaknesses of interviews, other selection techniques could be used alongside the interview, in order to build a better picture of the suitability of the candidate for the role. Psychometric/personality profiling and tests/case studies give a broader insight into the candidate's style and 'technical' ability. Group work may be used, where several candidates are set a task or asked to make a decision or consider an issue; this enables the opportunity to observe how the candidate works in a group, and whether they lead, contribute or dominate. Finally, work simulations could be used, which could include in-tray exercises or role plays.

There are many psychological aspects to recruitment and each candidate will have a different set of circumstances and motivations that have led them to enter the recruitment process. From the recruiter's point of view, the aim is to influence the candidates so that they will take the job if it is offered to them. There is an unusual mentality associated with job search and experience shows that it is important to get the balance between making the opportunity attractive without it being too good to be true, and making the process challenging enough without being too stressful.

Learning activity 7.3

Using the person specification you found in Learning activity 7.2, undertake a mock interview. In groups of three, one person takes on the role of interviewer and one person the interviewee. The third person can act as observer and give feedback on both roles.

The job offer

The final stage of the recruitment and selection process is the job offer and acceptance. In making the decision to appoint a candidate, salary/package details should have been considered. The offer made to the candidate will depend on many factors: their current job situation and salary, their expectations of salary for the role, what value they place on the opportunity on offer and what value the company places on them, how closely they match the needs of the vacancy.

It is not uncommon for this stage to be the most precarious aspect. Common sense would say that if a candidate has spent so much time and effort in attending interviews then they are bound to take the job. In reality, however, at the point of being made the job offer, the candidate has a real decision to make. Before then they only had to decide whether to go for interview or not. Now they are making a life-changing decision that may mean them leaving the security of a job and company they know well, leaving behind friends and colleagues who work for their current employer and sometimes the job move can entail a geographical relocation. It is at the point that the job is offered that these realities hit home. Also, it is not uncommon for a candidate to accept a job offer, hand in their notice, and then be persuaded to stay with their current employer, either through an increase in salary or promotion.

Once the candidate has accepted the job offer, then the organisation should keep in touch and be prepared to offer support and help if necessary. This is especially relevant if the candidate has to relocate; simple things such as recommending local estate agents and giving advice on the nearby regions can be invaluable.

Induction

Recruitment and selection is only the beginning of the employment relationship; the future of the relationship depends to a considerable extent on the degree to which the new employee has an effective induction that enables them to settle into the job.

Ineffective inductions can lead to poor integration into the team, low morale, loss of productivity and under-utilisation of the employee's potential (CIPD, 2007). The Advisory, Conciliation and Arbitration Service (ACAS, 2006) has identified that most labour turnover is among new employees, and this is supported by the CIPD recruitment and retention survey (2007a), which found that 19 percent of leavers had been with their employer for less than six months. Early leaving results in:

- additional costs for recruiting a replacement;
- wasted time for the inductor;
- lowering of morale for the remaining staff;
- detriment to the leaver's employment record;
- having to repeat the unproductive learning curve of the leaver;
- damage to the company's reputation.

There is little research into the levels and quality of staff induction in the sport industry. One indicator is the SkillsActive (2008) *Working in fitness* survey, which found that the majority of those who replied to the survey identified that they were quite satisfied with their induction.

A survey by *IRS Employment Review* found that effective inductions involve a number of factors (Rankin, 2006): a short initial and intensive programme followed by a longer, tailored learning process; support for line managers in delivering the induction effectively and the integration of induction with the main learning system of the organisation; finally, evaluation of the induction and regular updating of the process.

Performance management

Performance management is a process that enables a shared understanding of the objectives that need to be achieved, and then effectively managing and developing individuals and teams to attain them (Armstrong and Baron, 2004; Foot and Hook, 2005). These objectives should relate to the overall objectives and long-term goals of the organisation (Torrington et al., 2005). The process should enable performance improvement, and also involves the measurement of performance and feedback.

A key part of performance management is the review, which should be ongoing, with the manager providing the employee with regular feedback. However there should also be a more formal review, which often involves performance appraisal systems. This is an opportunity for an overall assessment of the employee's past performance, the agreement of objectives for the future and identification of their development needs.

An issue with appraisal systems is the possible conflict between the appraiser's role as both as the judge and helper to the employee (Foot and Hook, 2005). Another problem occurs when organisations try to use the appraisal system for too many different purposes, or where the process is linked with pay or the disciplinary process. Disciplinary issues should be part of the ongoing performance management process. A further common problem occurs where appraisal is seen as an administration exercise on behalf of the HR department that occurs once a year, rather than being driven by the line manager and employee. Appraisals should be viewed as learning events, where employees are encouraged to reflect on their development needs in order to create a personal development plan (PDP). The following section examines personal development and training in a little more detail.

Training and personal development

Training and development are crucial in ensuring the success of organisations and enabling industries to flourish; in the sport industry this has been signified by one of SkillsActive's six key priorities of increasing the sport sector's investment in its people. Sport England (2004a) identified that only 41 percent of organisations have a training plan and that the average spend on training is £2,336 per organisation and £117 per employee. In the *Working in fitness* survey, undertaken for SkillsActive (2008), 19 percent of the health and fitness workforce felt that they had not received enough training to do their job, although the report acknowledges this was an improvement on the previous year. The survey also found that 45 percent of respondents paid for their own training.

The terms 'training' and 'development' are often used interchangeably. Training is defined as 'an instructor-led and content-based intervention leading to desired changes in behaviour', while development is described as tending 'to refer to a longer process of learning, acquiring skills or knowledge that may include a number of elements such as training, coaching, formal and informal interventions, education or planned experience' (CIPD, 2005). There are a number of reasons for training and development in sports organisations:

- increased job satisfaction and morale among employees and volunteers;
- reduced turnover of employees and volunteers;
- increased employee and volunteer motivation;
- improved efficiencies in processes and procedures;
- enhanced capacity to adopt new technologies and methods;
- risk management in terms of better knowledge of compliance requirements.

(Taylor et al., 2008)

Some of these reasons are embodied in the *Working in fitness* survey finding that a third of respondents who had undertaken no training would not recommend their employer to others, 82 percent of those who had spent eleven or more days training would. It also found that, as the expectation of remaining in the industry rises, so do the average training days the respondent has received.

A sport organisation that is an example of good practice in training and development is Greenwich Leisure (GLL), which has won a series of accolades for its training and development programmes. An example is its trainee-management scheme: since 1997 it has trained 41 graduates to address the issue of a significant shortage of skills. The GLL HR director stated that: 'It became vital to recruit and mould managers who would spread GLL's ethos . . . It is recognised that the trainee managers of today are the senior managers of tomorrow.' The two-year training programme gives graduates hands-on experience, and they are also mentored and take part in presentations, lectures, workshops, shadowing and external visits. They are also able to obtain a number of technical qualifications, such as the YMCA Fitness Instructor, National Pool Lifeguard, First Aid at Work, Pool Plant Operators' Certificate, Institute of Sport and Recreation and Management Certificate. Seventy-eight percent of recruits have completed the course and 27 of the 41 graduates continue to work with GLL. All 27 gained jobs as assistant managers and 12 have become managers (Politt, 2006).

A key aspect of effective training and development is that it should be aligned to the organisation's mission and strategic objectives. For a more detailed overview of the training and development process see Taylor et al. (2008).

Managing diversity

Another key human resource attribute that a sport manager needs is the ability to manage a diverse workforce. Diversity is described as 'valuing everyone as an individual – valuing people as employees, customers, clients' (CIPD, 2006). It consists of both visible and non-visible factors, which include personal characteristics such as sex, race, age, background, culture, disability, personality and work-style.

It is important to manage diversity effectively for two key reasons. First, social justice – everyone should have the right to equal access to employment, and when employed should have equal pay and equal access to training and development, as well as being free of any direct or indirect discrimination and harassment or bullying. Second, there is a business case – if people are not treated fairly at work they will feel less than fully committed and will therefore under-perform. Organisations that take diversity seriously perform better financially, and the effective management of diversity enhances the reputation of an organisation, which means that a wider range of people are likely to want to work for it, thereby helping to address skills shortages (CIPD, 2006).

Sport England (2004b) has identified that an organisation that is more diverse, reflecting the community it serves in terms of staff make-up at management, executive, officer and volunteer levels, is likely to be more innovative and able to respond better to the varied needs of all members of that community. This increases market competitiveness and the organisation's appeal to large numbers of people, which can increase memberships and revenue, and attract revenue support This approach is reflected by Sport England's Sport Equality Policy, which recognises the need to 'address issues of fairness in the workplace and the way in which services are allocated and delivered'. It also identifies two other benefits as: increasing the number of volunteers and the number of people able to fulfil roles in administration, coaching and management; and ensuring that the organisation is working within the law.

Sports equity is supported by legislation including the Race Relations Act and Race Relations (Amendment) Act, the Sex Discrimination Act and the Disability Discrimination Act. Finally, it ensures that the organisation is working to the government's agenda and thus is more likely to receive or continue to receive funding to develop sport.

Learning activity 7.4

Choose a public, commercial and voluntary sport organisation and investigate whether or not they have an equity policy in relation to human resources. Reflect on why there may be differences between the organisations.

Review

This chapter has provided an overview of the processes of human resource management that are relevant to the sport manager. It can be seen that these processes are comparable to those used in other industries and much is drawn from generic human resource management theory. The chapter has also shown that the sport sector faces a number of issues that need to be addressed through effective implementation of HR processes; conversely, it has also identified the good practice that does occur within sport.

Review of learning outcomes

Having read the chapter and undertaken the various learning activities you should be able to answer the following questions.

- Identify the key issues facing sports organisations in planning their human resources.
- Outline the activities involved in the process of replacing a member of staff.
- Explain why interviews are perceived to be poor predictors of performance and discuss how sports organisations could address the problems you identify.
- Discuss the importance of effective induction, training and development processes within sport organisations.
- Outline the reasons why sports organisations should effectively manage diversity.

Further reading

Textbooks

Taylor, T, Doherty, A, and McGraw, P (2008) *Managing people in sport organizations*. London: Butterworth Heinemann.

This book provides an excellent, in-depth look at HRM theories and concepts applied to sport and thus is a good follow-up text for this chapter. Although the authors are based in Australia it does provide some UK case studies and examples.

Foot, M and Hook, C (2005) *Introducing human resource management*. London: Prentice Hall.

This is a good introductory textbook to generic HRM concepts and theories.

Websites

The ACAS website provides a number of resources for good practice in HRM **www.acas.org.uk**.

The CIPD website provides factsheets on a range of HRM processes and issues that have been written by HRM experts, see: **www.cipd.co.uk**.

As the Sector Skills Council for Active Leisure, SkillsActive has a number of interesting reports on its website that are relevant to HRM, see: **www.skillsactive.com/resources/publications**.

Chapter 8

Planning, monitoring, controlling and evaluating sports organisations

Caroline A. Wiscombe

This chapter examines the ongoing process of planning, controlling and evaluating the business of sport. The chapter will extend knowledge and understanding of the role of the finance function in all aspects of sports management and indicate how its importance has grown in today's economic climate. The chapter introduces the concept of management accounting and its different financial planning tools in order to provide sports managers with a system of monitoring, control and evaluation.

Learning outcomes

This chapter is designed to enable you to:

- understand and develop planning tools within the finance function;
- explain the importance of control in finance terms;
- describe the importance of financial evaluation for sports organisations.

Introduction

Strategic management, marketing, human resources and membership functions within sports organisations need to be developed using a strong planning process. These may be long-term (strategic plans), mid-length (which can be strategic or operational) or short-term (operational) in nature. The plans can also be capital in nature (buying or developing fixed assets such as building or equipment) or operational (increasing the workforce or marketing activity for instance).

To support the planning, function managers or department heads need to be able to estimate the costs and expenses involved in implementing plans. They also need to ensure that other resources (human or equipment) exist to support both capital and operational planning. Therefore financial budgets underpin all planning and development, in order to ensure that the resources (capital, human, equipment and finance) to implement those plans are available, controlled and evaluated. The process is cyclical in nature as illustrated in Figure 8.1.

Figure 8.1: The financial cycle

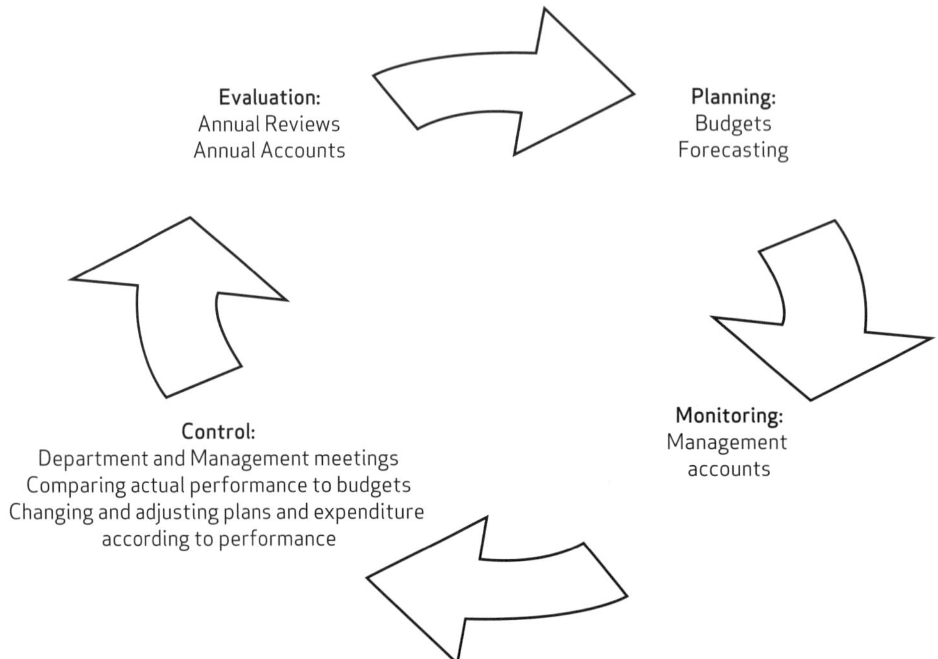

Plans are commonly monitored using performance measurement tools that encompass the key components of financial budgeting and financial measurement. This is true for both profit and non-profit making organisations. Profit and non-profit making organisations were described in Chapter 5.

Financial functions are perhaps the most crucial of all the management skills and thus taking the time to study and develop these is vital. This chapter considers the concepts of performance measurement using management accounts, and the minimum analysis needed to ensure that plans can be implemented, budgetary control is monitored and quantitative performance is evaluated, while understanding that, in many sports, performance or achievement of participants may also provide key evaluation tools.

This chapter looks at specific financial tools called accounts to help develop plans and subsequently to evaluate them. The funding of sport is not part of the content of this chapter. That is examined in Chapter 13. Here we make the assumption that funding or funds, cash investment or sponsorship has already been procured; however, revenue, or income from other sources than funding, is a direct responsibility of sports managers. All income streams are an essential part of the planning process.

Financial and management accounting

Financial accounting is largely developed for an external audience. Management accounting is for internal audiences, used on a daily, weekly and monthly basis to monitor activity. It is thus very detailed and will look at every nuance of the organisation's costs and expenses in all aspects of its planning functions. External audiences do not need to see all the 'lines' of account and therefore end-of-year accounts will be much less detailed that those used on a day-to-day basis. Financial accountability for external audiences was discussed in Chapter 5. This chapter concentrates on the detail that sports managers, heads of department and supervisors will need to undertake their daily activity; however, financial accounting also helps to inform the operational evaluation of the organisation. Therefore, the final section of this chapter brings together financial and management accounting, in order to supply the holistic overview which sports managers need so as to operate their organisations effectively.

Management accounts, unlike end-of-year annual accounts, are not a mandatory requirement, but they are an essential function which assists in planning, developing, controlling and evaluation. They follow the formal structures of financial accounting in order to help simplify processes. We can thus differentiate 'financial accounting' from 'management accounting' in terms of historical sequence, the former being about what has happened, the latter being about forecasting or what we expect to happen.

Financial planning tools

Strategic planning in sports organisations is part of the leadership and management function. The formulation of strategy will begin with a vision, mission and objectives based on demand for sport, the external or macro environment and the internal or micro environment, (see Chapter 6 for more information on these concepts).

To achieve the vision of the organisation, detailed planning will be needed both in the development of operational functions, such as marketing or human resources, and in the development of financial planning tools or 'budgeting accounts'.

Management accounts for any business, or budgeting for a project within it, will contain much more information (or lines of account) than the accounts submitted to shareholders or tax offices. They will be used on a weekly, monthly, quarterly or other time-bound parameter in meetings and discussions on monitoring business performance or project success. Differences from the plan, for instance in income, may lead to changes to expenses in order to ensure that income exceeds expenditure. Thus financial planning tools are used for monitoring ongoing business activity and for one-off projects.

The main financial planning tool is a 'cash flow forecast'. This is developed alongside a 'management budget'. Other tools or systems include 'individual project projections', 'budget trading profit and loss accounts' or 'budget income and expenditure accounts' and 'budget balance sheets', which are similar in format to the annual accounts but with more detail. All the documentation combines to form part of the management accounting process.

Cash flow forecasts

The most basic reason why any organisation monitors financial performance is to ensure that it remains solvent, i.e. has the ability to pay its creditors. If a company cannot meet the demands of its creditors then it would be wound up and the assets sold in the hope of meeting, at least partially, the demands (Wiscombe, 2009).

To monitor the cash position of the company, a cash flow forecast is prepared. Sports managers will estimate how much income, from ticket sales, entry fees, social functions, catering facilities, merchandising and so on that the organisation will receive in any given period. There may be cash income from government grants, sponsorship or income from investment of assets which should also be accounted for. Then the manager will carefully work out when costs and expenses are due.

'Costs' is the financial terminology for those items which will change with the sale, for instance the cost of the shirt sold as merchandise, or the food item as catering. 'Expenses' are those items which do not change, no matter how many sales are made, for instance the lighting in the retail shop, insurance or administration. From this analysis the manager can develop a cash flow forecast to ensure that monies are ready when creditors are due to be paid.

The standard format cash flow forecast is illustrated in Figure 8.2.

At first it may appear that the totals of each line in the cash flow forecast could be used to determine the overall profit or loss of an organisation (profit is defined as income less costs and expenses), rather than net cash flow. However there are some aspects of expenses which are not cash but are recorded in the profit and loss account (P&L) or income and expenditure account. This needs some understanding, but, once mastered, helps to underpin knowledge on profitability. The two most common terms in sports accounting are 'depreciation' and 'amortisation'.

When a fixed asset is used, for example gym equipment, it reduces in value. This reduction in value is termed 'depreciation'. Depreciation appears as a figure in the balance sheet to reduce the value of the fixed asset. It is also accounted for in the profit and loss account as an expense incurred during the course of the year. Generally accepted accounting principles (GAAP) are used to determine the amount of depreciation which should be charged against the asset value. One such concept is based on length of service. For instance a rowing machine may be expected to last for 10 years. At the end of the 10-year period the asset would probably be worth nothing if the business tried to sell it 'second hand'. If purchased for £15,000 then the asset would be written off over 10 years and the depreciation would be £15,000 divided by 10 or £1,500 per annum. Accountants will ensure that the concept of depreciation is explained in the 'notes to the accounts'. Whichever concept is used this will remain the same year on year.

Sometimes organisations buy business interests for more money than the worth of their assets. The price paid reflects the intangible assets which cause the business to run profitably (this could be location, reputation, skills of employees and so on). Thus a golf course may be worth £1 million in assets. The fact that it employs a famous-name golfer, such as Nick Faldo or Seve Ballesteros, as its 'professional' would undoubtedly raise the value of any sale to perhaps £1.5 million. The intangible assets are referred to as 'goodwill'. Goodwill has been bought and paid for but must be accounted for. The solution in accounting terms is to write off the goodwill (i.e. to reduce its value to zero) over a number of years. This process is called 'amortisation'.

Figure 8.2: Cash flow forecast statement

	Jan £	Feb £	March £	April £	Etc £
Receipts					
Ticket sales					
Entry fees					
Government grants					
Sponsorship					
Investment income					
Players' dinner dance					
Total receipts					
Less payments					
Insurance					
Secretary's salary					
Legal fees					
Electricity					
Gas					
Players' wages					
Merchandise					
Food, etc.					
Total payments					
Net cash flow	Receipts – payments				
Opening balance	From December closing balance				
Closing balance	Opening balance + net cash flow				

Learning activity 8.1

Write a cash flow diagram that represents your own personal income and expenditure for the next three months. Ensuring you start with an accurate opening balance.

Consider what you might need to do if you end up in a negative position at the end of the period. How does this relate to what a business would have to think about?

Management budgets

Management budget formats may take a long time to develop as the business or organisation grows. At a very simple level management will list all expected income, for the project or the year, and all expected costs and expenses. These will link to the planned or expected activity. If income exceeds the costs and expenses then setting the budget may not be too onerous. If income does not exceed the costs and expenses, however, consideration may be given to reducing the planned activity or finding cheaper alternatives.

Challenges include early monitoring of strategic plans which affect income and expenditure; gaining the engagement of department heads to ensure they include all operational activity in their area for over 12 months ahead; and being adaptable to changes (for instance, if income is not as projected, planning early what spending might be reduced in order to achieve overall success). When organisations begin their development all the 'lines of accounting' may not be complete enough for all avenues of control to be effective. The important factor is that, as they are discovered, those responsible should include them on an ongoing basis.

Learning activity 8.2

A group of friends have decided to put on a fundraising event for the local youth club. They want to host a sporting 'fun-day' using the local football club's grounds and plan to have a number of activities such as five-a-side hockey, table tennis, rounders and an 'egg and spoon' race; they have tried to choose activities in which everyone can have fun, so they want to include a bouncy castle and put on refreshments as well.

List all the costs and expenses you can think of that might be associated with the event.

What can they do to ensure a profit is made?

In advance of the accounting year, sports managers will spend time developing the budget or management account, which uses historical data from their organisations, data from competitors, company strategy and plans, for instance an increased marketing push for the sale of merchandise or season tickets. They also use evidence from the macro environment, such as demographic changes, government funding mechanisms, new legislation or the economic climate. This budget process is similar for both profit and non-profit making organisations.

CASE STUDY 8.1

Reductions in income

In December 2008 UK Sport announced funding for a number of sports organisations for the period running up to London 2012. Whereas it had been expected that athletics would receive a high proportion of the funding on offer, their poor performance in Beijing meant that the greater amounts went to rowing and cycling. This undoubtedly means that management will need to reduce their plans for the period, or seek private sponsorship for the £50 million reduction in expected funding.

Once set, the budget, which includes all expected income and expenditure, needs to be monitored or controlled to ensure the plans stay on track. An ideal format for a management budget cannot be given as this will differ according to the organisation but an example is given as part of the Pegasus Sports Association case study (8.2). The process of budgeting should be consistent across organisations and take the following approach:

- a timetable for each step should be prepared and circulated;
- preparation of key business objectives which have taken into account the macro and micro environment;
- analysis of resources to support the business objectives;
- preparation and circulation of a draft budget with explanations and highlighting key targets;
- plan of action prepared in case budget targets are not met, e.g. income streams are not on track;
- a discussion phase, which allows for changes to the budget;
- draft a consolidated master budget.

The master budget will always be termed 'draft' because, as we will see, it will be an evolving and changing document.

CASE STUDY 8.2

Pegasus Sports Association

Management accounting in practice

A section of the management accounts for the membership department of 'Pegasus Sports Association', as presented to the September management meeting, is provided in Figure 8.3. This section, which looks at the membership department, is only a part of the total management accounts system.

The plan in the membership department at the beginning of the accounting year, which runs from January to December each year, is to increase membership by around 20 full paying members. The association has struggled to retain

Figure 8.3: Section of the management accounts for the Pegasus Sports Association

1	2	3	4	5	6	7	8	9	10
Membership Summary									
Line No	Note		Yr to date budget	Year to date actual	Variance	Total budget for the year	Sept. of previous year	Previous Year end	Revised Forecast For year end
508		No. of members		17,427		17,406	17,389		
509				£	£	£	£		
510		Membership Summary							
511		Income							
512		Renewals	672,380	599,137	(73,243)	813,016	582,758	739,167	760,516
513		Upgrading	17,253	15,667	(1,586)	23,000	18,913	23,344	20,010
514		New Entrants	321,719	205,525	(116,194)	415,076	222,678	285,953	270,325
515		Membership services	9,000	9,001	1	12,000	6,750	10,617	12,001
516		Sports Association Magazine	111,500	109,128	(2,372)	160,000	106,732	152,951	145,000
517		Employment Contracts				2,000	8,176	8,176	2,000
518		Regional Support							
519									
520		Total Income	1,131,852	938,458	(193,394)	1,425,094	946,007	1,220,208	1,209,851
521		**Direct Expenditure**							
522		Renewals	2,250	2,265	(15)	3,000	2,497	3,440	3,020
523		Upgrading	14,750	12,034	2,716	20,000			16,045
524		New Entrants	186,773	120,276	66,497	243,525	126,223	174,679	160,408
525		Membership Services	5,994	6,839	(845)	8,000	6,200	7,755	9,119
526		Sports Association Magazine	315,873	298,583	17,290	449,730	293,539	414,991	431,496
527		Employment Contracts							

528		Employee Benefits	30,377	36,890	(6,513)	30,500	29,125	37,965	37,000
529		Other Membership Expenditure	16,000	25,336	(9,336)	84,500	30,028	82,522	87,000
530		Total Direct Expenditure	572,017	502,223	69,794	839,255	487,612	721,352	744,088
531		**Departmental Expenditure**							
532		Membership – General	226,020	251,285	(25,165)	331,359	223,425	310.060	369,016
533		Regional	260,088	198,397	61,691	344,293	198,685	265,010	297,287
534		**Total Dept Expenditure**	486,108	449,582	36,526	675,652	422,110	575,070	666,303
535		Membership deficit/Surplus	73,727	(13,347)	(87,074)	(89,813)		(76,214)	(200,540)
536		Cost per member		.77				4.38	
537									
538		**Membership excl magazine**							
539		Income	1,020,352	829,330	(191,022)	1,265,094		1,067,257	1,064,851
540		Direct Expenditure	256,144	203,640	52,504	389,525		306,361	312,592
541			764,208	625,690	(138,518)	875,569		760,896	752,259
542		Departmental Expenditure	486,108	449,582	36,526	675,652		575,070	666,303
543			278,100	176,108	(101,992)	199,917		185,826	85,956
544		Income per member		47.59				61.32	
545		Surplus per member		10.11				10.68	
546		**Sports Association Magazine**							
547		Income	111,500	109,128	(2,372)	160,000		152,951	145,000
548		Expenditure	315,873	298,583	17,290	449,730		414,991	431,496
549			(204,373)	(189,455)	14,918	(289,730)		(262,040)	(286,496)
550		Cost per member		−10.87				−15.05	
551		Cost per member per issue		−1.09				−1.51	

CASE STUDY 8.2 continued

members and while the increase is not large, it includes a plan to try to stop the drift of members to a competing association.

The current position of the department, as at September, three-quarters of the way through the period, is given here. Please note this is only a small section of the whole management accounts, as this association's budget actually runs to 1,205 lines (see column 1). Numbering the lines helps enormously in discussing figures at management meetings.

Column 2 includes any notes that are essential for understanding of the line of account. Column 3 is the description of the line of account. Column 4 shows the original year-to-date budget estimate for the current year, while column 5 looks at actual year-to-date performance. The variance, or differences, between expected and actual performance is given in column 6. The total budget for the year is given in column 7, followed in column 8 by the performance-to-date in the previous year. Column 9 shows the year end for the previous year and, finally, a revised year end estimate is provided in column 10. Variance is a crucial concept; if the actual figures differ from that budgeted, management may need to make further decisions on the objectives they want to achieve. The revised year end estimate in column 10 provides the 'new' budget based on variances.

The management meeting immediately starts by looking at line 520, which shows income into the department. The budget for the year to date was £1,131.852 and the membership director, whose responsibility it is to meet the budget target, reports an income of only £938,458; a variance of £193,394 (note that negative amounts are expressed in brackets). The target for the whole year, seen in the next column, is £1.4 million.

The membership director evaluates this performance against the different lines of account illustrated in lines 512 and 514, as being directly linked to the changing economic climate, the forceful marketing of the competition and staff changes in the department, which has left it without a recruitment manager (new members are down by £116,194). As a result the end of year forecast, column 10, is now predicted at £1.2 million.

Close monitoring of the department has allowed careful control of costs and direct expenditure. Line 530 of the accounts shows that the department was predicted to spend £572,017, but has come in under budget by £69,794. However, departmental expenditure, which includes the salary for the recruitment manager, gives a clear illustration of how not all savings result in a positive result. Line 532 indicates the salary saving, but, as this can be directly linked to a reduction in income, the variance is not to be welcomed. The overall performance is shown in line 535, where a negative variance of £87,074 against budget is recorded.

The membership director has long been irritated by the costs and expenses linked to the association's magazine, which is a responsibility of the department. Members welcome the magazine's content and it is provided free to all full members and to a wide ranging number of other close contacts of the association. The magazine is paid for by advertising space that the department knows does not cover the costs of production and distribution.

CASE STUDY 8.2 continued

In order to ameliorate this problem the membership director has set an income against expenditure target to reduce the costs of the magazine to members from a high of £15.05 in the previous year for a total of 10 issues. This target needs to be monitored and the additional lines to the accounts showing the income over expenditure of the membership division, excluding the income and expenses of the magazine, were requested in order to control and evaluate performance. This is shown in lines 538 through to 543. The magazine income and expenditure is shown in lines 547 to 549. The magazine staff are very happy that their income, which, while down on budget, is only £2,372 adrift of target (line 547). Expenditure has been well controlled; they have challenged the printing costs, stationery and distribution methods, and overall have a positive variance of £17,290 (line 548), but some bills are still outstanding. Overall, the magazine has performed well against budget, showing a positive overall variance of £14,918 to date, and their end of year target in column 10 shows a revised estimate of losses of £286,496 against an original budget of £289,730.

The membership director has been pleased to see that the extra work the finance team has done to extrapolate these figures can show just where difficulties arise; in previous years the team may just have blamed the magazine, whereas now the direct income figure in line 539 clearly and articulately shows non-magazine based consolidated performance.

Learning activity 8.3

As a member of the management team you are concerned about the variances in the accounts for the Pegasus Sports Association.

(1) What other lines of account would you like to be investigated and why?

(2) Are all your investigations on negative aspects of performance? If so are there any positive variances which would warrant investigation? Why might investigating positive variances aid the organisation?

Control systems

Control really means ensuring that what happens in an organisation is what is supposed to happen (Allen et al., 2005). The process of control is operational in nature and involves establishing standards of performance, identifying deviations (or variables) from the standards and, where possible, correcting those deviations. Control is a fundamental aspect of management accounting, as is planning and decision making, because any variables to the master budget could be very costly.

There are some challenges to the control cycle, first in anticipating where deviations could occur. When setting the budget there is an expectation of 'x' number of ticket sales at a particular price. If those sales are not happening according to plan then remedial action needs to be taken, perhaps in reducing the price, cutting costs or unnecessary expenses, or in spending more to promote the tickets. Doing nothing would not be an option or all the budgeting work would be futile.

In many organisations management meetings are held on a weekly, bi-monthly or monthly schedule. Each department would report on progress to date according to their planned activity. The current financial figures would be given and compared to the budget. Decisions will be taken based on the performance of those figures against the target. At a simple level the expected income will be compared with actual income. The expected costs and expenditure will be compared with actual costs and expenditure. However, corrective action is needed in order that the company continues to be able to perform effectively and this may not be so simple to achieve.

Project accounting

Planning one-off projects requires similar skill sets to those of overall management accounting. Before approving projects, a cost/benefit analysis is undertaken to ensure that the project is worth the outlay in time, risk, resources and manpower. In the sports sector we need to remember that benefits may not be wholly dependent on profit, or even targeted to 'break even' but could be linked to participation in healthy activity, perhaps by a group previously averse to exercise. Break even is the point at which a project makes neither a profit nor a loss.

Once started, the scope of work to be undertaken would be broken down into a work schedule underwritten by a financial plan. The financial plan may take the format of a cash flow forecast, management accounts, such as those already illustrated, or, depending on the time scale of the project, a series of 'trading, profit and loss accounts' or 'income and expenditure accounts'.

Most project management theory assumes a fixed or defined source of income and the management of the plan becomes concerned with the control of costs in order to ensure that the budget comes in as forecast; however, in the sports industry this may not be the case. Increased income may be available after the budget has been set through extra sponsors coming on board, more tickets being sold than estimated, or other income being more successful than anticipated (such as fundraising raffles or auctions). Further discussion on planning individual sports events is given in Chapter 12.

Evaluating performance

The budgeting process allows for the setting of targets, the control process allows for performance to be monitored, and the evaluation process allows for entry into a new phase of planning which is based on observation and research. In project management this may aid future developments, or reassessing the cost/benefit of repeating the process again. In management, evaluation is an essential function which allows operational activity to improve. This final element of the financial function allows us to see the cyclical nature of the process that was introduced in the financial cycle illustration earlier.

Without evaluation the company cannot review performance and set budgets for the following year, shareholders or funding providers cannot assess the value of their investment and planning cannot be set for future activities. Business reviews and post-project evaluation gathers statistics and data and analyses them in relation to the key objectives. These are termed key performance indicators (KPIs) and may, or may not, be financial.

All budgets will be analysed in both income and expenditure and considered in the light of other accrued benefits. For one-off projects a report would be given to the host organisation that might have different needs and demands of, say, sponsors, funding bodies, councils, participants or other stakeholders. The reporting process is vital for future demand for projects. The outcomes from the Sydney Olympics in terms of tourist numbers, regeneration and sustainability were vital data sets on which the London 2012 bid was generated.

For ongoing businesses, operational performance analysis should be carried out that moves beyond the variance analysis of the management accounts we viewed in case study 8.2. In-depth performance analysis is needed to ensure both a return on the investment into the sport or sports organisation, and that the assets are well utilised.

Operational performance analysis

In sports organisations return on any investment may not be seen as profit driven, however all operational performance must be cost effective. For non-profit making organisations operational performance will be analysed through user enjoyment or sport participation, and may be measured through one of a number of quality standards.

Financial performances, however, can highlight operational difficulties much quicker than quality systems can, and for that reason both profit and non-profit making organisations share a number of financial analyses for evaluation purposes. Where possible, all organisations should benchmark the results against competitors', or equivalent organisations', performances.

Analysis is done using consolidated 'income over expenditure accounts' or 'trading, profit and loss accounts' and 'balance sheets', which may be those used for mandatory financial accounting or be more detailed, according to the needs of the organisation. Examples of these formats were given in Chapter 5.

A number of financially measured areas should be evaluated, including growth and returns on investment. Other important analysis includes how assets have been used and whether the organisation has managed its income and expenditure effectively (through cash flow). Finally, the organisation will seek to evaluate its operational performance through looking at its 'activity'; this includes stock performance, management of debtors and asset utilisation. These areas of investigation are illustrated in Table 8.1.

Many sports managers do not feel they need to understand these elements of evaluation and it certainly can seem complicated. Once mastered, it becomes an integral and key part of management discourse and enables a very clear picture of the organisation to emerge. It also allows for remedial action to take place. For example if debtors are not paying their bills within the required time, usually 30 days, the organisation must put processes in place to make sure that, first, they are not sold more goods and, second, that the debt is chased and collected.

A chart explaining the operational area under investigation, the analysis needed, the calculations (called ratio analysis) and either a comment or the remedial action that management can take, is included in Table 8.2.

Table 8.2: The evaluation of operational performance (ratio analysis)

Area of investigation or key performance indicator (KPI)	Financial record	Analysis	Calculation	Remedial action or comment
Growth				
Income or Sales	• Cash Flow Forecast • Trading Account		+/− against budget	• Marketing • Reassess demand for services • Competitor analysis
Cost control				
Cost of Sales	• Trading Account	% of Sales	$\frac{\text{Cost of Sales}}{\text{Income or Sales}} \times 100$	• Reduce costs • Reduce wastage • Ensure wastage is recorded effectively • Investigate theft or pilferage
Profitability				
Gross Profit or Income less Cost of Income	• Trading Account	% of Sales or Income = Gross profit margin	$\frac{\text{Sales} - \text{Cost of Sales}}{\text{Sales}} \times 100$ or $\frac{\text{Income} - \text{Cost of Income}}{\text{Income}} \times 100$	• Check original estimate was realistic by benchmarking with competitors or equivalent organisations • Reduce costs • Increase sales
Operating Profit Margin	• Profit and Loss Account	% of Sales or Income	$\frac{\text{Gross Profit} - \text{Operating Expenses}}{\text{Total Sales}} \times 100$	• Reduce expenses where possible • Increase Gross Profit by reducing costs or increasing sales

				• Ensure productivity in salaries and other personnel costs • Ensure salary and wage costs are analaysed per head of population and dept heads are aware of 'on costs' such as pension provision and health benefits when employing more staff • Redeploy staff • Investigate production or development of sport within the organisation
(After Tax) Net Profit Margin or Surplus performance against budget	• Profit and Loss Account	% of Sales	$\frac{\text{Profit after deductions}}{\text{Sales}} \times 100$	• Ensure budget accuracy by Comparison with industry norms • Benchmark with competitors • Increase sales/income • Reduce costs and expenditure • Investigate other incomes, e.g. from investment, and ensure performance matches expected • Look at interest paid on long term loans and ensure best value for money • Ensure results are judged against operational, and not amortisation or depreciation income or expenditure.

Table 8.2: Continued

Area of investigation or key performance indicator (KPI)	Financial record	Analysis	Calculation	Remedial action or comment
Growth of Profits or Surplus	• Profit and Loss account	Growth of Profit or Surplus year on year.	$\frac{\text{Profit this year} - \text{Profit last year}}{\text{Profit last year}} \times 100$	• Check comparisons year on year to monitor growth or fall of organisation • Benchmark against competitorss or equivalent companies
Solvency Current ratio	• Balance Sheet	Ability of company to pay its short-term debts	$\frac{\text{Current Assets}}{\text{Current Liabilities}}$	• Usually an organisation is trying to achieve a figure of 1:1. For every £1 of debt there is a £1 of asset to cover it but dependant on the industry • Reduce current assets
Acid test	• Balance Sheet	Ability to pay debt without reducing current assets	$\frac{\text{Current Assets} - \text{stock}}{\text{Current Liabilities}}$	• Identifies if there is a stock holding problem • Reduce stock
Inventory ratio	• Balance sheet	Highlights stock problems in high inventory (stock) businesses	$\frac{\text{Inventory}}{\text{Current Assets} - \text{Current Liabilities}}$	• Reduce stock holding to release working capital

Activity Rates

Stock performance	• Balance Sheet and P&L	Unused stock costs money to store and ties up cash	(1) Average stock = ½ Opening Stock + Closing Stock (2) Stock Turnover = $\frac{\text{Cost of Goods Sold}}{\text{Average Stock}}$ x times (3) Days of Stock Holding = $\frac{365}{\text{Stock Turnover}}$ = no of days stock held	• Stock not turning over or too high needs urgent action • Reduce stock by investigating alternative 24/7 suppliers • Working to a Just in time (JIT) purchasing policy • Assessing what sales are forecast and only holding stock to supply these
Debtor management	• Balance Sheet and P&L	Debtors reduce working capital	$\frac{\text{Average Trade Debtors}}{\text{Credit Sales}} \times 365$ = x days	• All debtors should pay within 30 days • Send out reminder statements • Follow up with letters • Stop further supplies • Sell debt to a factoring company • Ask for cash on delivery in future
Asset utilisation	• Balance Sheet and Trading Account	Assets should earn their expense and maintenance	(1) $\frac{\text{Total Sales Revenue}}{\text{Fixed assets at book value}}$ = return on assets (2) $\frac{\text{Total Sales Revenue}}{\text{Total assets}}$ = total asset turnover	• Use all assets effectively • Sell unused assets • Ensure capital expenditure on assets is subject to a cost/benefit analysis in future

Table 8.2: Continued

Area of investigation or key performance indicator (KPI)	Financial record	Analysis	Calculation	Remedial action or comment
Performance of long term investments				
Return on Investment (ROI)	• Balance Sheet and P&L account	Profit return on Investment	$\frac{\text{Profit after deduction}}{\text{Total assets}} \times 100$	• Should always be above a bank rate that investors could obtain • In sports organisation and ROI may not be deemed financial
Debt to assets ratio	• Balance Sheet	Indicates the extent of borrowed monies in an organisation Protects another long term financial institution from lending too much or 'over gearing' the company	$\frac{\text{Total Debt}}{\text{Total Assets}}$	• Industry norms apply • Either lend or don't lend according to the result which would normally be no less than one third owned by the sole trader or partner(s)
Debt to Equity	• Balance Sheet	Indicates the division of shares of funds provided by creditors, to those of equity or share holders	$\frac{\text{Total Debt}}{\text{Total Equity}}$	• Industry norms apply • Either allows further credit or not dependant on the security illustrated by the result

Long-term debt to equity ratio	• Balance Sheet	The indicator of long-term debt as a part of total equity invested	$\frac{\text{Long -term debt}}{\text{Total Equity}}$	• Industry norms apply • This is a vital ratio for long-term lenders to assess the risk of the business. If too much long-term finance is part of the overall worth of the business then further funds may not be secured against assets if anything went awry
Times interest earner or 'covered' ratio	• P&L and Balance Sheet	Indicates how well the business can service the cost of the debt	$\frac{\text{Profits before deductions}}{\text{Total Interest charged}}$	• A ratio which shows long-term lenders how the business is situated in terms of paying the interst on loans
Shareholders interests				
Return on equity	• Profit and Loss account & Balance Sheet	Measures the net rate of return on the share investment	$\frac{\text{Profits after deductions}}{\text{Total Equity}} \times 100$	• Industry norms apply • Future shareholders will want to see an equitable return in order to risk investing
Return on common equity	• Profit and Loss account & Balance Sheet	Measures the net rate of return for common shareholders	$\frac{\text{Profits after deductions}}{\text{Total equity − preferred stock}} \times 100$	• Industry norms apply • Future shareholders will want to see an equitable return in order to risk investing
Earnings per share	• Annual reports	Indicates earnings per share	$\frac{\text{Total profits after deductions and dividends on preferred stock}}{\text{Number of common shares}}$	• Stock market industry norms • Shareholders will need to understand their earnings in order for the company to remain an attractive investment

Table 8.2: Continued

Area of investigation or key performance indicator (KPI)	Financial record	Analysis	Calculation	Remedial action or comment
Dividend on yield equity	• Annual reports	Actual rate of return to shareholders based on the dividend they will receive	$\frac{\text{Annual dividend per share}}{\text{Current market price per share}}$	• Stock market industry norms • Shareholders will need to understand their earnings in order for the company to remain an attractive investment
Price/earnings ratio	• Annual reports	Shareholders long-term view on the potential future income streams to grow against the risks	$\frac{\text{Current market price per share}}{\text{Earnings after deductions per share}}$	• Stock market industry norms • Shareholders will need to understand their earnings in order for the company to remain an attractive investment
Dividend/ payout ratio	• Annual reports	Indicates willingness of companies to distribute profit	$\frac{\text{Annual Dividends per share}}{\text{Earnings after deductions per share}}$	• Balance between payout to shareholders and retention of cash flow for future investment

Review

This chapter has examined the cyclical process of planning, controlling and evaluating the business of sport through the use of management accounting practices. The importance of this process cannot be underestimated in both profit and non-profit making organisations for the private, public and voluntary sectors. Planning tools have been shown to be essential to management success, and include cash flow forecasts and management accounts. Control systems are highlighted by using variance analysis to monitor performance, and operational evaluation is illustrated through the final stage in the cycle illustrating the differing measures which organisations can use to define project or organisational success.

Review of learning outcomes

Having read the chapter and undertaken the activities you should be able to answer the following questions:

- Select a sports organisation of your choice and examine its annual accounts. Comment on the operational evaluation of the organisation using at least four financial KPIs described in the Table 8.2.
- Using a spreadsheet, write a financial budget for the following financial year; so that the organisation can use to monitor its ongoing financial situation.
- Discuss the key factors that might affect the success of the financial budget.

Further reading

For further study of accounting and accounting techniques read:

Dyson, JR (2004) *Accounting for non-accounting students*. 6th edition. London: Pitman.

McKenzie, W (2003) *The Financial Times guide to using and interpreting company accounts*. 3rd edition. London: FT Prentice Hall.

Millichamp, AH (2000) *Finance for non-financial managers*. 3rd edition. London: Continuum.

Owen, G (1999) *Accounting for hospitality, leisure and tourism*. 2nd edition Harlow: Pearson Education.

For further understanding of the financing of sport read:

Wilson, R and Joyce, J (2008) *Finance for sport and leisure managers: an introduction*. Abingdon: Routledge.

For some further discussion of ratio analysis and its applications see:

Wiscombe, C A (2009) Financial awareness of travel operations management, in Robinson, P (ed.) *Travel operations management*. Oxford: CABI.

Chapter 9

Sports entrepreneurship

Karen Bill

This chapter provides an overview of what is meant by entrepreneurship and enterprise and how this can be translated into the sports business arena. Such enterprises could broadly include sports team owners, sports tour operators, sporting goods stores and health clubs. We start from the premise that there are some fairly broad characteristics that are generally accepted as being entrepreneurial and a set of practical exercises are included to help you gain an understanding of your personal entrepreneurship competencies. In order to think about starting a business venture, a good idea is required and, with this in mind, the chapter encourages creative thinking and explores idea generation techniques in order to facilitate opportunity recognition, creation and the harvesting of sports ideas. Finally, it explores how to evaluate and present your idea.

But what if you do not want to start a business? In a thriving and dynamic sports economy there will always be a need for innovation and a call for better entrepreneurial skills and abilities for dealing with current challenges and uncertain futures in whatever job you do. You may work, or want to work, for a sports organisation. In this situation, entrepreneurship does not necessarily have to imply the creation of a new business; rather it is about the entrepreneur working within the confines of an established organisation. Pinchot (1985) terms this an 'intrapreneur'.

Learning outcomes

This chapter is designed to enable you to:

- develop awareness of your own entrepreneurial abilities to equip you for the world of work;
- begin to develop creative business ideas;
- consider and evaluate your business idea;
- present your business idea.

Introduction

The national context

The Chancellor of the Exchequer stated in his 2006 Budget Address, and again in the Mansion House Speech of 2002 that there were: 'Too few skilled employees, too few men and women starting and growing businesses . . .', and this has been a failure by government 'to realize the educational and entrepreneurial potential of its own people.'

So it seems that: 'the need for enterprising capacities in individuals is fundamental to our future and economic and social well-being. An industry, such as the sports industry, worth £9.8 billion a year, needs graduates with all the critical thinking, entrepreneurial attitude and business skills' (UUK, 2006).

Defining entrepreneurship

The word entrepreneurship itself derives from the word *entreprendre*, relating to individuals who undertook the risk of a new enterprise. 'Entrepreneurship' is a term closely associated with the economic development and wealth creation of businesses. It involves 'the process of creating and developing new ventures' (Enterprise Insight, 2005, p23).

The term 'entrepreneur' was first introduced by the early eighteenth-century French economist Richard Cantillon. In his writings, he formally defines the entrepreneur as the 'agent who buys the means of production at certain prices in order to combine them' into a new product (Schumpeter, 1951, pp248–50). Nixon sees entrepreneurship as: 'fundamentally, about using enterprise to create new business, new businesses and "can-do" organisations and services' (Nixon, 2004, p1).

Here 'enterprise' is understood as, having ideas, making things happen and doing something about them in order to bring about change. However, today, there is still no agreed, universal, definition.

Defining sports entrepreneurship

Is there such a term as 'sports entrepreneurship' and if so, what does it mean? Or is it simply the application of entrepreneurial concepts to sport situations?

According to Bailey, manager of KPMG Tourism and Leisure Advisory Services (in Ball, 2005, p19): 'Entrepreneurship is critical to the hospitality, leisure, sports and tourism sectors, as with rapidly changing consumer demands and expectations, constant innovation by businesses is vital to meet and, hopefully, exceed these evolving demands and expectations.'

So how could we define sports entrepreneurship? My personal definition would be that of an individual who has the tacit industry-specific knowledge (e.g. personal trainer) and/or general business knowledge (e.g. football club owner), innovatory capacity and creative spirit to spot and generate openings within the sport sector in order to realise a market opportunity. An alternative definition is 'a person who organizes, operates, and assumes the risk for a sport-related business venture' (Changemakers, 2008).

Reflection 9.1

Let's consider the relevance of entrepreneurship to the sports industry.

One could argue that 'sports entrepreneurship' has become increasingly prominent within the sports business environment as a major route for sports graduates into the world of work and therefore a term in its own right. This has led to a growing number of university courses devoted to this field of study on the back of prior academic interest. The growth of the sports industry in terms of small businesses (89 percent of the industry workforce are employees, 11 percent are self-employed [Experian, 2005]), along with the increasing interest on the part of government, industry practitioners and academics in sports innovation, all point to this being an emerging field. This is further evidenced by the recent UK Sport's Ideas 4 Innovation programme, in particular the Garage Innovators Award (a competition open to any sports enthusiast with creative ideas that may have the potential to enhance the performance of British athletes). While regional headlines like 'Sports World entrepreneur casts an eye over Blacks Leisure' (*Yorkshire Post*, 21 July 2008) indicates that the media, too, recognise this emerging field.

Sporting entrepreneurs

If we agree then, that there is such a thing as sports entrepreneurship, who might we classify as our sport entrepreneurs? It is perhaps easier to think of more general entrepreneurs in society such as Bill Gates and Richard Branson.

Learning activity 9.1

Sport entrepreneurs?

Read the following case studies and think about them. Then compare the two individuals (Mike Ashley and Roman Abramovich).

(1) Using Cantillon's definition above of an entrepreneur, to what extent would you consider them both to be entrepreneurs? Explain your reasoning.
(2) To what extent would you describe them as sport entrepreneurs? Use the sport entrepreneurship definitions above to help you reach a decision. (Look at how they made their money and where their skills/knowledge lies in particular).
(3) Now look at case study 9.3 (John Wood) and discuss to what extent this individual might differ from the two above. Consider to what degree you might classify him as a sport entrepreneur.
(4) Of the three, which one might you most readily identify with? Why?

Learning activity 9.1 continued

Case study 9.1: Mike Ashley

According to the *Sunday Times* Rich List 2008, Mike Ashley is worth: £1,398 million.

He is an English billionaire entrepreneur who has made his money in the sporting goods market. After leaving school at 16 in the 1980s, Ashley began opening Sport and Ski shops in and around London. Ashley has made his money by buying a number of sport brands. He purchased sports equipment companies, including Donnay, Dunlop Slazenger (the tennis and golf brand), Kangol, Lonsdale (boxing brand) and Karrimor, the outdoor gear manufacturer. Ashley also owns Lillywhites, the London sports store, and Sports Soccer. Often derided as a 'pile it high, sell it cheap merchant', his main company, Sports Direct International plc, was floated on the stock market in 2007. He also paid £133 million to gain control of Newcastle United football club that year.

Case study 9.2: Roman Abramovich

According to the *Sunday Times* Rich List 2008, Roman Abramovich is worth: £11,700 million.

His source of wealth is derived from oil and industry. Abramovich, 41, started his commercial activity in the late 1980s when Soviet President Mikhail Gorbachev's reforms permitted the opening of small private businesses, known as co-operatives. Abramovich began his business career selling plastic ducks from a Moscow apartment, but within a few years his wealth spread from oil conglomerates to pig farms. In June 2003, he became the owner of the companies that control Chelsea Football Club in the UK. The club also embarked on an ambitious programme of commercial development, with the aim of making it a worldwide brand, and announced plans to build a new state-of-the-art training complex in Cobham, Surrey. As of May 2008, Abramovich has spent approximately £600 million on the club.

Case study 9.3: Teardrop Technologies

Teardrop Technologies designs cricket batting gloves and pads with an innovative design for wicket keepers. John Wood, who is managing director of Teardrop Technologies, joined the Enterprise Fellowship Scheme after he graduated from the University of Wolverhampton with a degree in Sports Technology and has continued to use the facilities and assistance available at the university through various projects ever since. Teardrop Technologies provides innovative, injury-preventative equipment for conventional and extreme sports. The company aims to keep its customers well protected during sporting activity; Teardrop provides technological solutions to improve equipment currently used in the sports industry, increasing product performance and reducing the risk of injury for sportspeople. In 2007 the company won the Entrepreneurial Spirit award at the Lord Stafford Awards for its innovative sports equipment, including newly designed and polymer based cricket batting gloves and pads.

Personal qualities and entrepreneurial abilities

> 'Entrepreneurship is not solely about business skills or starting new ventures; it is a way of thinking and behaving relevant to all parts of society and the economy' (CIHE, 2008).

This section is about your suitability for entrepreneurship and asks you to consider your personal entrepreneurship abilities. Changing career patterns require graduates who are able to move within the employment market in 'entrepreneurial ways' in order to cope with uncertainty and constant change, regardless of whether one wishes to start a business venture. This is discussed more fully in Chapter 3.

Learning activity 9.2

Entrepreneurial competencies

List the skills, behaviours and attributes that you think are needed by an entrepreneur then reflect on your own entrepreneurial competencies and complete the exercise below.

Table 9.1: Entrepreneurial competencies

Skills	Behaviours	Attributes	Indicate the extent to which you possess abilities in this area (low/ medium/high)	Provide examples demonstrating your abilities in this area

In order to help you complete the activity you may find the definitions below helpful:

- a skill is knowledge demonstrated by action; an ability to perform in a certain way;
- a behaviour is often seen as the way we act or conduct ourselves;
- an attribute is an inherent quality or characteristic which is representative of the person.

Some scholars (e.g. Gibb, 1993) have focused on what makes an entrepreneur in terms of defining sets of enterprising behaviours, skills and attributes. Some typical examples of the behaviours, skills and attributes required of entrepreneurial people are indicated in Table 9.2.

McGrath states that a key aspect of establishing an 'entrepreneurial mindset' is 'creating the condition under which everyone is energized to look for opportunities to change the business model' (McGrath and Macmillan, 2000, pp2–3). Entrepreneurs need to be able to identify new markets for a new product and in this sense they are using their skills to carve a path through uncertainty; or they might do old things in new ways, seeing problems as opportunities. They need to possess the ability to negotiate and sell, and be versatile when dealing with uncertainty and complexity.

Entrepreneur behaviours are naturally geared to opportunity seeking and grasping, taking initiatives to make things happen, using judgement to take calculated risks and solving problems creatively. Creativity is an attitude of mind which often involves lateral thinking (de Bono, 1990).

Reflection 9.2

So are entrepreneurs born or made? What are your views?

Some would say that there are innate, personality characteristics; others argue that it is possible to learn to be more entrepreneurial through experiential learning and entrepreneurial learning experiences.

The skills you have developed may have come from work placements, your personal life or your time in education. The following activity enables you to discover what your values and motivations are in preparation for becoming a sports entrepreneur.

Learning activity 9.3

Values inventory

In considering whether self-employment would be a sensible option for you, it is worthwhile assessing what your key values in life are. This exercise is designed to look at what factors are important in deciding your own future. This could help guide you in terms of the type and nature of entrepreneurial activity you might engage in. For instance, if citizenship is of importance then you may be more of a social entrepreneur (a social entrepreneur identifies and solves social problems, and seeks to generate social value rather than profits). If family is very important to you then you might wish to establish a lifestyle business rather than go for high growth. Or if you have a high moral responsibility to society then you may consider a business which echoes 'fair trade' principles such as Café Direct.

Select from the list in Table 9.3 your five most important values, but feel free to add others to the list! Now reflect on your learning and thinking in this task. If you were an entrepreneur, how might your values be seen in action in your business?

Table 9.2: Entrepreneurial behaviours, skills and attributes (Gibb, 1993, p14)

Skills	Behaviours	Attributes
Problem solving Creativity Persuasiveness Planning Negotiating Decision making	Acting independently Actively achieving goals Flexibility responding to challenges Coping with and enjoying uncertainty Taking risky actions in uncertain environments Persuading others Commitment to make things happen Opportunity seeking Solving problems/conflicts	Self-confident Autonomous Achievement orientated Versatile Dynamic Resourceful

Table 9.3: Values inventory

Recognition	Family life
Teamwork	Intellectual matters
Freedom	Social responsibility
Survival at all costs	Career
Competition	Well-being, health
Religious life	Honesty
Love	Independent mind
Citizenship	Politics
Power	Local community
Physical independence	Massive wealth
Creativity	Self-fulfilment

Reflection 9.3

Support can mean many things and involve many people when starting a business. For instance, in starting up a tennis academy you'd certainly need the following network.

- National Governing Body of sport – Lawn Tennis Association (LTA) (potential licence arrangements)
- Banks (e.g. borrowing arrangements, business account)
- The Council (e.g. provision of tennis courts, health and safety issues)
- Accountants (e.g. who is going to audit my income for tax purposes?)
- Suppliers (e.g. who is going to supply my tennis balls, rackets, etc?)
- Customers (who is going to attend my tennis classes?)

Learning activity 9.4

The network audit

The nature of support from different stakeholders will vary, and will vary over time, and you need to recognise this. Below are three examples of support based on the network audit. A network audit is a tool which enables you to identify the types and levels of individual support that are open to you. The nature of the support has been coded according to whether it is vital, its frequency, and the strength of the relationship using a scale of 1 to 10 where 10 is high. Coding may vary slightly according to the nature of the business.

Table 9.4: Network audit

Source of support	Vital	Frequency	Strength of relationship
Family	10	10	7
Bank	5	7	8
Local council	10	10	3

Imagine that you are just about to set yourself up as a self-employed football coach. Repeat the above exercise. Write down a list of the people you think you would need to support your business venture. Grade them on how vital they are, frequency and strength of relationship using a scale of 1–10. What does this tell you? Are you well networked?

Reflection 9.4

Are you in the 'know-who'?

All businesses need some form of support network and this may change over time. A key aspect of the entrepreneur's armoury is acquiring the 'know-who'.

Access the Shell Livewire web page. (It is a premier source of free information and advice for young people starting a business in the UK.) It can be found at **http://www..shell-livewire.org/promote-yourself/**. Have a go at searching for network contacts. You may also wish to join the Social Network or Discussion Forum.

Idea generation

In this section, we shall look at ideas. It is not easy to come up with good business ideas. Equally, you may think that you have a good idea but it may not be a good business idea because there are no customers or market for your idea. This section is designed to help you work this out.

There are many techniques used to assist with the generation of ideas. Idea generation techniques can determine how we may support the development of new business ideas or the recognition of market opportunities. Below are some examples.

Idea showers focus our attention on all the attributes of a product or service – its potential usages; customer groups, their needs, etc. The ideas shower enables us to create a list of the 'obvious', the 'fantastic' and the downright impractical by bouncing ideas off each other to create new ideas and opportunity identification.

How does it work? Using a tennis scenario, the activity could conclude with a number of ideas:

- meeting previously unmet needs – graphite tennis racket;
- needs being better met – wider tennis rackets;
- more needs being met – luminous tennis balls;
- different combinations of needs – tennis trainer gadget.

Negative idea showers can also be used, by identifying opportunities from problems, i.e. taking a problem, service or product and 'pulling it apart' in order to create a list of the negatives.

An example is inaccuracies in line calls at Wimbledon. From this, it is then possible to rethink the product/service by making it address all of the negatives associated with the existing product/service or company and drawing out the improvements required. The solution could be, for example, the Hawkeye Technology that is now used on Centre Court.

Rule reversal – this is where you challenge the norm. Rule reversal involves identifying the pattern of rules, conventions, assumptions and traditions and seeks ways to contradict them. A good example is Lucozade, originally marketed to poorly people but remarketed to healthy athletes as an energy drink.

When thinking of ideas often a good starting point is to ask yourself the following questions, which often provide a seed for new ideas:

- What annoys/irritates me? (Use your own experiences as a customer.)
- What's in the news?
- What would I buy?
- What type of business would I work for?
- What person do I most admire?
- What am I really good at?

For example, exploring what you are really good at often helps focus the mind on what you could do in business. Perhaps you have a really good skill and hobby that could become a lifestyle business as in the scenario below.

> I'd rescued and repaired several abandoned bikes for friends when I realised it was a great opportunity to make a living doing something worthwhile for the community and environment. (Dom Scholfield, 28, co-founder of the Oxford Cycle Workshop, on **www.makeyourmark.org.uk**)

The Oxford Cycle Workshop has repaired and recycled 600 abandoned bikes in two years (see **oxfordcycleworkshop.org.uk**).

Mind maps are diagrams used to represent words and ideas, which are linked to and arranged around a central key word or idea. Mind maps are used to generate, visualize, structure and classify ideas, and are often used as an aid to solve problems and generate ideas. The idea was invented by Tony Buzan, author of *The mind map book* (1995).

Figure 9.1: Mind map

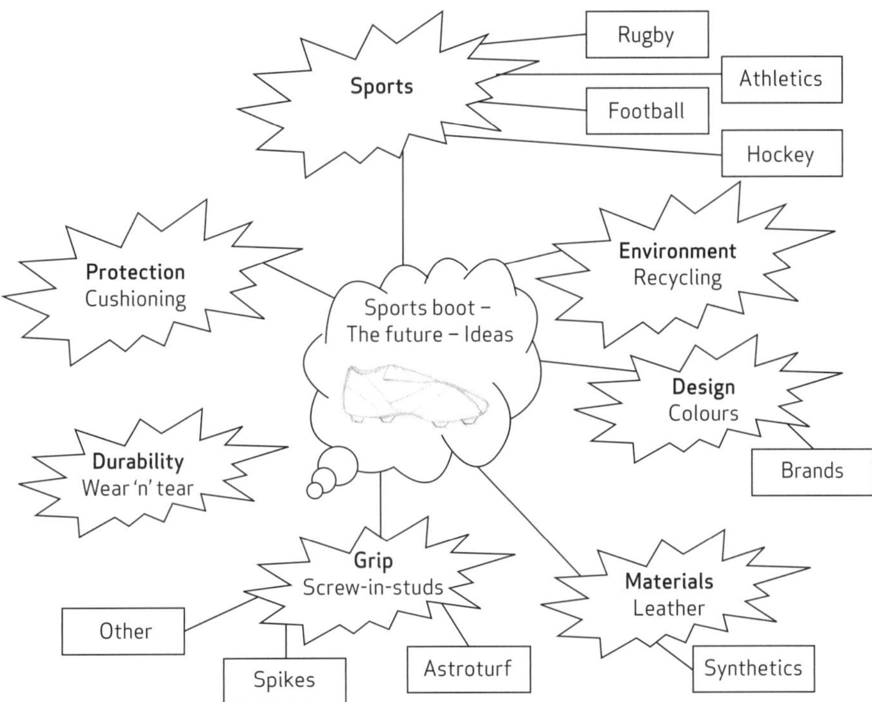

A mind map of a sports boot

If I was thinking about developing a new sports boot then a basic mind map might look something like Figure 9.1. The idea is to join up and see the relationship between the various sections in order to generate new ideas.

According to Barrow (Barrow et al., 2005, p16): 'It's a good strategy to have an idea which appears from the outset to have some compelling features, an addressable market and which you are likely to be interested in.' There are very few truly original ideas. Other ways of getting into business can, therefore, involve using ideas that already exist within the market. For instance, one method is to 'add value to an existing product', for instance table tennis balls that don't get squashed! Further examples are highlighted in Table 9.5.

Table 9.5: Ways into business

Ways into business	Examples
Franchising (The granting of a licence by a corporation to another, which entitles the other to trade under their trade mark/trade name.	Franchise from a major sport company to offer a particular service or product brand.
Taking a patent opportunity (A patent is exclusive rights, given by government, upon application, to protect your product from competitors).	Many products do not get patented for various reasons, sometimes financial. Go to a patent office and look at some of the ideas. The UK government Patent Office website is www.patentoffice.gov.uk.
Discount selling (Where you bulk buy products).	Look for bankrupt companies with excess stock or manufacturers with 'seconds', e.g. footballs.

Learning activity 9.5

Idea generation

Access the following weblink: **www.starttalkingideas.org/whoyouare/whats_bigidea.php**. This will take you through the steps involved in generating business ideas. You will need to have a go at generating a few ideas which you can then evaluate in order to help you decide upon the main contenders for your business. Capture all of your ideas.

Explore other relevant idea source websites to find other potential idea generation initiatives, such as:

- **www.thinksmart.com**
- **www.globalideasbank.org**
- **www.creativityatwork.com**
- **www.mycoted.com/creativity/techniques/index.php**
- **www.springwise.com**
- **www.ideacafe.com** (a fun approach to serious business)

Not found a good business idea yet? Here are a few examples of possible sport businesses that you might like to use throughout the remainder of this chapter.

What about starting up as:

- a sports coach to offer holiday sports coaching programmes;
- a personal trainer to deliver bespoke fitness programmes;
- a sports clothing print company to offer embroidery and print screening for sport clubs.

The next sections are about evaluating your business idea. It is difficult to quantify ideas and opportunities. According to Kaplan (2007, pp32–58): 'the world is full of ideas, but ideas are not opportunities and opportunities are not ready-made to build a business around'.

Evaluating your business idea

Marketing an idea

While you may think that you have a good idea, it may not be a good business idea for various reasons, as discussed earlier. Therefore, once you have some ideas, they will need building upon and analysing as real business opportunities before being tested in the market. There are a few specific, relevant marketing questions that you may wish to ask yourself at this stage:

- Does the idea work? Is it valid?
- What needs does it meet? (What are its features and benefits and unique selling point?)
- Who are the customers?
- How many customers are there? Are there sufficient?
- What is the competition?

There are a number of marketing tools which can help you quantify your business idea such as a SWOT and PESTLE analysis. Essentially, a SWOT analysis is a summary tool used to gauge the particular internal strengths and weaknesses of a product/ service as well as the external opportunities and potential threats. A PESTLE analysis provides a framework for looking specifically at the global, external drivers and influences on the business, such as political, social and economic forces. These marketing tools are explored in more detail in Chapter 4.

Financing an idea

It is important to ascertain whether the business idea is financially viable. While you do not have to have A-level Accounting, knowing the key financial procedures is essential to staying in business and growing your business. Chapter 8 provides information on key financial concepts based around a business venture. However, suffice to say that, at the very least, you need to estimate how much money is needed to get the business off the ground, that is, what your start-up costs are (expenses, assets and funding).

By now you should have an innovative sports business idea that offers a unique selling point. You should have researched the market for this idea by identifying suitable target market segments and potential competitors. You should also have identified the resources and capabilities, as well as providing a cost breakdown for the new venture. Future sales projections and cash flows should also have been considered.

There are various tools which can be used to test market viability.

Learning activity 9.6

Market viability (Venture Navigator)

Access the Venture Navigator Programme at **www.venturenavigator.co.uk** and test out the validity of your new business idea. What does the report tell you? (Venture Navigator is a free online service helping start-ups and small businesses improve their chances of success. You will need to sign up but it is free.)

Another useful website is **businesslink.gov.uk**. Use the Business Link checklist to help you research and test the market for your goods or services.

Presenting your buisness idea

This section is about how to present your business idea. You are now ready to present all of this information to key stakeholders, whether they are potential investors such as bank managers or venture capitalists (High risk investors). This can be communicated by a business plan. Table 9.6 provides information on what should be included in a business plan.

Table 9.6: What goes into a business plan

Contents	Information
Mission	Mission statement that defines the business.
Business plan objectives	Strategic objectives: achievements in the market and gains to be made in market position.
	Financial objectives: the turnover and profit targets for the period of the plan; the growth desired over the previous period.
Summary of business	Provides a snapshot of all business aspects.
Market environment	Background to the market – size of the market, key trends, buying behaviour, etc.
	Competitors – analysis of principal competitors.
	Competitive advantage and strategy – 4 Ps or 7 Ps (if it is a service-based idea).
Management team	Expertise, roles in the company, CV.
Financial information and forecasts	Income, routine and capital expenditure, cash flow.
Conclusion	
Appendix	

The key benefit of a business plan is that it is a relationship management instrument. It is a means of communicating, projecting and providing a deeper understanding of your business. According to Bygrave 'it is more than just a document; it is a process, a story' (Bygrave and Zacharakis, 2007, p263).

Wickham (2006) recognises that a business plan is an essential tool for the entrepreneur as it provides four mechanisms which aid the performance of your business:

- analysis (in order to gather and process information);
- synthesis (in order to create a strategy);
- communication (in order to gain support, i.e. fund managers);
- action (in order to define what you are going to do, i.e. objectives etc.).

What goes into a business plan?

Learning activity 9.7

Business plan/role play

Have a go at writing a business plan for an idea that you have developed or using one of the examples provided earlier in the chapter.

Consider using the following websites to support you in the process of writing your business plan:

- **bplans.co.uk** – offers business plans;
- **Smallbusinesspro.co.uk** – offers help and advice for starting up;
- **Teneric.co.uk** – is a business planning website, offering sample business plans by industry.

Then, in small groups, exchange your business plans and assign one of the roles below to each member. Undertake a role play, creating empathy with each respective role. You may wish to brainstorm first with panel members to ascertain what each person will be looking for in the proposal. Think about the particular questions that you might ask, for example,

- An investor/business angel (What are your networks like? What is your commitment? Is it a concrete opportunity? Can we work with you – likeability?
- A lender/bank manager (Is it a good plan, idea? Does the money asked for match with the plan? What are the risks? How much is the entrepreneur putting in? Have you run a business before – track record?)
- A customer (Is it a good service/product? What are its qualities? Is the company reliable and sound financially? Will I get a good after sales service experience? Reputation?)
- A family member (What is my risk? What might be my role? What happens if the business has to fold?)

Elevator pitch

Another communication method is an 'elevator pitch'. The elevator pitch is named after the opportunity to pitch someone an idea in a short period of time, i.e. the length of an elevator ride.

An elevator pitch is a quick and concise way to communicate who you are, what you're trying to do and why you do it better. It's much more than a mission statement, it is understanding your business in a way that gets people excited and thinking. The term is typically used in the context of an entrepreneur pitching an idea to a venture capitalist to receive funding rather as one sees on the business reality TV programmes such as *Dragons' den*.

The types of questions that need to be considered when presenting an elevator pitch are:

- What is your product or service? Provide a quick, concise and clear definition of your idea. Visual information is often useful.
- Who are your customers? Introduce the market sector and what its potential is.
- How do you expect to make money?
- Who runs the company? Explain the expertise and skills within the company to demonstrate credibility. The old adage 'bet on the horse not the jockey' often runs true.
- Who are your competitors? Clarify who they are and what market share they own.
- What is your competitive advantage? Articulate your unique selling point, how your service/product is differentiated and how (pricing, distribution?).

Learning activity 9.8

Elevator pitch

Imagine you are in an elevator that goes up 40 storeys. You are in the elevator with a potential funder of your business idea who is getting off at the top floor. You know the lift will take two minutes to reach the 40th storey. You have this time to convince the potential investor of your business idea. In other words, you have to sell both yourself and your idea. Prepare your brief.

Now that you have worked through the chapter, you will have more of an insight into what entrepreneurship is and its meaning within sport business management and value in both societal and economic terms. You will have a greater insight into the entrepreneurial mindset in terms of the associated characteristics, skills and attributes. You will have had experience of generating a raw idea and opportunity spotting, as well as formalising your idea and testing it out in the market, and communicating your plan.

Review of learning outcomes

Having read the chapter and undertaken the various learning activities you should be able to answer the following questions.

(1) Undertake a poll on a number of your peers and ask them to define both entrepreneurship and enterprise. Record your answers. What are the most common buzz words used? Can you distinguish between both terms? Analyse your findings and see what patterns emerge. Consider also the definitions provided within the text and create your own definition of each. Try to apply these definitions to sport and create your own definition of sports entrepreneurship.
(2) Identify three reasons why entrepreneurship is both relevant and important to the sports sector.
(3) Demonstrate your understanding of one of your business ideas that you have developed by completing the following:

Having analysed your idea in relation to its market, try filling in the blanks for your new sport service or product.

For	____________________	(name the customer group)
Who	____________________	(has the problem/desire)
The product/service	____________________	(is new)
Offers	____________________	(results)
Different	____________________	(competitors or substitutes)

(4) Do you think that you have the right abilities/attitudes/values to make a success of your proposed business? Provide explanations for your choices.
(5) Reflect on the reasons whether and why you may be (a) a sports entrepreneur or (b) a more enterprising person. Highlight your qualities, skills and experience.

Further reading

This chapter has directed you to a variety of resources within each learning activity. Additional resources are listed below.

- The Global Entrepreneurship Monitor (GEM) provides high-quality international research data on entrepreneurial activity readily available to as wide an audience as possible. GEM is the largest single study of entrepreneurial activity in the world.
- National Council for Graduate Entrepreneurship (NCGE) – **www.ncge.com** is not only focused on graduates starting businesses, but understanding, developing and promoting a culture of entrepreneurship within Higher Education through research, education and facilitation.
- The International Entrepreneurship Educators Programme (IEEP) for those teaching enterprise education, to which I must attribute much inspiration for this chapter.

- **www.princes-trust.org.uk/** – this is a charity that supports youth enterprise
- **www.shell-livewire.org** – Shell Livewire has a comprehensive guide on business start-up.
- **www.sife.org** – SIFE (Students in Free Enterprise)
- **http://www.simventure.co.uk** – the ultimate business start-up experience; this website is subscription based, however it also has a useful learning zone. In the 'Other Resources' section there is 'Entrepreneurs on Film', which shows e-clips of business entrepreneurs.

For further reading on the skills and employability aspects to entrepreneurship read;

Gibson, DA (2006) *The e-factor: increase your career, business or social enterprise prospects*. London: Enterprise HQ.

For further sports entrepreneurship education material see:

Bill, K (2008) *Sports entrepreneurship interactive learning and teaching resource*. Oxford: Higher Education Academy, HLST.

Bill, K (2006) *Supporting entrepreneurship: the development of entrepreneurship education within UK sport*. Birmingham: National Council for Graduate Entrepreneurship Working Paper 026/2006.

For information on business ideas see newspapers, which increasingly provide special or regular features on enterprise and entrepreneurship, and offer useful up-to-date examples and sources of information.

The *Sunday Times* offers features such as 'How I made it', 'Idea of the week' and the 'Business doctor', which answers business related queries. The Monday *Daily Telegraph* has a start-up section. The *Financial Times* has articles of relevance and a sponsored report on understanding entrepreneurship. See also: **www.bbc.co.uk/**, which contains information on small businesses in its Business and Money section

For further information on business planning and plans see:

- **Startups.co.uk** – for articles which will help you understand what's involved in writing a business plan, as well as the latest news on the topic of business planning.
- **Businesslink.gov.uk** – Business Link offers practical advice and lots of links to assist with writing your business plan.
- **smallbusinessadvice.org.uk** – Small Business Advice has a number of free business planning templates for you to download.

Chapter 10

Risk management and the sport manager

Mark Piekarz

'Risk' is a term commonly referred to in management, business and by the media, but is frequently misunderstood. Perhaps the most common associations with risk are with the notions of dangers and accidents, whereby any mishap, no matter how minor, can be followed by legal action. The result is that there can sometimes be a constant demand for organisations to reduce or remove all risks in order to prevent expensive claims for compensation. Stories of conkers being banned in playgrounds, or school sports being stopped because of fears of injuries and legal action are often used to illustrate this trend.

Yet, without risks, there would be no challenge, and a life without challenge is a much duller one. One just has to think of animals caged in zoos, which, while having their basic needs of food and security met, can develop many psychological problems, such as manic pacing or even self-harm. Simply put, part of the problem is the lack of stimulation; and a key part of stimulation comes from risks. This idea is also extended to the business world, whereby it is sometimes said that without risk, there are no profits for commercial businesses.

What this chapter will therefore illustrate is how important it is for the contemporary sport manager to have a more complex understanding of risk in a sport management context. It is shown that risk management is not only used in operational related health and safety assessments, such as inspecting equipment for signs of wear, but also in a more general, strategic sense, for example as part of a SWOT analysis. It is emphasised throughout this chapter that a key management challenge is about striking a proper balance between controlling negative dangers and threats, while also maintaining sufficient challenge and opportunities for the activities to be enjoyable, or profits and social gains to be made.

Learning outcomes

This chapter is designed to enable you to:

- recognise the importance of risk in the management of sport operations;
- explain why it has grown in significance;
- identify and explain the difference between a notion of a risk culture and a practical risk process;
- adapt and apply a variety of risk approaches to the context that they are needed for.

The growth of risk management

For the sport manager, it can be difficult to ignore or avoid dealing with notions of risk. The use of the term has become ubiquitous in every aspect of our lives, with an increasing usage in sport and adventure activities. Grainger-Jones, in his chapter on sport risk management, makes the provocative comment that:

> In no other sphere is risk management so essential but so problematic. In no other sphere is legislation becoming so onerous, licensing so substantial, insurance so important, and litigation so worrying. (1999, p175)

It is an argument that is difficult to disagree with, particularly when one considers the many factors that are *driving* the adoption of risk management processes and concepts, which are explored in Learning activity 10.1, and can be summarised around the following areas:

- *Increased regulation affecting operational sport management*. The 1974 Health and Safety at Work Act and its various subsequent amendments and additions have been key pieces of legislation driving the adoption of risk assessment practices at an operational level for all of the UK. This legislation helped clarify the principle of the *duty of care* of employees and employers to ensure as far as is *reasonably practicable*, that the work environment is safe and healthy, which over the years has encouraged a process of assessing risk in the workplace. This, in turn, has been steadily extended to participation in sport and adventure activities.
- *Increased regulation affecting strategic sport management*. In many developed countries, corporate organisations (an organisation is defined by legal regulations, which limit corporate governors' and shareholders' liability to the losses a firm may incur) also have a responsibility for the annual reporting of the future operating conditions of the organisation which could generate risks for the organisation, whether they are good or bad. The type of risks, the time scales involved and the level of management at which this review is conducted has helped drive the adoption of risk practices at a *strategic level*. For the UK, this requirement was established by the 1999 Turnball Report and in the USA by the Sarbannes Oxley Act in 2002, which gives clear guidance on corporate governance and the importance of developing risk management systems (RMS) and holistic risk cultures (i.e. it covers all aspects of the organisations functions and operations). In addition, the Lyme Regis court case in 1994 helped clarify the principle of *corporate manslaughter*. This tragic incident, where four school children were drowned during a canoeing trip in Lyme Bay, in Dorset, resulted in the managing director of the parent company of the activity centre being prosecuted and jailed for four years, even though he was not directly leading the activities on the day. This case acts as an important reminder of a senior manager's responsibility for ensuring that regulations and systems are properly adhered to by all staff leading sport activities.

Learning activity 10.1

Conduct a search on the Internet to find out more about the following areas.

- Health and Safety at Work Act 1974
- Management of Health and Safety at Work Regulations 1992
- Control of Substances Hazardous to Health Regulations 1988 (COSHH)
- Health and Safety (First Aid) Regulations 1981
- Reporting of Injuries, Diseases and Dangerous Occurrences Regulations 1985
- Fire Safety and Safety of Places of Sport Act 1987
- Disability Discrimination Act 1995
- Activity Centres (Young Persons' Safety) Act 1995
- Adventure Activities Licensing Regulations 1996
- Turnball Report 1999
- Lyme Regis canoeing disaster in 1993.

For each area, try to clarify where the role of risk management is identified and how this has affected sport management.

- Growth in a blame culture and litigation
  Some argue that there has been a growth in a *blame culture*; the notion that any incident or accident can always be attributed to someone else's fault, which can allow for compensation to be claimed, and so has become an important part of the legal system (Frosdick, 1999, p36). This culture is much stronger in the USA, but is a growing problem for the UK sport industry. It has encouraged organisations to conduct risk assessments not only to comply with regulations, but also to reduce further the negative exposure of danger and harm, which can lead to lawsuits. In this sense, Smessen and Gregg (1999, p285) and Cloutier (2000, p98) argue that the risk assessment process acts as a 'protective shield' against litigation.
- Media amplification
  The all-pervasive media and their desire to find new, provocative stories, means they can play a significant role in distorting and inflating (*amplification*) people's perceptions of risk, which can have little grounding in the actual chance of the risk occurring. In the sport, tourism and adventure industry, when accidents occur, particularly if the victims are vulnerable (such as children), then the media have been instrumental in articulating notions of moral outrage, which has subsequently helped drive the demand for new regulations. This was certainly evident after the Lyme Bay incident, mentioned earlier.
- A rational response to a complex world
  The use of risk management in all aspects of our lives can also be attributed to its value as a tool for helping us understand the world and the problems managers face. A sport manager can face a complex business world, which constantly needs to be scanned for opportunities and threats, such as new legislation, economic trends, political changes and technological developments. Risk management

simply represents another means to frame or view these changes, offering a step-by-step guide to what is looked for and how changes can be dealt with. In that sense risk management is a rational response to a complex world, as it is based on ideas of being logical and developing reasoned arguments.

- On grounds of ethics and morality
  In essence, ethics relates to principles of what is right and wrong. Ford et al. (1992, p243) make the important point that, regardless of the other drivers for the adoption of risk practices, such as the legal requirements, all organisations should have the 'moral concern and welfare' of their participants at the centre of their operational ethos, with Cloutier (2000, p98) arguing that these ethical arguments represent the 'highest' justification for risk management. In other words, risk management is undertaken because it is viewed as right and proper that staff and participants are kept safe and free from unnecessary dangers and harm. These ideas of organisations operating in an ethically sound way have been extended in recent years to businesses being seen to operate in an environmentally friendly and sustainable way, because failure to do so risks the organisation's brand or image being damaged, which ultimately can affect the revenues it receives.

Defining risk management

So risk touches everyone and can now be regarded as a vital function of the sport manager, but what exactly is it? Despite the increased use of risk management, this does not mean that it is consistently applied or understood. Examining risk related literature and the definitions offered, one soon finds numerous confusing variations. This is illustrated in Learning activity 10.2, where a number of different definitions are given for comparison.

Learning activity 10.2

Reflection on what risk means

Look at the following different definitions of risk and highlight the key themes that emerge. What can one conclude from this reflection?

- Sample 1: 'Risk is the potential to lose something of value, or simply the potential accident.' (Brown, 1999, p274)
- Sample 2: 'Risk (is) the probability that a particular adverse event occurs during a stated period of time, or results from a particular challenge. As probability in the sense of statistical theory, risk obeys the formal laws of combining probabilities. Explicitly or implicitly, it must always relate to the 'risk of (a specific event or set of events)' and, where appropriate, must refer to a hazard specified in terms of its amount or intensity, time of starting or duration.' (Royal Society, 1992, p3)

Learning activity 10.2 continued

- Sample 3: 'Risk management is a rational approach to the problem of dealing with the risks faced by a business. It is about managing or optimising risks; it is not necessarily about eliminating them, because risk is inherent in adventure activities – and should remain so.' (Cloutier 2000, p241)
- Sample 4: 'Risk management refers to the "the culture, processes and structures that are directed towards the effective management of potential opportunities and adverse effects".' (Australian/New Zealand Risk Management standard, cited in Tarlow, 2002, p207)

Looking at the various definitions presented in Learning activity 10.2, together with any number of additional definitions of risk which can easily be found, a number of important features soon emerge in relation to risk and risk management which are:

- Risk is often defined around *two central categories* (Klinke and Renn, 2001): the *probability* of occurrence and the *severity* of impact. The notion of probability, or likelihood, relates to estimating the chance of a risk occurring, which is sometimes represented in numeric or percentage terms, such as a risk event being given a 10 percent chance of occurring, or using a qualitative descriptor, such as describing the risk as having a high or low likelihood of occurrence. The second concept relates to the notion of a *severity* of outcome, or *magnitude*, or *level of threat*, which refers to how people or the organisation may be affected, such as the physical harm which could occur to people, or the scale of the financial loss or gain, and even the damage or enhancement of an organisation's reputation.
- Although the notion of *frequency* is sometimes used interchangeably with notions of *likelihood*, these are not the same concepts as frequency refers to the number of times an event or situation occurs, which can *then* be used to help formulate the probability of occurrence. A simple example of this may be to use a work accident book to look at the occurrence of past sporting injuries in order to formulate the likelihood of occurrence of incidents in the future.
- Risk is often distinguished from *uncertainty*, whereby if the outcome of a project or event is not known, or highly subjective, then this can be categorised as *uncertainty*. If, on the other hand, the outcome can be given some degree of assessment as to its probability or likelihood, then this is classified as a risk. Some writers question this distinction, arguing that in practice all risk assessments are highly subjective and uncertain.
- Risk involves a *hazard*. Perhaps rather confusingly, in some literature the idea of a 'hazard' and a 'risk' are used interchangeably, but it is important to recognise that they are different concepts in the risk management process. The Royal Society's influential 1992 report on risk offers clear conceptual distinction between the two terms, referring to a *hazard* as any property, situation or indeed anything which has the potential to cause harm, which can become '*realised*' under certain conditions (Royal Society, 1992, pp2–3). It can be useful therefore to see the *hazard* as the source of the *risk*. For example, the large floats that might be used

for a family fun swimming session are the hazards, but the risks relate to the possibility and severity of injuries, which can range from minor abrasions, to the most severe, that of someone drowning.

- Risk can be understood as both a *practical process* and as a *risk culture*. As a *culture*, this relates to how risk is viewed and understood, such as whether it only creates threats and dangers, or if it can also include opportunities. This should already be apparent from Learning activity 10.2, where some definitions focus just on dangers and loss, while others emphasise that risk also creates opportunities. For example, if one refers back to the example of the pool floats, then it is possible not only to consider the negative risks, such as injuries, that might result, but also more opportunistic ones, such as the fun that people can have and the increase in usage which may occur.
- As a process, risk management refers to the practical step-by-step actions that are used to collect and analyse information on risks, in order to produce an assessment, then the measures that are used to deal with these risks.

What an analysis of various risk definitions does is to help distil the key conceptual themes of risk and risk management, which can be preferable to trying to reduce risk management down to a single-sentence definition. These key themes relate to ideas of *probability, severity, hazards, uncertainty* and the differences between risk *cultures* and risk processes.

Changing risk definitions and cultures

How we understand risk shapes our business organisational culture, which in turn influences what is and is not identified as a risk. It is this organisational risk culture that is crucial in driving the more practical risk process discussed in the next section. Yet it is important to recognise how our understanding of risk has changed over time.

These differences in how the understanding of risk has changed over time have already been hinted at in earlier sections. For example, if one compares the sample 1 definition with the sample 4 definition back in Learning activity 10.2, it should be evident that whereas the first definition focuses just on notions of loss and can be defined as *symmetric*, the second identifies both threats and opportunities, and can be defined as asymmetric.

So why do these differences in risk occur? In essence this relates to how our understanding of risk has changed to meet the needs of a particular time. The word *risk*, in terms of its origin, has its roots in the Arabic word *risq* (to be given by god), and the Latin *riscum* (the challenge of a barrier reef for sailors, with connotations of a fortuitous or unfavourable event), but it was in the pre-industrial seventeenth century that the word *risk* was increasingly used in business. At this time it became strongly associated with the growing insurance industry, whereby ship owners would take out policies to cover against the perils of a sea voyage, such as ships, their goods and crew being lost in a storm. The odds of a safe voyage were calculated by insurance brokers, such as Lloyds, who would consider the seas sailed in, or the time of the year the voyage was to take place, in order to work out how much the ship owners should pay for their insurance cover. Over time, the view of risk evolved to focus on not only the natural environment generating risks, but also people. The main focus came to be on trying to control or remove risks from activities and the business environment. This period is often described as the *second age* of risk and develops with the process of industrialisation. More contemporary understandings of risk are now regarded by some to be in a *third post-industrial age*, whereby risk is characterised by its complexity in origin, and seen to create both opportunities/up sides as well as the more familiar threats/down sides, which are generated by the complex interaction of forces.

It still may not be clear why it is important to recognise why these different viewpoints of risk are important, therefore an example will be used to illustrate the value of recognising these different risk cultures. The weather for a sport event would be a key *hazard* identified as part of any practical risk assessment process. If one conducted the assessment using a second age risk culture, one would just focus on the negative consequences of adverse weather conditions, such as storms causing damage to equipment or injuries to people as debris is blown off structures. If, however, one used a more contemporary third age risk culture, one would not only focus on these negative factors, but also more positive ones, such as what would be the impacts of a spell of very good weather. Here the actions adopted would relate to not only dealing with adverse weather, such as ensuring that extra measures are taken to secure equipment in case of high winds, but also considering the actions needed to deal with a spell of very good weather, such as ensuring extra parking and refreshments are available because of increased visitor numbers.

In the context of this chapter, while aspects of the operational health and safety risk assessments will always tend to focus more on the negative aspects of risks, it is encouraged that the third age understanding is adopted when analysing and reflecting on hazards and risks.

Identifying the key process stages of risk management

When looking at the actual practical process of a risk assessment, one can again find many variations as to how one should begin, and how each stage is described. There can also be confusion between the different operational and strategic levels of management (see Chapter 2 for an explanation of these terms). What is recommended here is an approach which can be utilised at both these levels, such as a health and safety assessment, or as part of a strategic environmental analysis. The advantage of utilising a broadly similar approach is that it can help in the communication of risks, because without effective communication and understanding of risk assessments or plans, then they can remain useless documents.

An overview of the risk process is presented in Figure 10.1. Before each stage is explained it is important to examine a number of key underpinning concepts. In the framework presented in this chapter, the terms risk *analysis*, *assessment* and *management* are used in quite specific ways, which may differ from how others writers may refer to them. Although the concepts of analysis and assessment are often used interchangeably, here it is recommended that they are treated as separate concepts. Risk *analysis* is therefore used to refer to the identification and examination of the origins, or causes, of the possible hazardous events and risks. *Risk assessment*, however, relates to considering the level of probability of a risk happening and the

Figure 10.1: Risk management process summary table

Risk management process (encompassing)		
	1. Risk context process stage	
		What is the purpose of the organisation?
		Who are the key stakeholders/clients?
		Identifying what in the organisation is exposed to risk and the manner of its exposure.
	2. Risk analysis process stage	
		Identification or discovery of the key hazards and risks.
		Identifying the factors that create or cause the risks.
		Analysis of suitable indicators of causation and the critical paths indicated for events/scenarios.
	3.Risk assessment process stage	
		Record data in appropriate formats to help in assessment.
		Categorise key risks.
		Ascribe a value to the political risk based on severity and likelihood.
	4. Risk control process stage	
		Categorise risks into basic control matrix.
		Develop risk plan.
		Develop crisis plan for extreme risks.
		Implement plan at a strategic and operational level.
		Communicate plan throughout all levels of the organisation.
		Reappraise risks in light of any new control measures.
	5. Risk monitoring process stage	
		Continue to monitor and update records.
		Amend assessments and control measures as appropriate.

severity of impacts on the organisation, which often involves ascribing some measure or value to the risk. These differences between *analysis* and *assessment*, while small, are nonetheless important, because what most organisations want or need is the risk *assessment*; yet it is in the *analysis* of the risks that the most important work takes place.

The term *risk management* can also be confusing, whereby it is sometimes referred to as a separate process stage from the *analysis* and *assessment* stages, focusing on the possible actions and control measures developed to deal with the risks identified. This seems a limited way of understanding the concept of management, however, as a number of writers argue, such as Frosdick (1997), who notes that the term can either refer to an encompassing process, or one specific process stage. To overcome this confusion, he highlights that one can distinguish between *risk management*, used to refer to the control of risks, and the *management of risks* (MoR), used to refer to the whole risk process, which includes the analysis and assessment stages. In order to avoid confusion, the preference here is to use the more specific term of *control measures* (see the overview of the risk management process below) to refer to the actions developed to deal with the risks, with the term *management* used in the more general sense, rather than as a specific process stage.

Each of these key stages of the risk process are described below:

- *Stage 1: Context*. This stage is often ignored in risk processes, but it is vital to appreciate how the nature of the organisation, its services and its clients can all affect the *risk exposure* of the organisation (i.e. the scale of the impact the risk has upon the organisation). These impacts can be considered in relation to the: *financial* losses or gains; the *physical* injury or damage which may occur; the enhancement or damage to *reputation* or brand; and the *ethical* tensions created. Many writers who identify this stage emphasise the importance of having a clear understanding of the organisation's aims, objectives or operational ethos, which subsequently helps to frame both *what* assets may be at risk, together with *how* they may be at risk. For example, a sport facility which has a social orientation, such as encouraging active recreation for children to try to help combat obesity, would need to consider carefully the risks of sourcing funding from organisations which can be associated with poor diet, such as sweet or chocolate manufacturers. The risks generated relate to the risks of financial deficits if the money is not sought or accepted, to the potential risk of reputation damage, as accepting the money could undermine the credibility of the sport facility's social objective and the message it attempts to convey.
- *Stage 2: Risk analysis*. A key part of this process is the initial identification of hazards and risks. This can be done through a variety of techniques, ranging from creative thinking techniques (e.g. thought showers), and physical inspection of premises and equipment, to scanning news databases as part of a strategic risk planning process. Part of this process is an analysis of what factors may lead to the occurrence of a hazardous event and subsequent risk which could be generated.
- *Stage 3: Risk assessment*. While the *analysis* stage is the most complex of the process elements, it is in the *assessment* (some use the term *evaluation*) that the analysis is turned into something more tangible to aid decision making. It is here that the hazards are considered in relation to the risks they could pose to the

organisation in terms of their likelihood and severity of impact. A variety of techniques can be used, such as conducting frequency profiles of past accidents and near-miss events, to what-if scenario techniques, where the consequences of the organisation interacting with a hazard are mapped out.

- *Stage 4: Control measures.* After the hazards and risks have been identified, analysed and assessed, it is then vital that decisions are taken as to how to *control them*, thereby dealing with the threats and dangers, or helping to seize the opportunities. The range of possible actions are usually categorised around four broad possibilities. The manager can decide to *take* or *retain* the risks, for example, when they have a low probability and severity of impact. Alternatively, the decision can be taken to *transfer* or *reallocate* the risks, for example by taking out insurance against possible losses or litigation. Another alternative is to *treat* or *reduce* the risks, such as placing extra staff to supervise activities. Finally, there is the measure of simply *terminating* the activity to *avoid* the risk. When the control measures have been implemented, then, where appropriate, the assessments should be reappraised.
- *Stage 5: Monitor and review.* This will be done after the initial control measures are developed, whereby assessments are reviewed in terms of their value. As new programmes are developed, or changes occur in the business environment, the risk assessments need to be constantly reappraised. Risk assessments should be regarded as living documents that staff can consult and modify as circumstances change, whether this is because of changed weather conditions, new equipment or in response to international events, such as a terrorist attack or a financial market crisis.

A number of examples can be used to illustrate how the concepts highlighted in the previous sections are utilised in the practical risk process. The first relates to the example of an *operational* based risk assessment for a swimming pool, which is done in order to comply with Health and Safety regulations. As part of the *analysis* stage, it was identified that because of the design of the pool, it was possible for a young child to run out from the changing rooms and jump into the middle of the pool. The *hazard* in this instance is the pool. The *risk* relates to the probability of drowning, which is increased the younger the child, as they are more likely to be out of their depth, or less likely to be able to swim. Such an incident could also generate many other risks to the organisation, such as damage to their reputation and risks of litigation, both of which can increase the risk of financial losses. At *Stage 3*, an assessment of the risk is given, which will vary depending on the scale used. For example the risk of an incident could be given a high severity in relation to drowning, but a medium likelihood rating. This assessment value may be informed by staff relating their experiences, or looking at past incidents or near misses (i.e the times when children have actually jumped in, but where they were quickly rescued), to even using scenario mapping or 'what-if' analytical tools. In *Stage 4*, the control measures are formulated, which could range from reducing the likelihood by placing a lifeguard near the point where children could run into the pool, or placing a simple physical barrier by the pool, to stop children running straight in, in much the same way that barriers are placed by school entrances/exits, in order to stop children running straight out of school onto a road. An aspect of the risk can also be *transferred* by ensuring adequate insurance cover is obtained to help protect against litigation if an accident was to occur. After these control measures are implemented, then the risk assessment can be reappraised and modified, such as giving it a low likelihood rating.

The second example relates to using a risk framework to complement a strategic planning process, which may have to be done in order to comply with corporate governance regulations. Here, understanding the nature of the organisation is vital, particularly if it wants to emphasise its ethical ethos (see Stage 1 in Figure 10.1), such as wanting to operate in a sustainable manner (see Chapter 15). In the second process stage of analysis, the identification of hazards in the external business environment can be scanned for using a PESTLE framework (see Chapter 6). If one adopts a more contemporary third age risk culture, then hazardous events are considered in terms of the opportunities and threats they may generate, where someone's loss, may represent someone else's gain; for example, during an economic recession, membership to more expensive private gyms declines, with some of the demand being diverted to cheaper public sport facilities. It is also important not to confuse hazardous events with risks, as these events are only significant when the organisation *interacts* with the hazardous situation. (In much the same way that a cyclone is a hazard, but it does not follow automatically that it is a risk to people; the risks, such as the risk of physical injury or death, only come about when the cyclone hits human habitation). These risks can then be given an assessment, which helps focus the type of control measures that will be written into the strategic plan, which are constantly monitored and reviewed.

A key part of the risk management process is how information is recorded to help with the analysis and assessment. Once again there are numerous variations in the possible approach which can be adopted, as the sample operational risk assessment form extracts used for Learning activity 10.3 illustrate. It is key to recognise how all the previous concepts help to explain the mechanics of the forms and their underlying principles.

Learning activity 10.3

Comparing sample risk form extracts for operational risk assessments

Look at the sample extracts from four operational health and safety risk assessment forms and highlight their similarities and differences. Try to apply each of the forms to a specific sport activity or facility, and consider which is easiest to use, clearly justifying your answer. See the earlier section for further explanation of each of the concepts.

Finally, when recording information it should be appreciated that this analysis and assessment process is not always so neat and structured. As one collects data, one may move back and forth between the stages, particularly if one reviews and reassesses the risks after certain control measures may have been implemented.

Sample risk assessment form 1

1. Hazards	2. Person at risk	3a. Potential outcome (severity)	3b. Frequency	4. Risk rating ($a \times b = r$) 1 to 5 low, 6 to 12 medium 12 + high	5. Risk low, medium, high

Sample risk assessment form 2

Hazard	Control measures in place	Risk factor	Further control measures

Sample risk assessment form 3

Step 1	Step 2	Step 3	Step 4	Step 5
List potential hazards here	List groups of people at risk from hazards; include those most vulnerable	List existing control measures or note where information may be found	Calculate the residual risk taking the presence and effectiveness of existing measures into account: severity (1 to 3) × likelihood (1 to 3) = risk rating	List further control measures necessary to reduce risks to an acceptable level *and* date of their proposed introductions

Sample risk assessment form 4

Analysis		Assessment		Control	Review
Hazard(s)	Who or what is at risk?	Probability (H/M/L)	Severity (H/M/L)	Prevent (eliminate, guard or warn against) Alternatives Response to occurrence	Means of monitoring, communication, reporting and reviewing

Key issues in sport risk management

Despite the growing importance of risk management practices in the sport management process, risk management is not without its problems. It can be useful to recognise these inherent weaknesses, as this can help the manager to better reflect on the value of the risk process, and so help in improving risk management practices. The key problems are listed below:

- *The problems of communicating risks.* As has been highlighted, there are numerous variations in the vocabulary used to describe key risk concepts, together with many differences in the practical processes of collecting, analysing and assessing data. All of which can become further confused by the amplification effect of the media, which can distort people's perceptions of hazards and risks, which can have little grounding in reality.
- *There are many new hazards and risks.* One example relates to the impact terrorism has had on large sporting events. Although such an act is still low in terms of probability, the severity of outcome is such that many large sport events need to consider it as a serious risk, hence the huge increase in costs of security for events such as the Olympic Games.
- *Risk management is highly subjective.* Despite all the attempts to develop more scientific models and processes which attempt to quantify risks, it will always remain a possibility that two people can look at the same information but produce two different risk assessment values. This should be apparent after Learning activity 10.3.
- *The quantitative/qualitative debate.* While a critical part of risk is the notion of probability, how this is represented is fraught with difficulties. While for certain areas of risk, developing clear confidence intervals based on past frequencies and statistical profiles is possible, for many other areas there remains much doubt as to how possible it is to quantify them with any real degree of accuracy.
- *Inherent messiness to causality, environmental complexity and interaction of the business environments.* The term *messiness* is used to stress that causality tends to be multiple, not singular, with Allinson noting that causation rarely operates in 'splendid isolation', and going onto say that a cause cannot operate singly as it will always operate as 'an ingredient in a network of connections' (1993, p8). For example, if one were to examine the Hillsborough disaster in 1989, one sees that it was the complex interaction of ticketing, policing, crowd behaviour and stadium design, which led to the deaths of 96 people. Indeed, some of the factors that contributed to the disaster were not just rooted on the day, but went back many years. For example, the fences against which people were crushed were designed in response to problems of football hooliganism, violence and pitch invasions going back to the 1970s.

Review of learning outcomes

Risks are generated when people and organisations interact with hazardous events and situations in some manner. While there are some differences between operational and strategic type risk assessments, it is important to recognise that, in terms of the broad underpinning concepts and descriptors, it is possible to utilise a more consistent language and process of risk management.

When looking at the many different ways that risk can be understood and risk management can be applied, it should be appreciated that there is no one definitive approach. A cultural outlook is recommended, based around a notion of a third age risk culture, which has as a key feature the view that risks can create opportunities as well as threats. The problem is that when one utilises this in a real setting, it may not be quite so neat or straightforward, particularly if one has to utilise many existing risk forms, processes and cultural outlooks. This is not as big a problem as it may initially seem; the key is to use this chapter as a lexicon (i.e. as a form of dictionary) which helps to translate and explain the differences in how various books, articles or organisations approach risk. If one can understand the basic principles involved with risk management, then it is easier to adapt risk practices and approaches as the situation requires, whether this is part of a business plan or a risk assessment of a sporting activity. With greater understanding it is also hoped that risk assessments will be written with purpose, rather than just as a mechanical paper exercise conducted simply to comply with regulations.

Further reading

The Health and Safety Executive provides a useful explanation of the Health and Safety at Work Act, which can be found via: **www.hse.gov.uk/legislation/hswa.htm**.

The BSI (British Standards Institution) publishes a number of important guidelines which managers should be aware of; it can be found via: **http://www.bsi-global.com/en/BSI-UK/**.

For a useful overview of how the different ages of risk have developed, one can read: Tarlow, PE (2002) *Event risk management and safety*. New York: Wiley.

A very good case study, using a sociolegal perspective, of the Hillsborough tragedy is given in Hartley, H. J. (2001) *Exploring sport and leisure disasters: a sociolegal perspective*. London: Cavendish Publishing Ltd.

Chapter 11

Sports development

Andrew Pitchford and Richard Colman

This chapter considers how sports are currently managed by major organisations in order to help participants develop lifelong participation. With the help of learning exercises and case studies, the chapter will explore the various ways in which agencies such as Sport England, the National Governing Bodies (NGBs) of sport and County Sports Partnerships (CSPs) attempt to structure and organise the efforts of the clubs and volunteers who look after the majority of our sports performers and participants.

Learning outcomes

This chapter is designed to enable you to:

- understand a range of different concepts of sports development;
- explain how the major sports organisations attempt to manage and structure sports development processes;
- evaluate the extent to which partnership working can enhance these structures and systems;
- identify some of the key skills for effective partnership working in this sector.

Introduction

Although sports development is now a recognised occupation, the term itself is relatively new. It first appeared in discussions about the future of clubs and services for young people in the 1960s, and has since been used to describe any action or initiative which aims to increase or enhance participation in sport. As Chapter 2 demonstrated, all sorts of individuals and organisations have an interest in this process, because the apparent benefits of sport are so many and varied. Government departments as diverse as the Home Office (2003, 2004), the Department for Education and Skills (2003), the Department of Health (2002), the Office of the Deputy Prime Minister (2002) and the Department of Culture, Media and Sport (2001, 2002a, 2002b, 2003, 2004) have all identified sport as important to their aims in the past decade, demonstrating its considerable value in modern society.

When the government, and the rest of us for that matter, talk about sport, we are often describing a wide range of leisure and cultural activities. Walking and dance, kite flying and horse racing, motor racing and darts, visits to the gym and martial arts feature in many people's conceptions. Others prefer to restrict the use of the term to descriptions of institutionalised, competitive, physical activities that have traditionally featured in the physical education curriculum. No one conception is right or wrong, they are simply different interpretations that have emerged over time. Such a breadth of understanding does cause problems, however, when an organisation is charged with making sense of the structures that support these activities. A single organisation would be unlikely to harbour within its staff sufficient expertise to oversee and manage such a hugely varied range of practices. Often, though, those responsible for sport have tried to carry such a broad range of concerns on their shoulders. As a consequence, the management of sport in the UK has proved to be enormously challenging, some would say impossible, in the past 30 years.

Learning activity 11.1

Use the list of government departments in the 'Introduction' to identify as many reasons as you can to explain why the UK government has an interest in developing sport.

Access the websites of the following government departments and identify those who have a direct responsibility for delivering or organising sport in the UK:

- Home Office
- Department for Culture, Media and Sport (DCMS)
- Department for Children, Schools and Families (DCSF)
- Department of Health
- Department for Transport

How do the lead agencies in the delivery of sport and physical activity in Britain, for example the DCMS, Sport Scotland and Sport England, define the concept of sport?

Which activities do these definitions exclude, and what are the implications of this exclusion?

These challenges have been compounded by the historical position of sport in the country widely regarded as the birthplace of many modern forms of the activity. British sport has always been organised on a small-scale, local basis. Participation, coaching, training and competition has typically been the reserve of locally based clubs, which tend to be organised around single activities and run by committees comprising prominent members of the club at any particular point in time. This is second nature to us; we imagine it to be the way sport has always been organised, and that it is likely to be the way sport is organised in other cultures too. However, this is not the case. In countries like China, for example, there is no broad tradition of collective self-help and 'volunteering' as there is in Britain. In fact, self-interested collectives or groups were often discouraged by the powerful elites in the Eastern bloc. In their place, government and state agencies have taken the lead in introducing, establishing and developing sport. As a result, the models of sports development created in these countries appear clinical, systematic and even sometimes quite ruthless in comparison with our own experiences.

Where some other countries can look at sport and see clarity, systems, progression and development, we, in Britain, tend to see fog. This is largely the residue of all the hot air produced over the centuries by the thousands of voluntary sports clubs and their committees, who have spent an infinite number of hours scrutinising the minutiae of their own experience while rarely looking up to see how the rest of sport, and the rest of the population, has been getting on. In one sense, these small, local, democratic clubs represent a great strength in our society, offering people influence and interest and a connection to others in their neighbourhood. In another, they represent a minefield for anyone who wants to make sense of them, to somehow draw them together into a coherent system that will maximise participation and help the talented to achieve their potential.

The rest of this chapter is therefore focused on the attempts of the leading British sports agencies to create some order out of the chaos.

The desire to manage sport so that it can be developed in various ways has really come from the government in its different incarnations, at local and national level. Sometimes, as we have already seen, this has been motivated by a desire to utilise the ability of sport to bring people together and forge a sense of identity, sometimes it has been driven by a desire to see British athletes performing on a world stage. While these underlying motives have been examined and criticised by a range of authors (see for example Henry, 2001; Houlihan and White, 2002) the purpose of this analysis is to identify how the major government and state-aided organisations have tried to shepherd sport into some meaningful formation in recent years.

CASE STUDY 11.1

The role of a sports development officer

The work of sports development officers (SDOs) can be extremely varied. Much depends on the type of organisation they work within. SDOs are most commonly employed by local authorities in their leisure services departments. However, this will vary between local authorities and is often influenced by the remit of the post. If the emphasis is purely on 'sport for sport's sake' then leisure is often the host area. If the post has a strong focus on social cohesion or youth engagement then the SDO may find themselves based within another department of the local authority such as Safer and Stronger Communities for example.

SDOs are also employed by other organisations which feel that improving the provision of sport can help meet their objectives. These organisations can include universities, charities, youth services, church groups and even professional sports clubs or commercial enterprises. Then there are also those development officers who are linked to specific sports and in many cases are employed directly by the NGBs. Depending on the size and resources of the NGB, these

CASE STUDY 11.1 continued

development officers can cover geographical areas ranging from counties to regions.

Most SDOs work in a co-ordinating or management role. Some still engage directly in coaching and leadership, but increasingly SDOs are expected to be able to manage projects, oversee budgets, hold meetings, negotiate with other organisations, mentor staff and find ways to monitor and evaluate the impact of their activities. The work of an SDO can therefore be extremely challenging but also hugely enjoyable.

A management model for sports development

For most of the past decade, the British government has been pressing for sport to be organised in a single, simple, unified system that all stakeholders and participants can understand and access. In order to invest in sport, the government needed to be certain that the system would deliver what was required. Years of intransigence and in-fighting in the sporting world had made it clear that, left to its own devices, the sporting world was unlikely to achieve such clarity. Change was necessary, and this change started at the top.

Being the Minister for Sport in the 1970s and 1980s was not an easy job. Nobody above the minister was duty bound to listen to anything he or she said, and nobody below the minister was duty bound to listen to anything he or she said, let alone do anything about it. The minister did not hold a Cabinet position, and so held little weight in the government ranks. The Sports Council, which was the closest thing the minister had to a department, was in an advisory position. In other words, it didn't really do very much apart from tell the minister that he or she wasn't in a position to do anything. Beyond the Sports Council were a series of very amateur NGBs, which were keen to ensure that neither the minister nor the Sports Council interfered in any way with their business.

The many changes in the landscape of sport since this time are all due, in one way or another, to demands for a single sensible system to be put in place, and for the government to be in charge of it. A detailed explanation of these changes can be found at the main sports development portal on the Internet – **www.sportsdevelopment.org.uk** – but for the purposes of this chapter, here are the key building blocks.

1. The DCMS holds the most significant position, creating policy and funnelling government monies into those areas of sport deemed in greatest need of investment. The Minister for Sport is appointed to serve in this department.
2. Below the DCMS, Sport England remains in an advocacy role, offering support, guidance and expertise to all players in the new system. Its other major role is the investment of funding from the government and, significantly, from the National Lottery.
3. At a local level, CSPs are charged with co-ordinating the delivery agencies and with driving forward government targets for increases in participation in sport

Figure 11.1 Sport development structure

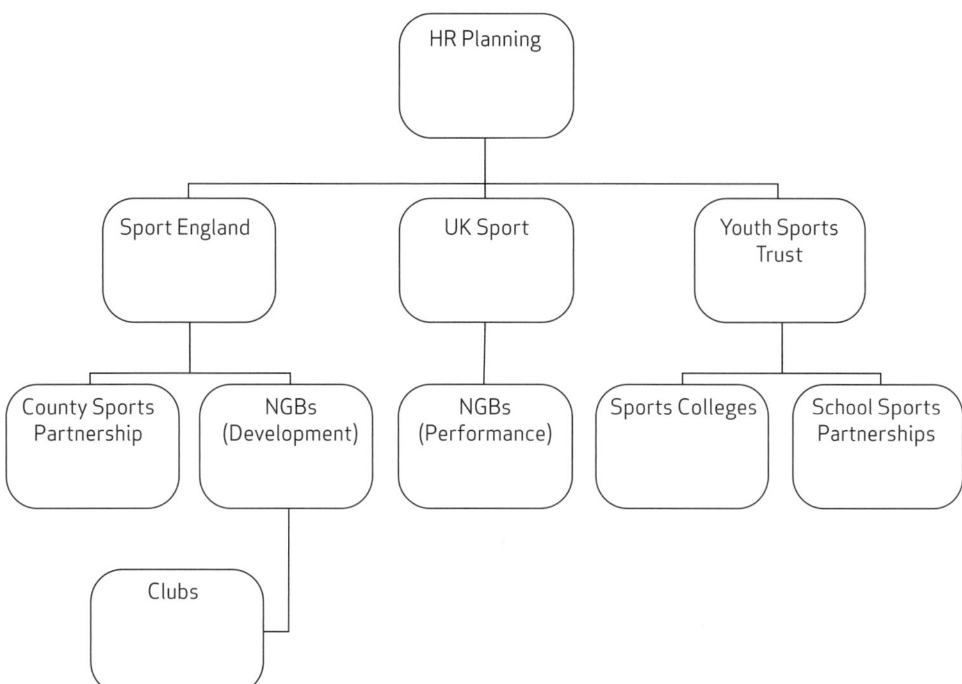

and physical activity. There are 49 CSPs, which are normally managed by representatives of all of the major sports agencies, including local authorities and NGBs.

4. In parallel with each of these developments is the work funded by the DCSF, which is summarised in the *Physical education and sport strategy for young people* (2008). This strategy relates to aspirations for high-quality physical education and school to community links, and funds the network of School Sport Partnerships (SSPs) across the country.
5. Providing the mortar for all of these elements is the Youth Sport Trust, a charitable agency established in 1994. The Trust advises all agencies involved in the new delivery structure and has been the preferred advisor to the government in the past 10 years.

While these five broad changes have undoubtedly shifted the scenery, other characters have arrived in the wings to complicate matters further. A new state-funded body, UKSport, is responsible for the management of performance and excellence systems, primarily in relation to Olympic sports. Alongside them, Sports Coach UK leads on matters relating to coaching and leadership. Both of these agencies then liaise with the NGBs, many of which have now shed their old amateur clothes in preference for something rather more snazzy and professional. So although the fog may have lifted to a certain extent, some parts of the picture still remain rather fuzzy.

Learning activity 11.2

1. Use an internet search to determine whether there is a CSP in your area. If no provision exists, where is your nearest CSP?
2. Focusing on the CSP you've located, try to identify any Community Sports Networks (CSNs) that they host or encourage. Sometimes the CSNs are known as Sport and Physical Activity Alliances or Community Partnerships.
3. What kinds of individuals and organisations appear to be involved in these networks or partnerships? Are all possible organisations represented, and if not, what are the implications – does it matter if some people are missing?

The need for partnership working

Beyond these high-level organisations are many other local agencies which have an interest in delivering and enhancing sport. A survey of 899 sports development workers by SkillsActive (2005) identified 40 different kinds of organisations which employed people with related job titles (see Figure 11.2). Of these, by far the most influential were local authorities, which continue to employ thousands of sports development workers across the country as they have done for 15 years or more. Many urban councils retain sports development teams that include 20 or more workers. Then there are charities, trusts and social enterprises which employ sports development workers, and professional sports teams and clubs which consider themselves to be in the same business. Increasingly, educational establishments and Primary Care Trusts are employing people in similar roles, and so too do the NGBs themselves and some more progressive voluntary sector clubs.

Clearly, many of these agencies will be trying to use sport for different reasons – to develop communities, to support high performers, to counter inactivity and obesity, to raise their own profile – but the fact remains that they all share an interest in promoting

Figure 11.2: Employing agency of sports development workers: most frequently cited (%)

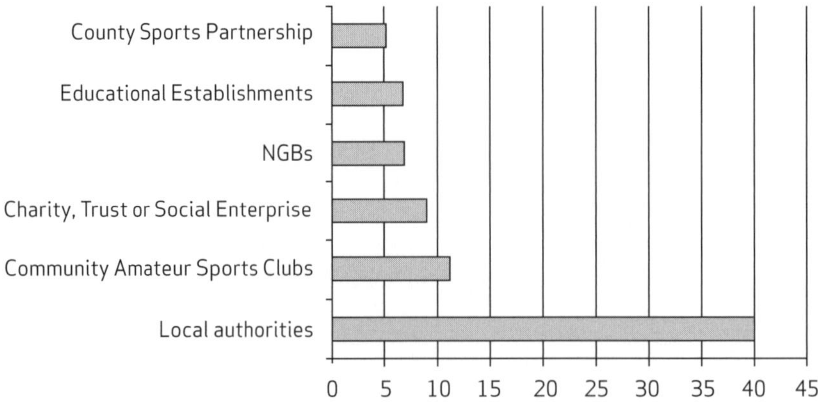

and developing the same kinds of activity. The established, traditional sports organisations have not disappeared as a result of the new system described here. They are still there, sometimes charging forward, sometimes stumbling on, sometimes in need of a helping hand to keep going.

The key to the success of the new structures for sport is the extent to which they can draw all of the various contributors into the new vision. If all of these agencies can work in partnership, can share their resources and work in unison, then a great deal can be achieved. If not, the presence of so many different stakeholders means that progress will be slow. If too many cooks can spoil the broth, too many sports organisations can lead to abandoned matches.

The CSPs, with their commitment to the involvement of all of the major local sports organisations, are one expression of this desire to foster focused and co-operative working. In 2006, the CSPs were further tasked with establishing CSNs. These networks operate on a local level, normally based around local authority boundaries. The idea was to bring together local organisations, which can identify ways of working and investing collectively in order to build capacity that helps to increase participation in sport. The CSNs were designed to be a hub for action rather than a further layer of bureaucracy and red tape. Below these networks are the people who deliver at grassroots level to the local population.

At this level, all of the major players agree that the key aim is to help clubs, coaches and volunteers to maximise their effectiveness. The aim is to have the right people delivering the right activities in the right place in order to increase and enhance participation. We will now look at each of these elements in turn to see whether partnership working can deliver more effective sports development.

Developing clubs

According to the Central Council for Physical Recreation (2006) there are over 100,000 community amateur sports clubs (CASCs) in the UK. There are then hundreds of professional sports clubs, all of which offer sporting opportunities at different levels. This is an enormous resource but, as noted earlier, the tendency of these clubs to focus on their own immediate business means that they have not always looked to join forces with others in their locality. Furthermore, there are so many of them, and so many of them compete for participants and competitors, that it's actually very difficult to know which of them are best suited to the needs of children and young people in particular. Selecting the most appropriate club for a child has, for the most part, been something of a lottery until recently.

In the early part of the 2000s, Sport England tried to foster more collective, European style multi-sport clubs as an antidote to our single sport, single area, often single gender CASCs. These were known as 'multi-sport hub clubs'. A number of these have received lottery funding, and there may be some in existence in your locality. However, progress in this area has been slow, for the same old reasons, so the major agencies have turned their attention, instead, to finding a way of regulating the chaotic world of clubs and to helping new members understand more about the potential services on offer.

Increasingly, workers in Sports Development Units and in the School Sport Partnerships (SSPs) are being encouraged to make links with local clubs, in order to foster and sustain sports participation. Without some guide to the quality of clubs, and some kind of marker of minimum standards, this has been an arduous process. To create more effective pathways for participants to follow, Sport England and the major NGBs have started to introduce quality 'kitemarks' that indicate where a club meets certain key standards.

Some NGBs have their own approach, for example the Football Association has an initiative called the Charter Standard for clubs, but Sport England's kitemarking system is called 'Clubmark' (see case study 11.2). The Clubmark programme provides clubs with a template to implement the minimum standards that a club should have in place in order to operate effectively and safely. The four areas covered are Club Management, Sports Equity and Ethics, Child Protection and Playing Programme. The core elements are the same across all sports, with the NGB for the respective sport then determining the sport-specific elements of the criteria. Once a club has achieved this minimum standard it then provides others with the confidence that the club will provide a positive experience for those who attend. Caution should however still be exercised as the standards implemented are only the minimum standards expected.

An example of how the use of Clubmark has been encouraged is highlighted in case study 11.2, and is outlined within the Sport England West Midlands Regional Review document for 2005–07.

CASE STUDY 11.2

Clubmark

The CSP in Herefordshire and Worcestershire identified a need to support clubs at a local level to achieve Clubmark. A generic 'Club Health Check' was devised and is now in circulation with all their partners. When a partner, for example School Sport Co-ordinator (SSCo), makes contact with a club, they provide the club with a brief introduction to Clubmark and ask the club to carry out a complete health check. The SSCo then returns this to the CSP which then contacts the club and initiates the Clubmark process.

This allows for greater contact with clubs and support for the partnership development managers (PDMs) and SSCOs. And it has allowed an agreement to be finalised with each SSP to ensure that they will only engage in school club links with clubs that have achieved Clubmark, or which are actively working towards the standard.

Meetings were held in each district within the CSP area. The evening meetings allowed clubs to network and to also have the opportunity to meet the CSP, PDM and SDO in their area. Through discussions, the clubs were able to realise the benefits of Clubmark and become aware of the help and support available to them to go through the process of obtaining the standard.

Learning activity 11.3

1. List five community sports clubs with which you have had an association – through playing, coaching, spectating or links with family or friends. What were the characteristics of these clubs? Were they single or multi-sport? What was their geographic focus? How good do you think these clubs were in terms of working in partnership?
2. Can you identify any common ground between the clubs you have listed? Is there anything that they share that could be the basis for useful partnership working?
3. Using an Internet search or a trawl through a telephone directory, can you identify any multi-sports clubs in your locality? How old are they? Why do you think they have combined?
4. To what extent do you think that kitemarking schemes, like Clubmark or the Charter Standard (see the section on Developing Clubs, p. 000), encourage partnership working? Is there any more that they could do in this respect?

Developing coaches

Sports coaching is central to developing, sustaining and increasing participation in sport. It drives better performances and increased success, as well as supporting key social and economic objectives throughout the UK. At all levels of society, coaches guide improvement in technical, tactical, physical, mental and lifestyle skills, contributing to personal and social development (Sports Coach UK, 2008). There have been many initiatives to increase the quality and quantity of coaches delivered both nationally and locally. There are also many new schemes emerging.

Sports Coach UK is the lead agency for developing the *UK coaching framework*. This framework aims to create a cohesive, ethical, inclusive and valued coaching system, where skilled coaches support children, players and athletes at all stages of their development in sport, and which will become the best coaching system in the world by 2016. According to Sports Coach UK (2008), the *UK coaching framework* will enhance the quality of coaching at all stages and provide active, skilled and qualified coaches to meet demand. This will lead to sustained and increased participation, improved performances in sport underpinned by clear career structures for coaches within a professionally regulated vocation.

The Community Sports Coach scheme was begun in 2003. It aimed to establish 3,000 paid, qualified community sports coaches working at a local level to increase the number and range of coaching opportunities according to strategic and local need by 2006. This scheme succeeded in providing funding for full-time coaches, and therefore provided employment opportunities which provided a salary to a coach. The coaches employed have delivered to more than 1 million children across a wide variety of sports and activities.

The intention of the scheme was to create a major change in developing a career structure for coaching: an increase in the number of qualified coaches employed at a local level; quality standards for the recruitment, employment, management and development of coaches; managed, quality continuous professional development support for employed coaches; and high-quality coaching with a focus on young people.

However, for all of the scheme's successes, it has masked an underlying problem that is prevalent throughout sport. This problem is the short-term funding of initiatives and also the constant swinging of focus for bodies such as Sport England and NGBs. With the majority of funding being provided for three years, it can be said that this provides a regular opportunity to review the system and therefore make changes. This could be seen as a positive opportunity but tends to lead to disruption and 'transition years'. This in turn leads to a reduction in productivity as sports development professionals and the voluntary sector realign themselves.

Within the context of the Community Sports Coach scheme, this has meant that many coaches arrive at the end of their contract with uncertain future funding and have no viable career route to follow. Until long-term funding is secured, this particular route into professional coaching looks to be uncertain.

This issue should not detract from the fact that the majority of coaches coach on a voluntary basis. The issue with these coaches is then not how to provide future payment for them but how to maintain and ensure the quality of these coaches. In the case of many Continuing Professional Development opportunities, the challenge is to reduce the cost for those coaches who often end up spending money to enable them to coach.

This problem has nowhere been more evident than with the current cost of NGB coaching awards. The introduction of the UK Coaching Certificate has meant that the cost of many coaching qualifications has risen in order to meet the requirements of raising the standards of these coaching awards. It can take up to 10 years to produce an expert coach, and yet the current system struggles to provide an environment that allows a coach to develop as a full-time employee knowing that they have a long-term future with an organisation.

The *UK coaching framework* has also begun to challenge the perceived pathway that coaches must travel along as they gain knowledge, experience and qualifications. As coaches develop, they have often been pushed into working with better performers. The *UK coaching framework*'s '4 × 4' model challenges this and allows for movement within certain areas of speciality. The model divides coaches into four distinct areas of Children's coach, Participant coach, Performance coach and Elite Performance coach. Within these areas it then classifies coaches' abilities as apprentice coach, coach, senior coach or master coach (see Figure 11.3).

Learning activity 11.4

If you are a coach, plot yourself on the 4 × 4 coaching model. Think about your own experiences and knowledge of coaching, and the type of coaching you deliver. What stage are you at now, and where would you like to be in five years time?

Think about particular coaches or leaders who have inspired you in your sporting or leisure journey. Where would you plot those individuals on the same model?

Select three areas of the 4 × 4 model. List what you think the key skills and competencies would be of a coach in these areas. How do these competencies vary throughout the model?

At which levels of the model do you think working in partnership is most important?

Figure 11.3: The UK Coaching Framework 4x4 model

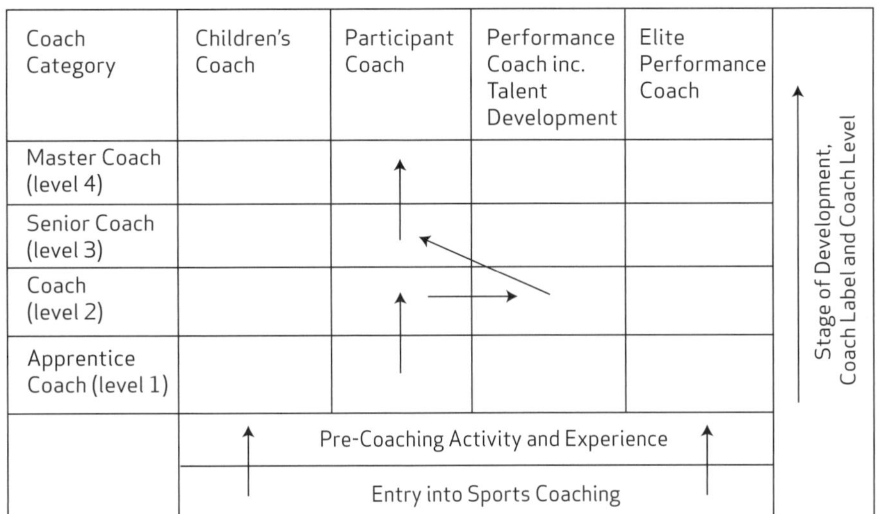

Developing volunteers

It is can be argued that volunteers play a pivotal role in running sport. There are an estimated 5,821,400 volunteers in sport, contributing 1 billion hours each year – this is equivalent to 720,000 additional full-time paid workers in sport (Sport England, 2005). The challenge for sport is how to best support this vast workforce. With a massive variety in roles, expertise and the number of hours committed by individuals, this is not an easy task. There is a real need to balance pressures placed on volunteers in areas such as Child Protection with an acknowledgement of the time being given up by these individuals to support their sport.

With the London 2012 Olympic Games on the horizon there has been a new focus on sports volunteering. Even with the vast number of volunteers that will be required for the games, it is unlikely that many people will get the opportunity to volunteer at the event itself. Many organisations have realised this and are using the Games as a tool for inspiring people to volunteer in their local communities.

The recruitment of young volunteers into sport is a focus of many organisations with the most prominent programme being the Youth Sport Trust led 'Step into Sport' programme. Step into Sport aims to integrate volunteering and leadership into young people's lives. This is done through providing training and experience through the young people's Physical Education programme. As the young people develop through school they have the opportunity to gain Sports Leaders UK awards, so that their knowledge base is increased. Upon reaching 14 the young leaders are then encouraged to volunteer for sports events within the school environment. Upon reaching 16 the volunteering then moves to community activities, usually based within a local sports club. This could for instance be as an assistant to the local tennis coach while delivering Mini Tennis sessions.

Schemes like this have two purposes: first, to make young people aware of volunteering and the satisfaction that it can provide; but, second, it also provides a level of work experience with excellent skills that can be transferred to other industries if a career in sport is not followed (see Chapter 3 for further discussion). However, while clubs and coaches are championed by various agencies, sports volunteering does not enjoy the backing of a single major agency. Instead, local agencies like CSPs have to create networks to help them support volunteers. Again, partnership working is crucial to sustaining sport, as case study 11.3 demonstrates.

CASE STUDY 11.3

V in Herefordshire and Worcestershire

The CSP in Herefordshire and Worcestershire made strong links with the Volunteer Centre network in Worcestershire and had aligned their volunteer recruitment process with that of the five Volunteer Centres/Bureaus in the county. When the national volunteering organisation called 'V' then launched an application process to establish a V team within the county, it provided a perfect opportunity for sport to contribute to such a project. The project had a target audience of 16–25-year-olds and sport was identified locally as a key activity that could attract this age group into the project. The CSP contributed financially to the project and strengthened the overall bid. This project then added to the infrastructure and support for sports volunteers and also sports clubs in the county. The V team consists of four members of staff who work across all sectors to enhance volunteering, but also access the CSP for specific advice on sport and the brokerage of links to local sports clubs and organisations.

Learning activity 11.5

- Visit the National Volunteering Database at **www.do-it.org**
- Search for sports volunteering opportunities in your local area.
- Select three of these opportunities. Would you sign up for them?
- If you would not sign up to these volunteering opportunities, what are the barriers that are stopping you from taking part?
- Who do you think would be attracted by these volunteering opportunities?
- How do you think some of the partner agencies could work together to make these opportunities attractive to a wider range of people?

Review of learning outcomes

In recent years sport has attracted large sums of money from the government in order to create a new structure to help participants and performers. This chapter has detailed some of the features of this new structure, and has also demonstrated that, in order to maximise the impact of the funding, there is a need for individuals and agencies to work in partnership. Because of the number of organisations involved, there is a danger that money is spread too thinly across a range of different stakeholders. These small pots of money need to be linked up in order to ensure that the most is made of the overall investment.

At first sight, this seems sensible enough. However, a system like this requires people with very particular skills. Sport is a 'political' arena, where people sometimes have big egos and can be reluctant to listen to other people or to recognise other people's needs. Sometimes arguments or disagreements can boil down to personality clashes or misunderstandings or age-old allegiances. To overcome this requires openness, honesty and bags and bags of patience.

The new structure for sport in the UK means that, to a greater extent than ever before, sport can be managed for the good of participants and performers, but our future success in this realm relies to a great extent on those involved having both the willingness and the skills to work collectively for a greater aim.

Learning activity 11.6

Reflection

1. The following list identifies some skills, experiences and aptitudes which may be useful for partnership workers in sport. Based on your work on this chapter, rank these from most to least important:
   - High-level sports coaching experience
   - High-level sports performance experience
   - A good knowledge of systems and structures for sport
   - Passion and enthusiasm for sport
   - Listening skills
   - Good verbal and written communication skills
   - Enterprise and imagination
   - Honesty
   - Openness
   - High-level sports officiating experience
   - A related degree
2. Now rank these skills in relation to your own capabilities. Which of these skills do you have most of, and which are in most need of development?
3. Would you like to work in a partnership position? If so, how would you need to develop your skills and experience in order to be a success in such a role?

Further reading

The most comprehensive collection of sports development resources is held at **www.sportsdevelopment.org.uk**. The site also includes a series of introductory guides for various aspects of sports development policy and practice, including *Government policy for sport*, *Sport and social enterprise*, *Sport and youth crime* and *Sport and neighbourhood renewal.*

Chapter 12

Managing events

Fiona Phoenix and Rob Wilson

The purpose of this chapter is to present an overview of the sport event industry in the United Kingdom and to provide practical guidance for students to understand the planning and processes that are involved in event management. Industry related case studies are used throughout to illustrate these processes in practice. Even though each event may be unique, the tools that are used in successful event management will be the same, whether the event being managed is major or minor.

Learning outcomes

This chapter is designed to enable you to:

- understand the importance of event management within today's sport and leisure sector in the UK;
- appreciate how sport events are managed successfully;
- apply planning tools and concepts to events that you may have the opportunity to manage.

What is event management?

Event management is becoming a well established professional field in the UK. Over the past few decades the status of event management as a legitimate and widely recognised profession has grown (Goldblatt and Schiptsova, 2002). Events constitute one of the fastest growing forms of leisure, business and tourism related phenomena (Getz, 1997). As well as sporting competition and development, events also involve entertainment, business and economic impacts (UK Sport, 2005).

Events differ from normal, everyday routines. An event can be defined as: a one-off or infrequently occurring finite activity or series of activities, which is outside the normal range of everyday experience. Events will normally; include specific terms of reference and are usually unique (Emery, cited in Trenberth, 2003, p272). Most events, regardless of their size or scale, will have common characteristics such as:

- a clear-cut starting and finishing point;
- fixed, absolute deadlines;
- one-off organisation, normally superimposed on other work (Torkildsen, cited in Trenberth, 2003, p271).

These characteristics require effective management with careful planning and a lot of hard work. It is important to take a step back, however, before embarking on planning for an event, and to take the time to create an overall events strategy and framework (UK Sport, 2005). Managing an event will often be time-consuming, tiring and sometimes frustrating, but, providing it is carefully planned, the rewards can be substantial for all parties involved (Running Sports, 2007). This chapter will explain the requirements of successful event planning in relation to the sports industry by breaking down the process into manageable sections on:

- the history and context of event management;
- defining events;
- economic impact of sport events;
- the sport event planning process;
- staffing;
- financial planning and control;
- marketing;
- managing risk;
- post-event evaluation.

Learning activity 12.1

Think of the last sports event you attended. This may have been anything from a local football match, a festival, a sports day or a championship competition at county, national or world-class level.

Write down all of the different aspects of the event that you think would need to be managed. Repeat this task again at the end of the chapter and see what difference in understanding you have of event management.

History of sport event management

Sports events have been in existence from early Greek, Chinese and Egyptian cultures. 'The ancient games of Olympia may have existed as early as the 9th or 10th century BC where they were part of a religious festival in honour of Zeus, the father of mythological Greek Gods' (Masterman, 2004, p9). The popularity of activities such as sports events taps into fundamental human needs for emotional and exciting experiences. This need has stayed with us for thousands of years.

The first modern Olympics were held in Greece in 1896 with the Frenchman Baron Piere de Coubertin becoming the founder of these modern games. The Winter Olympics started in 1924 and in 1948 the first Paralympic Games were held in Stoke Mandeville to coincide with the hosting of the Olympic Games in London that year.

Sports events throughout history have reflected or encapsulated wider issues in society for example on Christmas Day, 1914 First World War enemies took part in an inter-trench football match. At the 1968 Mexico Olympics, Tommie Smith and John Carlos, gold and bronze medallists in the 200 metres, took a stand against racial discrimination by staging a silent protest. The athletes stood with their heads bowed and a black-gloved hand raised as the American National Anthem played during the victory ceremony. Smaller, local events are also often important from a social perspective, as they have the ability to bring communities together and, with the influx of different cultures and nationalities to the UK, social inclusion is vital to the well-being of communities.

There has been a rapid growth of sports events over the last decade which has seen the formation of an identifiable event industry. This growth has come at a time when the globalisation of markets has had a significant impact on the nature and behaviour of large organisations. In the UK, for example, the growth of the broadcasting market has forced companies such as the BBC to develop 'in-house' event teams to stage or cover events. Consequently, in order to appraise events, their resource requirements and their associated value, a series of event definitions have been developed.

Classifying events

As mentioned earlier the size of events can vary considerably, from small summer village fetes to the Olympic Games. The complexity of events ranges along this scale. Events that are *special (planned)* are either *major* or *minor*. *Minor* events will attract limited audiences and may take the form of, for example, festivals whereas *major* events attract large audiences, for example the Olympic Games. Such major events may also be divided into *mega* and *hallmark* events. Hallmark events are infrequent, and often belong to one particular place; mega events are one-off and on an international scale (see Figure 12.1).

Mega events are so large they affect a whole economy and reverberate in the global media. They are often open to a competitive bidding process and the events are staged once in a particular location: for example, the Olympics, the Rugby World Cup, the FIFA World Cup. However, to complicate things a little, there are non-transient mega events, i.e. events that do not change their host location, for example the tennis grand slam held at Wimbledon is always held at SW19.

Hallmark events, on the other hand, are those that become so identified with the spirit and ethos of a city that they become synonymous with the name of the place and gain widespread recognition and awareness. The Carnival in Rio, the Tour de France, the Grand National at Aintree, are such examples.

Learning activity 12.2

Think of as many different events as you can under the headings of mega, hallmark and minor.

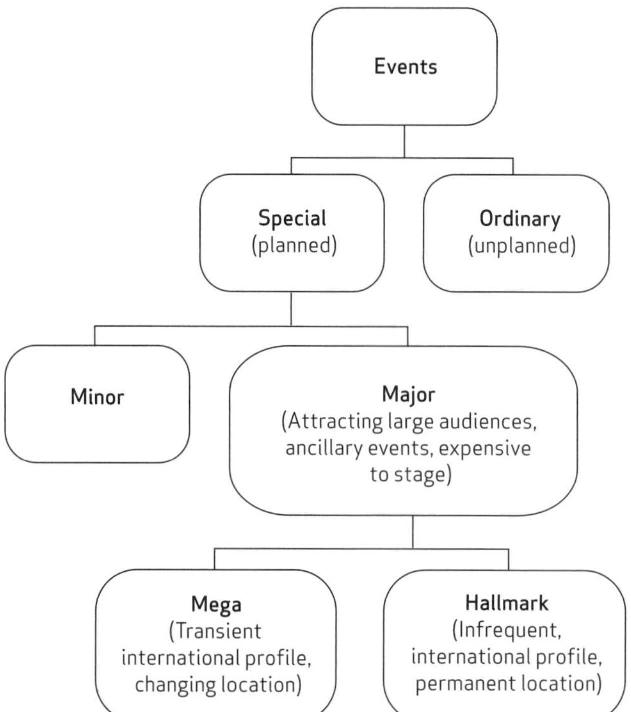

Figure 12.1: Classifying event type

Source: Adapted from Masterman (2004).

Economic impact of sports events

Once events have been defined or categorised, event planners, managers and broadcasters can begin to appraise the added value that they can bring. Gratton and Taylor (2000) suggest that events can be categorised into four 'types' with regard to level of economic impact that they have (types A–D). Wilson (2006) extended this typology by adding a fifth type (type E). This typology of events attempts to indicate that not all events labelled as major are actually economically significant (Gratton and Taylor, 2000). These are illustrated in Table 12.1.

The Los Angeles Olympics in 1984 was the first Olympics not to use public money, which transformed the whole funding process of major events. An example of their innovative funding was to have fewer sponsors who paid more to gain the rights. Through the private funding, the Games made a surplus of £215 million. This trend then continued at subsequent Games, culminating in the generation of $5.1 billion of economic activity at the Atlanta Games in 1996. Prior to the 1984 Olympics, cities were not generally encouraged by their governments to host major events, as prior organising committees had recorded significant losses, for example £178 million (1972 Munich Olympics) and £692 million (1976 Montreal Olympics) (Gratton et al., 2000). Today, the bidding for events has become extremely competitive due to the recognition that major sports events can generate significant economic impact on host communities. These impacts range from £0.18 million of additional expenditure attributable to the half-day IAAF (International Association of Athletics Federations) Grand Prix athletics staged on a Sunday in Sheffield, to the £25.5 million attributable to the Flora London Marathon in 2000 (UK Sport, 2004).

Table 12.1: Typology of sport events

Type A	Irregular, one-off, major international spectator events generating significant economic activity and media attention
Type B	Major spectator events generating significant economic activity, media interest and part of an annual cycle of sports events
Type C	Irregular, one-off, major international spectator/competitor events generating limited economic activity
Type D	Major competitor events generating limited economic activity and part of an annual cycle of sports events
Type E	Minor competitor/spectator events generating very limited economic activity, no media interest and part of an annual domestic cycle of sport events

The benefits of hosting a major sport event are hard to deny when considering the economic findings of the Euro '96 championships. To date this event has been the most successful in economic terms in the UK, generating £120 million and attracting 280,000 overseas visiting supporters (Dobson et al., 1997). This evidence builds on that of both the Los Angeles and Atlanta Olympics, and highlights the importance of considering any potential economic benefit before bidding to host such events. Furthermore, the recognition of local economic benefits has sparked fierce competition from cities to host major events (UK Sport, 1998).

CASE STUDY 12.1

Benefits to a city of hosting sports events

Sheffield, one of the UK's first national cities for sport, was one of the pioneers behind the establishment of a major sport event strategy. Sheffield's Major Sports Events Unit (SEU) states the benefits of having a major sports events strategy, suggesting that such events improve the local economy of the city, and enhance the national and international image of the city and the region, as well as increasing the bonds between people in local communities through encouraging their involvement and the regeneration of the community's identity.

The SEU provides a set of aims that are central in achieving their vision to 'promote the city as a European city of cultural distinction, positioning the city as a leader in hosting and delivering major sports events'.

In 2006 SEU achieved the following:

- delivery of 42 events: 13 international; 19 national; 10 regional, with 6 events for athletes with a disability;
- delivered 8 events that received national television coverage;

CASE STUDY 12.1 *continued*

- over 16,500 local people involved in major participation events such as the Half Marathon, Race for Life, Sheffield Festival of Athletics, the Lord Mayor's 10K and Think Pink walk;
- successfully bid for and awarded the 2011 UK Schools Games, which will bring over 5,000 athletes, officials and staff to the city;
- developed a working relationship with UK Sport, the government backed international sports events organisation;
- attended and displayed at Sport Accord, the world's number one major sports events conference in Seoul, South Korea, generating interest in a least one world-level event;
- bid for major high-profile international event, the European ice figure and dance skating championships 2010.

(Major Sports Events Unit, Activity Sheffield, 2007)

Once events have been staged certain legacy benefits can be left behind. This legacy can take many forms, including facilities and tourism. If managed properly, the facilities that are used during events can be used as a platform to host or compete for major events in the future, for domestic purposes like the training of young and professional athletes or for local community projects (regeneration, crime reduction, participation). Furthermore, the associated tourism impacts, post-event, have been found to generate an important source of income (UK Sport, 1998; see also Chapter 15 for more information).

These reasons are used to justify major sports events being part of a city's strategy to raise its profile, or to aid the re-imaging of a city. The recognition of the importance of hosting major events encouraged the development of a governing body in the UK in 1994, which helps cities bid for and organise major events. This is the Major Events Support Group (MESG) (UK Sport, 2004).

CASE STUDY 12.2

UK Sport's World Class Events Programme

Through its World Class Events Programme, UK Sport distributes approximately £3.3 million of Lottery funding each year to support the bidding and staging costs of major events on home soil, as well as providing specialist support to organisers.

The programme has grown from strength to strength, with the catalyst for change being the announcement on 6 July 2005 that London had won the right to host the Olympic and Paralympic Games in 2012. This has changed the sporting landscape in Britain forever, including the ability to expand the World Class Events Programme and bring even more strategically important events to these shores.

This expansion has been exponential; while five events were supported in 2006 (with an investment of £1.6 million), 19 events were supported in 2007,

CASE STUDY 12.2 continued

with some 17 events being supported in 2008, including a record six World Championships, despite this being an Olympic and Paralympic year.

A fantastic example of the success of the programme was seen at the 2008 UCI World Track Cycling Championships, where the British team swept the board, winning 50 percent of the gold medals available, a feat never achieved before. Chris Hoy, winner of two golds and a silver at the championships, commented on the significance of competing at home: 'It's been a significant factor for the whole team and it may sound silly but it's like having a hand pushing you and all you're aware of is this volume of sound the whole way round the track and I haven't known this in any championship.'

The priority of UK Sport's Events team is to support events based on their likely performance impact, but the broader impacts of events are also examined, to maximise the wider sporting, social, cultural, economic and environmental benefits, as well as sporting performance and legacy.

The sport event planning process

Whether an event falls within the mega, hallmark or minor category, there will be a planning process that will need to be adhered to if the event is to be a success. Events can be expensive, time-consuming and extremely hard work, so effective planning is essential. It is common to represent the key project event stages through a five step process: research, design, planning, co-ordination and evaluation (Goldblatt and Schiptsova, 2002). When managing an event it is recommend that planning for a small event starts at least six months in advance. For major events, planning can take a matter of years. The British Olympic Association (BOA) had been working on the 2012 Olympic bid since 1997. It was first shown to government in 2000 and a formal decision to bid was not taken until 2003.

UK Sport offers some useful guidelines when creating a new event. It is essential to ask the following questions.

- Why is this event needed/what is its purpose?
- Will there be interest from participants, supporters, the media and sponsors?
- What are the risks?
- Will it have credibility?
- What will it cost and do you need to make a financial gain?
- Where can you look for some successful examples?
- Who can help make it work?
- Will it have a future?
- What do you want to achieve by hosting the event?
- Who are your target audiences?
- How much do you know about previous events?
- Who are the key partners?
- Have you evaluated all the risks and opportunities?

Setting aims and objectives

An event should be focused on a specific purpose such as to raise funds, present awards, generate awareness about a sport or club or build support from a specific audience. Whatever the purpose, it is vital that aims and objectives are established in order to provide a direction for the event organisers. Any decisions made during the planning process should take the event aims and objectives into consideration.

Aims vary in complexity but they act as a focus for the planning group. Projects will often have more than one aim. Aims will be further refined and developed with specific objectives. An aim is more strategic, a broad or general statement. Objectives should be much more specific and measurable, and relate to the aims – they should still be about *what* is going to be achieved; *how* should also be in action plans. Objectives should be SMART (Specific, Measurable, Achievable, Realistic, Timed). For example:

> To raise £1,000 in sponsorship by January 2009

The £1,000 target, in turn, can form the basis of a performance indicator which can be used to evaluate performance. The evaluation of the performance could take the form of assessing how much has been raised by, say, September 2008, to gauge if the organisation is on course to raise £1,000 by January. If, say, only £100 has been raised, then that would give cause for concern, and decisions and actions would be taken accordingly, such as considering alternative sources of funding or reducing the cost of the project.

Learning activity 12.3

Create some SMART objectives for an event.

Event planning

With any event, many activities tend to be going on simultaneously, so there are many details which will need to be checked. A checklist will provide a step-by-step guide to organising and executing the event, and should include a timeline that will ensure that all deadlines are met. It is vital, therefore, to have a practical structure in place for managing the event that caters for every area of operation. Event planning must determine the key areas of responsibility, with effective reporting mechanisms and systems in place for when things go wrong. As the event plan develops, there may be a need to create additional functional areas.

A Gantt chart is the suggested layout for event planning, although there are alternatives. A Gantt chart is ostensibly a flow chart; it has each functional area as a main heading with each responsibility or task listed below. The dates and time-lines are then plotted along a calendar scale to give an illustration of how the event planning process will progress. An event flow chart brings together details from all the different event planners to establish an overall time frame for the event (Running Sports, 2007).

Figure 12.2 gives a very basic example of how to use a Gantt chart. Most event charts will be far more detailed and possibly organised slightly differently, for instance, dates may be shown as days rather than weeks and it may be reversed in the way you count (i.e. count down to the event rather than count up). Note that the highlighted (grey) boxes represent the act of working on a specific task.

The objectives should constantly be reviewed alongside the event plan and overview to ensure that the plan is on track. Continuous monitoring against quality guidelines enables the control of the eventual output through the planning process.

Figure 12.2: Event planning Gantt chart

Functional Area	Week 1	Week 2	Week 3	Week 4	Week 5	Week 6	Progress
Budget and finances							In progress
Venue and facilities							Completed
Health and safety							In progress
Perform risk assessments							Completed
Event catering							Completed
Staffing							Completed
Marketing and promotion							In progress
Monitoring and evaluation							In progress

Source: Adapted from Running Sports (2007).

Key skills of effective event managers

The nuts and bolts of running events centre around managing relationships in order to deliver a product within a given time frame and budget. Effective internal and external relationships are essential to the event's success. No event co-ordinator should be irreplaceable, so it is important to implement a succession policy, or a mentoring scheme, to allow others to learn the ropes and ensure sustainability

The event coordinator needs to:

- plan carefully and critically, paying attention to detail;
- communicate with key stakeholders;
- delegate effectively and manage workloads;
- motivate staff;

- disseminate information and provide opportunity for the team to feed back;
- meet deadlines and support others in meeting theirs;
- keep accurate and up-to-date administrative records.

Staffing events (volunteers)

Sports events would not happen without volunteers. From the estimated 70,000 volunteers required at an Olympic/Paralympic Games, to the community spirit shared by the 10,000 people who volunteered during the Manchester Commonwealth Games (2002), which will be seen on a larger scale across the UK in 2012, through to the five or six volunteers who may be required for a small community activity, they are vital to all events (Running Sports, 2007). Volunteers invest on average 1.2 billion hours each year. This is equivalent to 720,000 extra full-time workers in UK sport (Leisure Industries Research Centre, 2003).

If volunteers are a key component for an event, it is essential that they are treated as a valuable asset. Many advise that a role outline (role description) for each position is created, which will give a brief breakdown of activities the volunteer will be asked to undertake and the skills/qualities required to perform them.

The following issues should be considered:

- what type of roles will be required to deliver specific tasks?
- what skills are required to ensure the roles covered?
- how many people are required to facilitate each role?
- what will the organisational structure be (e.g. who will be in charge of what, and which roles are represented by the team on the ground?)

Learning activity 12.4

View some volunteer role outline templates by visiting *www.runningsports.org* and clicking on 'Manage sports volunteers', then 'Role descriptions'.

CASE STUDY 12.3

Volunteer recruitment at the Tour de France

The Prologue of the Tour took place on 7 July 2007 on the streets of London and Stage One – London to Canterbury – on 8 July 2007.

Within five weeks of the route announcement more than 1,200 people had signed up to marshal the race in London and Kent. Around 2,000 volunteers were needed for the whole event.

Transport for London was responsible for recruiting volunteers for this event. Recruitment received a large boost at the Herne Hill Good Friday event, which was affected by heavy rain. Many spectators took shelter in the Transport for London marquee and a large number signed up to volunteer for the event. In all, over 3,000 volunteers signed up for the event.

Financial planning and control

Exercising sound financial planning and control is of fundamental importance in running a successful event. A lack of knowledge regarding the cost of the event will lead to almost certain failure. It is essential to plan, budget and monitor finances throughout the planning and execution of an event to avoid any implications of cost variation or changing economic conditions.

Before an event progresses too far in to the planning process, it is essential to assess its financial viability. This will mean setting out a financial plan to balance the cost of running the event against any existing funds and prospective income. Several draft budgets may need to be compiled before the final version is produced. Initially, the budget will be based on estimates, but it is important to confirm actual figures as soon as possible to keep the budget on track and to exercise something resembling financial responsibility (Running Sports, 2007).

Budgeting will play a central role in keeping event finances on track and ensure that debts are paid as they fall due. A budget is often described as a quantified statement of plans, i.e. the event's aims and objectives explained in financial terms. The budgeting process will include costing, estimating income and the allocation of financial resources (McDonnell et al., 1999). Normally a budget will be based on the following information:

- financial history of previous identical or similar facilities/events;
- general economy and your forecast for the future;
- income and expenses you reasonably believe you can expect with the resources available.

Budgeting effectively forces managers to think ahead and implement any corrective action required or explain any variance to the original predicted costs (see Figure 12.3). The budget will cover a defined period of time (usually from start of event planning to post-event evaluation) and will normally be written up as an income and expenditure account (see Figure 12.3) once the event has taken place. To help with cost planning and control the following questions may be asked when developing a budget for an event.

- What are the timescales for the event budget?
- What did previous event budgets contain?
- Who managed the budget and the cash flow?
- What are the consequences of over-spending?
- Are the cost and revenue projections achievable?
- How will costs be met should the event be cancelled?
- Are there any cancellation penalties that need to be considered?
  (For further detailed discussion of financial planning and control see Chapter 8)

Managing income

The key to managing a financially viable event is obviously to make sure that income exceeds expenditure and the event makes a surplus. However, in most cases, it is acceptable for the event to break even, i.e. the income covers the expenditure, because of the associated economic benefits discussed earlier. Therefore, when managing

Figure 12.3: Income and expenditure budget for a residential sports camp event

Expenditure				
Description	**Units**	**Costs**	**Original budget**	**Actual cost**
Facility hire	1	£6,000	£6,000	£6000
Accommodation and catering				
Residential campers B&B	130	£60	£7,800	£7,800
Residential staff	10	£60	£600	£600
Staffing				
Coaches' salaries	12	£250	£3,000	£3,500
Assistant coaches' salaries	8	£100	£800	£800
Physio	1	£500	£500	£500
CRB checks	25	£36	£900	£900
Equipment				
Physio equipment			£200	£326
Radio hire			£300	£146
Van hire			£500	£325
Media equipment				
Media equipment			£150	£455
Marketing and promotion/printing				
Merchandise	100	£7	£700	£700
Promotional material	1	£1,058	£1,058	£1,058
Certificates design and printing	1	£1,000	£1,000	£574
Trophies			£-	£240
Prizes	1	£400	£400	£350
Staff uniforms	25	£30	£750	£850
			£-	
Contingency 5%	1	£4,000	£4,000	
Total expenditure			**£28,658**	**£25,124**

Income			
Description	**Units**	**Fees**	**Total income**
Residential campers	130	£295	£38,350
Merchandise	100	£20	£2,000
Total income			**£40,350**
Surplus/deficit			**£14,836**

events, no matter what their size, it is vital to create income streams as these will help to generate sufficient money to cover the costs. These can fall under the heading of 'internal' and 'external' (see Figure 12.4).

Sponsorship

Sponsorship is not new but the scale of it is! Each year, £30 billion is spent on sport sponsorship. European companies account for approximately 28 percent of that spend, making Europe the second largest region in the world after North America (IEG Sponsorship, 2005).The amount spent on sport sponsorship in the UK has increased dramatically over the past three decades:

1971	£2.5 million
1983	£100.2 million
2002	£500 million.

As a promotional tool, sponsorship is used by a variety of businesses for commercial reasons, i.e. financial gain (McDonnell et al., 1999). Simplistically, companies that provide sponsorship to sport events do so for a specified benefit, for example, brand exposure to improve product sales (Getz, 1997). Due to the growing scale of the sport sponsorship industry, sponsorship is no longer regarded as just 'entertainment' or 'goodwill' but as an effective and powerful marketing tool.

Companies sponsor major sporting events because these provide the opportunity for their brands to be exposed to a global audience. For example, the World Cup has a global audience of 40 billion viewers. Coca-Cola, as a world-wide, leading brand, wants to associate itself with such excellence and ubiquity and has chosen the Olympics and football World Cups for its sponsorships. But in order to personalise and localise its image and activity, Coca-Cola also supports grassroots sport to reinforce its global message.

Smaller events can also gain income through sponsorship. Backman (cited in McDonnell et al., 1999) discovered that for 200 UK sponsors the key benefit sought through the sponsorship was to reach the target group and gain 'added value' for their brand. Sponsors are looking for sports properties that can make a valuable and

Figure 12.4: Breakdown of costs

Internal	External
Ticket revenue/entry and participant fees	Sponsorships
Programme sales	Grants
Merchandise	Advertising
Concessions/food/bar/hospitality	Fundraising
Transportation	Donations/charities
	Local authorities
	Television/radio

quantifiable contribution to existing or planned brand communications. To do so the sponsorship must have a good fit with the event and its target audience.

Any prospective sponsor must be approached professionally as commercial sponsorship can be extremely difficult to find and requires a lot of work to service it (Watt, 1998, p52). Event managers need to carefully target prospective sponsors and then design an approach specifically tailored to each sponsor's needs. The number of sponsors an event has depends on the size/type of event. For more detail sponsorship please see Chapter 13.

CASE STUDY 12.4

Norwich Union and UK Athletics

Norwich Union began its sponsorship with UK Athletics in 1999; initially investing £10 million for a four-year sponsorship deal, this then being increased to a £20 million deal over five years (UK Athletics, 2007). In 2006, Norwich Union renewed this sponsorship deal, making a £50 million commitment to UK Athletics until 2012 – the biggest sport sponsorship deal in the UK outside football (Norwich Union, 2007 cited in King, 2008).

Norwich Union's 2007–08 sponsorship objectives:

- Awareness;
  - build mass market awareness of UK Athletics sponsorship in a way that delivers on a new brand proposition;
  - enhance Norwich Union's credentials;
- Engagement
  - build deeper connections with consumers, delivering interaction that drives data capture and involvement;
  - actively engage our broad target audiences to raise their emotional connection with the brand to increase trust and advocacy;
- Sales
  - utilise this engagement to promote products and drive consideration, retention and sales;
- Research
  - Norwich Union World Indoor Trials and UK Championships, broadcast on the weekend of 9–10 February 2008, from the Sheffield English Institute of Sport (EIS) and was one of 12 athletics meetings for the 2007–08 season where Norwich Union were the headline sponsor.
  - Quantitative research was conducted at the event by King (2008), in the form of respondent completed questionnaires, in order to determine the level of awareness and knowledge that spectators had of the Norwich Union brand. The results of the research suggested that Norwich Union's sponsorship objectives were being met, with 88 percent of the spectator sample at the World Trials Athletics recognising Norwich Union as the main sponsor. The overall recommendation of the research was for Norwich Union to continue the sponsorship of UK Athletics until the 2012 renewal date, as all sponsorship objectives were being met.

Marketing the event

Having the best-quality event product is one thing; unless there is a strategic plan for promoting the product, however, it will remain the best kept secret in the world. One of the major sources of income of an event will be the participants and spectators themselves, so it is important to attract as many as possible. As with other aspects of event planning, it is important to allocate enough time and resources to plan and distribute publicity effectively (Running Sports, 2007). Developing an event marketing strategy should include answers to the following key questions.

- What are the key markets for the event?
- What are the unique or key points in the event that would be attractive to a sponsor?
- What is the overall marketing strategy?
- Who are the main competitors in this field?
- What image does the event have?
- Who is the publicity aimed at?
- Will sponsors help publicise the event?
- Will advertising need to be paid for?

It is important that event managers carefully choose the right type of marketing that will precisely target the market segments that are appropriate for their events. For example, an event targeted at students could be marketed through flyer distribution near halls of residence or on social networking sites such as Facebook. Key marketing principles can be used to ensure that the message gets out, for example, AIDA will help ensure that event publicity is effective:

- Attention – does the publicity attract attention?
- Interest – does it arouse interest in the event?
- Desire – does it create a desire to go to the event?
- Action – does it cause action (i.e. going to the event)?

The principles of AIDA will apply throughout the planning process, from attracting attention early (e.g. distributing leaflets and application forms), to issuing follow-up information if the initial response is poor (e.g. reduced entry fees, to remind existing applicants about the event nearer the time, and continuing to attract further participants) (Running Sports, 2007). Making sense of this will help establish effective publicity, which will be simple and eye-catching and include essential information, for example, what, where, when and who to contact (Running Sports, 2007). Simple methods can be used in event marketing such as:

- a website;
- advertising in national newspapers, specialist sports publications, newsletters and magazines;
- posters and leaflets in shops, clubs, doctors' surgeries, libraries, sports centres and sporting facilities;

- radio and TV at local, regional and national level;
- letters/direct mailing which target specific people;
- sport NGBs.

Using effective marketing strategies will enable the event to secure the income required for it to run smoothly. It is also a vital tool in persuading sponsors to back an event. These simple techniques can be used in a variety of situations as case study 12.5 illustrates.

CASE STUDY 12.5

marketing 4orce student events

Formed in 2006, 4orce is an event management and marketing organisation, initially set up by a small group of students for a second-year 'Fundraising and event management' module within the Sport Management degree at Sheffield Hallam University (SHU). 4orce Student Events, which 'aims to provide events that everyone can enjoy!', had its first successful event, a Pro Evolution Soccer (PES) Tournament, in January 2007. The event, which took place at the SHU Student Union had over 200 participants and made a healthy profit which was used to fund further events.

The marketing strategy developed for the first event incorporated the development of a brand, logos (which appeared on all promotional material including clothing, tickets and posters), a website and utilisation of social networking sites. 4orce was granted permission to use the PES logo on all of their promotional material, such as posters and flyers (which were distributed around the areas that the target market of students resided, such as halls of residence and around the university campus). At the time of the event, a new PES game had come onto the games market; the timing was perfect for the event as PES Game advertising was in magazines, on buses and on television, which helped to create extra interest for the event.

4orce created an event that the target market had a strong interest in and hosted it at a venue that the target market associated with, as well as relating all the promotional material to the needs of the target market. Because of all of these factors, the students ran a very successful event resulting in the formal set-up of the 4orce Student Events Company.

For more information go to **www.4orce.org.uk**

For more detail on marketing as a management technique please see Chapter 4.

Managing risk

All events carry a certain amount of risk. This could be manifested in terms of actual physical risk, to financial risk, to the consequences of cancelling an event. It is therefore important to consider the basics before an event is staged. These basics cover three discrete areas; safety, child protection and cancellation. Further information about managing risk can be found in Chapter 10. Two areas within managing risk that are particularly prevalent to events and projects are child protection and cancellation.

Child protection

If an event involves young people, there will be a requirement to take appropriate measures in relation to child protection. These include:

- a clear code of conduct for all staff/volunteers, police checks, registration details for the young people, emergency contact details for parents/guardians, contact details for support services,e.g. local authorities and social services;
- a procedure relating to photo capturing equipment.

Further information on child protection is available in *Safeguarding and protecting children: a guide for sports people*, published by Sports Coach UK.

Cancellation

Sport England (2007b) suggests that it is necessary to consider the implications of cancelling events. In reality, events are cancelled on a regular basis and for a variety of reasons, for example, a lack of finance, a low projection for the number of attendees, the requirements of the event, etc. It is worth considering the point during the planning process at which the event should be cancelled, and who will be responsible for this decision? Key factors that will influence the decision to cancel will include:

- penalties/charges to you that you would still have to pay (e.g. the venue);
- income targets;
- number of entries/bookings.

Post-event evaluation

The final stage for any event should be a thorough post-event evaluation. This will allow the organisers sufficient space to reflect on the planning and running of the event, and the positive and negative lessons learnt. It is worth noting that an evaluation of the success of the event could also be a requirement of sponsors. Hall (1997) states that evaluation is not an afterthought for event management. It is a strategic necessity in order to achieve organisational change required for future success. It helps the event become more successful and supports professionalism.

It is also an opportunity to establish what went well and what you need to improve next time. Post-event evaluation must link to the original aims and objectives set for the event as the event is not over until evaluation and feedback has been disseminated. It is important to take time to evaluate right after the event, while the details are fresh. Gaining feedback from participants and spectators, both in verbal and in writing, will benefit the development of any future events.

Sport England (2007c) has outlined key issues to consider when evaluating an event.

- Did the event fulfil its goals and objectives? Why or why not?
- Identify what worked and what needs improving?
- What was missed off the original checklist?

- Was the event well attended?
- Was informal and formal feedback about the event positive?
- Given all that went into staging the event, was it worth doing?

A debriefing will also be important and the timing of it imperative. The appropriate people will need enough time to prepare for it, but it will also need to be close enough to the event to be relevant. The purpose is to gain constructive evaluation that should feed into enhancement of performance. Evaluation should not become 'self-congratulatory' – it should be highly critical and objective. Finally, after the event, it is important to thank all of the volunteers and people involved.

Review

This chapter has established the journey that successful event management should take. It represents the lessons learnt over a long period of time, and considers a variety of arguments and key tools for planning, managing and evaluating an event. Only by understanding and applying each of the tools can an event be thought of as a success, although it will never guarantee that it will be. There are many obstacles that can prevent an event from even being planned, let alone running smoothly – financial resources, human resources and event security, to name but three. If the event management jigsaw can be put together, then the odds will be stacked in favour of the event organiser. Key themes are: Planning, People, Pounds, Publicity (Running Sports, 2007).

Review of learning outcomes

Having read the chapter and undertaken the various learning activities you should now be able to answer the following questions.

- What are the key steps in running a successful event?
- What are the different categories of sport events?
- What types of impact can sport events have on communities?
- Why is the management of finance important to hosting a successful event?
- What will sponsors need to get from being associated with an event?
- What are the key factors in managing risk?
- Why is it important to evaluate the event once it has ended?

Further study

Masterman, G (2004) *Strategic sports event management: an international approach.* Oxford: Elsevier Butterworth-Heinemann.

This book constitutes a more detailed resource for the planning and managing of events within the sport industry. Both large and smaller-scale events are discussed, including both UK and international case study examples.

Chapter 13

Funding, investment and sponsorship in sport

Caroline A. Wiscombe

Many participants in sports activity, whether as part of a voluntary, public or private organisation, would rather avoid facing the challenge of funding their sporting pursuits. This chapter faces head-on the task management faces in funding, investment and sponsorship of sports against a background which has seen diminishing financial resources supplied by governments and a strain on the availability of voluntary assistance to support many clubs and sports organisations. Understanding the financial constraints of providing sports activity is, in many instances, about adding value and this chapter, while considering profit for some organisations, begins a discussion about the funding of sport to provide wider social benefits.

Learning outcomes

This chapter is designed to enable you to:

- understand the contexts of government funding for sport development and participation;
- explain the role of funding in private sports organisations;
- analyse the return on investment needed for sports funding and sponsorship;
- discuss the importance of a variety of income streams to the future of sport.

Introduction

Sport is very expensive to organise, develop and sustain. Land and buildings are challenging to build and maintain, while equipment needs constant replacement. Sport is heavily weighted toward human resource demands, with participants needing coaching, coaches requiring training, while matches and competitions require organisation. Sport management therefore requires a large amount of capital to develop an infrastructure and ongoing investment to maintain it.

Funding and investment comes from a number of sources. Both public and private organisations are reliant on government funding, which is driven by public policy decisions. In 2007 a total of £175 million was given by the Department of Culture, Media and Sport (DCMS) toward the development of the London 2012 Olympics, and £180.2 million to other sporting activity. This resource is spent on both capital projects, maintenance of organisational structures and public facilities.

In the United Kingdom the National Lottery provides further funding by providing the National Governing Bodies (NGBs) for sport with funds from their resources, channelled via the non-department public bodies organised by the DCMS, such as Sport England and UK Sport. Further lottery funding for sport is distributed by a bidding process to the National Lottery, and many voluntary organisations make application for funds under this process. NGBs are formed when like-minded groups agree to such associations being unified under a holistic umbrella in order to promote, regulate and monitor sports activity.

CASE STUDY 13.1

Horse Sport Ireland

Horse Sport Ireland is the NGB for equestrian sport in Ireland. It was formed in 2004 following discussions by the Equestrian Federation of Ireland, the Irish Horse Board, the Irish Sports Council and the Department of Arts, Sports and Tourism and Agriculture and Food. These groups agreed to work towards the establishment of Horse Sport Ireland in order to strengthen the horse sports sector, bringing common purpose to future development and create organisational efficiencies. Measurement of its success would be an improved Irish equestrian performance in future Olympic Games.

Voluntary organisations are vital in sport development. They are mainly funded by membership fees and have a wide dependence on volunteers to provide organisation and management skills. They continue to exist by using pay-to-play policies and trying to ensure that income is greater than expenditure, saving surpluses to achieve growth targets.

Commercial enterprises in sport can apply for government and lottery funding as well as reaping financial benefits from sponsorship and broadcasting deals. In all funding, investment and sponsorship for sport is part of a complicated network of affiliations and relationships created by the enjoyment of watching, participating and regulating a hugely entertaining industry. The concept of profit from sport takes on wider connotations than the purely financial, with health, regeneration and economic multipliers being just some of the acknowledged benefits of supporting both one-off projects such as London 2012 and continuing maintenance of existing supply.

Sport managers who have received funding, investment or sponsorship will have to show how monies spent have generated the results the provider was promised. Evaluation of both organisation and one-off project results was provided in Chapter 5. Where funding is received managers should ensure that careful records are kept in order to show any or all of the following performance measures: new participants in sporting activity, perceived health benefits, positive lifestyle changes, social networks, qualifications awarded, adherence/drop-out rates, attendances, increased self-esteem and voluntary support. Sometimes case studies are recorded. These indicators will provide evidence that can increase partner satisfaction and thus provide continued relationships that can provide continuity in funding streams.

Government funding and investment

There are a number of ways of defining the scope and sectors of the sports industry (Beech and Chadwick, 2004; Stewart, 2007; Torkildsen, 2005). Overall the consensus indicates that the drivers of sport provision and development provide a key to an analysis that includes voluntary, public and private organisations (Watt, 2003). However, it is also apparent that sports organisations comprise a unique industry where public funding is important to private organisations as well as solely publicly funded organisations. Public funds are also vital to the sustainability of many voluntary organisations. Public funding is distributed to sports organisations through three main conduits:

- Sport England, which is responsible for building community sports systems;
- The Youth Sport Trust, which focuses on enhancing the quality of physical education (PE) and sports opportunities for young people;
- UK Sport, whose responsibility is focused towards world-class elite performance.

Local and national governments also have specific roles in both sports policy and funding.

Local government

In the United Kingdom, government funding for sport is driven in a number of ways, one of which is through its devolvement to local government. Local government is funded through council taxes, which account for approximately a quarter of their needs. This income is supplemented by a series of government grants, revenue from non-domestic rates, and property taxes on business and non-domestic properties. From these funds, local government delivers services and facilities, which include sport and leisure activity, through the direct provision and management of services, for instance through leisure centres contract management. They also enable other organisations to provide services through planning provision, grants or rate relief and by partnering institutions, private and voluntary sector organisations and members' clubs. Such organisations benefiting from planning provision might include community halls and venues, and those from partnerships such as bowling clubs using municipal parks as their host green. The local authority network is illustrated in Figure 13.1.

Legislation does not compel local authorities to provide sport or leisure services and because of this there is a large difference between the quality and the quantity of provision and support in different regions. Leisure budgets may provide for parks and pitches, and contribute to swimming pools, and an increasing number of local authorities provide 'healthy' programmes of activity led by their employees such as 'Walsall Walk On', which encourages walks in local parks and countryside and has won a '3 heart' award from 'Walking the Way to Health'.

Figure 13.1: Local authority networks

<table>
<tr><td>Central government in England</td><td colspan="3">Office of Deputy Prime Minister
Department for Culture, Media and Sport</td></tr>
<tr><td>Scottish Parliament</td><td colspan="3">Deputy First Minister with mandate for Sport</td></tr>
<tr><td>Welsh Assembly</td><td colspan="3">Deputy First Minister/Minister for Culture, Sport and the Welsh Language</td></tr>
<tr><td>Local government</td><td>Unitary or single-tier authorities</td><td colspan="2">London boroughs
Metropolitan councils
Unitary councils, e.g. Rutland, Bristol, Isles of Scilly</td></tr>
<tr><td></td><td>Two-tier authorities</td><td>County councils</td><td>District councils</td></tr>
</table>

Drivers for sports expenditure within local authority leisure services provision are based on perceived benefits to communities, which can include promotion of health, regeneration, education, tourism and civic pride, while heritage and culture may also play a part in strategic development. To assist development plans, local authorities will often seek to provide community structures for sport as part of existing provision, especially where these have been provided by district councils. This is particularly noticeable in plans for community use of school provisions. Schools that have facilities provided by the local education authority, however, must ensure that community use is not subsidised from the 'delegated' school budget and therefore such use must be self-financing.

National government

The DCMS, as part of the national government, is responsible for developing national policy on sport, along with the arts, culture, libraries, museums, the National Lottery and many other aspects of socio-economic life. It has responsibility for 63 public bodies, including 57 non-departmental public bodies (NDPBs) that help deliver the department's aims and objectives. Over 95 percent of DCMS expenditure is spent on providing NDPBs with grant-in-aid for their operations and further distribution.

In 2005–06 sport received £134 million from the DCMS through the four national sports councils (Sport England, Sports Scotland, Sports Council for Wales and the Sports Council for Northern Ireland) and UK Sport. A further £1.3 million was given to the Football Licensing authority and £12.1 million to the Gambling Commission. Direct sport funding was expected to rise in 2006–07 by £21 million and additionally reach £180.2 million by 2007–08. The DCMS provided funding to the 'London 2012 – Olympic Delivery Authority' in 2006–07 of £106 million and this rose to £175 million in 2007–08. The figures in Table 13.1 allow a comparison of this funding with other areas of cultural development.

Table 13.1: Funding for cultural developments 2005–08 (£ thousands)

	2005–06 outturn	2006–07 estimated outturn	2007–08 plans
Museums, galleries and libraries	451,834	484,907	513,032
Arts	408,305	427,861	416,955
Sport of which	*135,297*	*156,669*	*180,229*
Sport England	*104,627*	*102,500*	*115,963*
UK Sports Council	*29,305*	*52,995*	*63,005*
Football Licensing Authority	*1,365*	*1,174*	*1,261*
London 2012 – Olympic Delivery Authority		106,026	175,000
Historic buildings, monuments and sites	164,102	161,788	166,997
Tourism	52,500	53,500	53,500
Broadcasting and media	31,660	29,480	27,010
Regional cultural consortiums	1,810	1,632	1,885
National Lottery Commission	7,562	9,200	14,001
Gambling Commission	12,132	18,741	4,220

Source: DCMS (2007).

Public bodies also receive money from the exchequer or the National Lottery for distribution throughout sport mainly by NDPBs. In total, Sport England distributed £87 million in grants and £9.9 million through the Active England Programme awards during the year ended 31 March 2008, helping 31 priority sports (through 'whole support' or 'one-stop plans') and 37 different governing bodies (Sport England, 2008).

The Office of the Deputy Prime Minister (ODPM) also has a contribution to make to the sports agenda. It has a wide remit that covers policy areas including transport, housing, planning, devolution, local government, social exclusion and regeneration. The ODPM is the link between government and the English based regions (while Scottish and Welsh regional authorities now deal directly with the devolved parliaments). Although it is not a funding provider, the ODPM will provide clear guidance and influence over the provision of sport, particularly in policy which aims to improve delivery and value for money in local services.

The impact of planning regulations, devolved through the ODPM, upon sport policy and development should not be overlooked. In 2008 Sport England was consulted on 1,216 planning applications, resulting in either improved or protected sports provision. As a result of these plans it is estimated that £28.2 million was generated for sport.

The National Lottery

The UK National Lottery was launched on 14 November 1994 and now raises money for sport, the arts, heritage, charities and innovative programmes in education, health and the environment. Previous challenges had included promotion of the millennium and future developments will include direct funding for the London 2012 Olympics.

The lottery is regulated by the National Lottery Commission and the Office of the National Lottery (OFLOT), while operational control lies with the current contract holder, Camelot. Camelot's licence will run out in 2009 whereupon a bidding process will be undertaken to determine the next operator. While DCMS has responsibility for the policy framework of the National Lottery, the distribution of funds lies with several independent distributing bodies. For sport these are directed through New Designs For Growth (NDFG), the Big Lottery Fund and the Millennium Commission.

Early distributions of funding from the National Lottery brought a number of publicly raised complaints. These included aspects of regional differences in benefits, combined with a focus on large projects. Management structures of large organisations with well-developed administrative functions and therefore better able to deal with the actual process were also high on the list of recipients of funds and many smaller voluntary groups felt the unfairness of this situation. The lottery distributors are now focusing on areas not previously funded. Sport England has responded to this challenge by seeking to prioritise applications for deprived inner-city areas, through its 'Priority Areas Initiative', and groups that provide opportunities to encourage people to retain an interest in sport post-16.

Local authorities can apply for lottery funding or can use their expertise to assist smaller organisations to make bids, using its administrative experience to 'match fund' the project. Lottery funding has its own peculiar network, however. Projects are not always funded by the NDPBs directly, or they may combine more than one source of lottery funds. Funding can be for capital projects (buildings, land and redevelopment of facilities) or for other resource needs.

CASE STUDY 13.2

North Cornwall District Council

North Cornwall District Council launched CREST (the Coastal and Rural Extreme Taskforce), which aims to create opportunities for extreme sports including surfing, climbing, surf kayaking and many others. The project won an Active England award that enabled it to fund a coastal recreation officer who co-ordinates programmes of activity which include coaching, free sessions, local competitions and pathways to performance. The Active England awards are jointly funded by Sport England and the Big Lottery Fund. CREST has become a truly community based development project that employs the private sector to deliver some outcomes and by 2008 had attracted over 7,000 participants.

Voluntary organisations

Historical studies of sports and their development highlight the amateur nature of the beginnings of many cricket, tennis and football clubs, as well as the independent athletes who boxed, rowed or ran to early success. Even now, in the age of mega-sporting events and commercial operations, a great many of us develop sporting lives using local clubs run by volunteers.

Volunteers take up roles within local and charitable organisations for a number of reasons, giving the gift of their time, not taking payment for services and maintaining an element of free choice in their elected contributions. While there are now some paid volunteering schemes, most provide a non-paid service in order to benefit others. Volunteers are vital for the future of sport in the UK. However, their role can become much more complicated than once was the case as compliance with health and safety legislation, coaching qualifications and child protection issues have become important concerns, which can result in (sometimes costly) legislation.

Despite the difficulties for volunteers 4.7 percent of all adults over the age of 16 are estimated to be involved in sport for at least one hour per week, with football alone dependent on the efforts of 500,000 volunteers. Despite the major funding of well-known events, such as the Commonwealth Games or the Olympics, volunteers are essential for their success. The Beijing Olympics in summer 2008 enjoyed the services of 400,000 Chinese volunteers.

Learning activity 13.1

You have recently become a member of the local rugby club, which is an amateur organisation solely run by volunteers, although a professional coach is paid to organise training sessions. The Annual General Meeting explained that the club was in severe financial difficulties and, if money is not raised soon, it would have to consider closing. You don't want this so you start to write a plan to provide some ideas for fundraising.

- Write a list of fundraising ideas that the club can use to raise cash.
- Write down some ideas about how costs and expenses can be controlled in order to ensure that income is greater than expenditure.

The scope of voluntary organisations is vast and, even in a sporting context, it is extremely hard to give a total number of such groups in the UK. It is also interesting to see that even the smallest club is joined, by affiliation fees, to the sports governing bodies. NGBs are themselves dependent on volunteers, while having paid management and officials. Other organisations, for example the 'Great Britain Wheelchair Basketball League' or the 'Keep Fit Association', have much smaller organisational structures.

It is important to understand that while some large organisations may have paid administrators, many management boards are still volunteers. The interrelationship between the large umbrella associations with much smaller clubs without administrative support to operate their sports activities is an organisational conundrum that sports managers need to manage.

Voluntary sporting organisations, such as a local football or netball club, will be funded largely by membership fees. Participants in the sport will also expect to pay-to-play within their league, and will also support the club by holding and hosting fundraising activities. As clubs grow in size they may have catering facilities which can earn them some income but are unlikely to charge supporters for viewing the game. Further income streams are difficult to generate, although some small clubs do successfully gain sponsorship from local companies and donations from long-term club stalwarts. Growth strategies for small sports clubs are therefore dependent on keeping expenses low in order to achieve a surplus which can be reinvested into equipment or fees for the following season. Ideas for creating income in small organisations are often innovative; quizzes, 'bonus ball', race nights, dinner dances, fairs and car boot sales have all been used to generate funds.

Generating a surplus for a major capital expenditure through development of income over expenditure is very difficult and very long term. Where major refurbishments are needed, applications to communities, local authorities and funding bodies is the only way forward. For voluntary organisations this is a difficult journey to take.

Financial resources are available under schemes such as the 'Community Club Development Programme' (CCDP). The funding for this scheme was provided by the exchequer rather than the National Lottery. Sport England undertakes CCDP distribution and in 2007–08 the £18.5 million of funds provided 330 projects with resources. These included new gymnastics halls, golf equipment and fabric halls for netball courts.

CASE STUDY 13.3

Lyme Regis Football Club – innovation in fundraising

Lyme Regis Football Club, 'The Seasiders', an amateur football club in the south-west of England, mounted a campaign to move its ground from an area of coastal erosion to an inland development site in December 2003. It would be a hugely expensive development and planning began in order to turn the dream into a reality. The club is run by volunteers whose families have been associated with the organisation for generations. The club, which once hosted only a first and reserve side, had improved its playing performance and wanted to enter a higher division of play. The club did not have the width of pitch necessary under the regulations. In addition, its success promoted playing interest. The club had grown and accommodated novice, youth and bantam teams, with many parents helping to coach and transport youngsters to games. In order to prepare a lottery bid funding was needed to prepare all the documentation necessary. Innovative thought was necessary and a number of fundraising events were held. The mayor of the town, and a large number of local councillors, supported the project and this helped to create a real 'feelgood' factor about the possibilities, as did a council donation of £4,000 toward the funding bid.

CASE STUDY 13.3 continued

Further funds to pay for architect's plans and for the administrative support for a lottery bid were found by 'selling' a square of the proposal to local community patrons. Local shops and businesses, along with everyone who had ever played for the club, their friends and families, were persuaded to donate to the 'strawberry fields' project, buying one tiny portion of the football field, to support the club's growth strategy. In an 'area of outstanding natural beauty', and in trying to develop a green-field very rural site, the club failed to win the planning permission needed and ultimately had to forego their plans. As a result the team cannot develop its youth football to the level it would like as its pitch continues to suffer from ongoing drainage problems and cannot be widened to accommodate the requirements for playing in a higher division.

Charities

To register as a charity an organisation must satisfy the Charities Commission that it satisfies one or more 'heads of charity'. These are to relieve poverty, advance education or religion, and to be purposeful to the community. Sports are not charitable if they exist to promote an individual sport or only to benefit their members, thus designated community amateur sports clubs (CASCs) can only apply for the financial benefits of charitable status, such as reduced rates on club premises, if they are open to the whole community and are organised on an amateur basis. In addition they must provide and promote facilities in one or more eligible sports.

The largest sporting charity in the UK is the Football Foundation. Its mission is to 'improve facilities, create opportunities and build communities throughout England'. The charity has funded over 5,000 projects worth over £637 million, which look to improve facilities for grassroots football working in deprived groups and communities. In addition, the charity seeks to develop women's, girls' and disabled football. In 2007–08 the charity received investments from Sport England totalling £18.5 million, to be spent across a variety of activity that included multi-sport facilities and community and education projects. In addition the Football Foundation receives funding from the Football Association (FA), the governing body of the sport. These additional funds are raised by the development of the FA work in promoting football, income from Wembley Stadium, and the majority from income raised by selling the broadcasting rights to football games.

Commercial enterprise

Commercial or profit making organisations exist in all aspects of sport and sports services. Professional sport and coaching occupy one end of a spectrum, where amateur status was the norm until 50 years ago, while related industries of sports equipment and manufacture, footwear, clothing and retail merchandising are growing in size and sit in the 'associated' spectrum. At the non-participant end of the spectrum profit making organisations will be funded along the same lines as other industries.

In order to start a sports equipment manufacturing company an entrepreneur will need to assess market demand for their product, develop a business plan, self-finance some part of the project or provide assets to cover long-term borrowings. Long-term lenders will be banks or financial institutions and they will seek assurance that the development is sustainable and probably has a unique selling point, given the plethora of manufacturers already in the market (see also Chapter 9).

Capital will be spent on premises, plant and equipment, stock to make the equipment and provide working capital for on-going expenses. These assets will be used to make products which sell for either cash or credit, and pay the costs and expenses of the business, such as marketing, research and development, administration and distribution. The operating surplus from all this activity generates profits for shareholders.

Where the sports team or elite athlete used to be exempt from any capitalist notions, today's sports industry finds itself populated by personalities whose income off the playing field is greater than that from participating in the sport. Examples include the footballer David Beckham, whose image has helped sell such brands as Brylcream® and Pepsi Cola®.

Alongside the change from amateur to professional has been the growth of broadcasting and media influences on sport, both in providing valuable income streams but also in changing some sports rules for increased viewing pleasure and, some would say, to increase advertising opportunities. Some sports, by their mode of play, have provided ideal broadcasting sports. American Football, for instance, is a game made up of a succession of set plays. Instead of focusing on the interaction between coach and players, except in a most superficial way, the television viewer is treated to a series of advertisements by the broadcaster. As the viewing audiences globally are enormous for many of the American Football games, advertising will sell at a premium and thus broadcasting fees to the clubs involved have risen. In the UK, the FA received an income of £110 million for broadcasting rights in the period 2005–08, a 40 percent increase on previous years, with £37 million of this money distributed to the football league clubs.

Venues themselves have grown and increasingly diversified to incorporate not just sporting arenas but a plethora of events which may or may not include entertainment. Each of these areas, if managed effectively, will increase profitability for shareholders of the organisations. Not all venues make profit however. Wembley Stadium was opened after a multi-million pound upgrade in March 2007. Despite 25 major events and visitor numbers of 1.5 million, and while gate receipts and ticket sales are selling healthily, high operational costs and expenses mean the venue is currently running at a loss. Management targets are to cut costs and expenses while maximising capacity in order to begin to pay back the huge cost of the venue's development.

As discussed in Chapter 5, some sports organisations are now facing the difficulty of reporting their performance and results to many different stakeholders. These include participants, fans, the public, shareholders and NDPBs. Interpretations of performance that could attract or deny more funding and investment will differ according to who the stakeholder is. NDPBs will be interested in performance of teams or participation of players, depending on the nature of the funding provided, while shareholders look to balance this with financial profitability, thus reaping a return on financial investment.

Commercial or profit making organisations within the sports sector can be divided into those which play or participate in sporting activity and those which don't. Those which don't are limited in funding opportunities to those accessible to all profit making organisations. These can be loans and borrowings, both short- and long-term, new share issues or retained earnings. Those who do participate in sport, no matter how profitable their clubs or teams, may have access to government grants or funds, which reflects government policy but also the likelihood of international success. This is illustrated by the London 2012 bid by the British Olympic Association. Government funds backed the bid and will underpin the networked development of international standard venues, housing and transport infrastructure, as well as supporting, through the DCMS and UK Sport, the provision of elite sports training facilities, medical supervision, professional coaching and an array of additional services.

Non-government funding and investment

Revenue sources are available to sports organisation on the premise that much of sport is regarded as entertainment. In the UK the most popular sport is association football, while in second place is horse racing. Each of these sports provides a number of sports providers with maximisation of profits by the development of ongoing income streams that cover a number of areas. Few profits come from spectators alone (Gratton and Solberg, 2007; Torkildsen, 2005).

Sports organisations' members are willing to pay annual membership fees, which may, or may not, allow them discounts on spectator admission charges, premium seats, advanced or guaranteed bookings with or without additional benefits. Most race tracks, for instance, have a members' tent and/or enclosure, prepaid ticket advances and access to areas of the stadium where they can get the best views of the parade ring and course. Members' access may also extend to the training rings or viewing areas of pre-parade activity.

At both premier football stadiums and in racing venues, a large proportion of the floor area will be given over to corporate hospitality, including restaurants, bars, boxes or marquees. Premium rates for corporate hospitality venues can be charged but the service must engage the market, which is very specialised, on match or race days. In addition, developing this aspect of a venue's business provides additional non-match or race day funds. Capital investment in these facilities may cost more to develop but the return on investment is high.

Merchandising is an essential element now for the average football fan. While many have complained about the costs of new team strip or colours, particularly for young fans, the hardy faithful will always pay a premium for the latest shirt, scarf or hat. Racing is not quite so dependent on merchandising, although every outlet will have shops and stalls with a variety of memorabilia. The largest race meetings, such as the Epsom Derby or Cheltenham Gold Cup, will attract additional revenue from the plethora of stands offering all kinds of retail goods that appeal to the market, not just racing merchandise. This ranges from high fashion, jewellery, riding paraphernalia and equipment, to wellington boots and cloth caps.

Sponsorship

Sponsorship is a valuable part of the investment structure in sport to overarching organisations, individual clubs and teams and to individual athletes. In 2005 101 different companies invested in football with Barclays Bank giving £57 million to the FA premier league and Vodaphone £36 million to Manchester United Football Club.

An interesting range of companies consider sponsorship of sport as part of their marketing communications technique. The aim of sponsorship is to affect the behaviour of a target audience and this takes considerable thought and planning on behalf of the sponsor business. It is seen as much more than an opportunity for advertising and corporate hospitality, and is used to drive sales growth and develop strong brand association. In the area of sport the integration of team, or athlete, with the brand links to their success and the viewers or audience. Strong sponsorship relationships can build lucrative returns both for sponsor and sponsored, with the market for sport sponsorship estimated to be around £848 million in 2008 – although that forecast was made prior to the credit crunch. The audience for sport provides a relationship of bringing buyer and seller together, providing a conduit for verbal and visual acknowledgement or promotion using a number of media.

Formula One motor racing has a huge number of sponsors so many that viewers might find it difficult to see the colour of the cars, the helmet of the driver and the hoardings around the track. The sponsor's message however is not limited to the advertising conduit in which they engage. While there are many opportunities for the sponsor to create sales promotions and to engage in more personal sales tactics or direct marketing through accessing the audience, there are other aspects to be considered. These include public relations where engagement through education and charitable donations provide powerful corporate social responsibility messages.

For the sports organisation choosing the correct sponsor may also be crucial in purveying ethical and moral messages about their company. During the 1970s and 1980s many sports organisations were sponsored by tobacco and drinks companies. The Martell Grand National, held at Aintree each April was a fixture in both the racing and social calendar of a wide audience. Benson & Hedges sponsored a major one-day county cricket tournament. While in some cases advertising legislation has changed the opportunities for companies to sponsor (television advertising has now banned tobacco products) other decisions have been taken based on associating with a healthier image of the recipient.

CASE STUDY 13.4

Sponsorship of the Olympic Games

The Beijing Olympic Games 2008 had a global audience of 4 billion. The games cost US $43 billion to stage, with venues alone costing US $1.8 billion. Funds, expertise and knowledge were contributed by 63 official sponsors and 12 worldwide partners, while 6,000 official retail products were launched. Agreements for sponsorship are based on the Olympiad or 4-year cycle, but not all sponsorship contracts start and finish at the same time, for instance Coca-Cola has signed sponsorship deals which run until 2020, while some others are contracted to 2010 and 2012.

Sponsorship can consist of official suppliers to the Games, or sponsors recruited for their ability to provide direct support, services or expertise.

CASE STUDY 13.4 continued

Sponsorship is sought by both the International Olympic Committee, through their TOP sponsors and official suppliers' programmes, and through Games organising committees. While sponsors receive the rights to using the famous five rings brand, returns on investment are hard to gauge. For the first time in Beijing separate broadcasting rights were sold for television and for new media, Internet and mobile technology. This provided additional revenues to support the 10,708 athletes competing in 31 Olympic venues across seven cities.

British Airways provided sponsorship for Team GB by providing flights and services in transport of equipment to Beijing. In exchange they had the benefit of the huge media welcome for the team as it returned to UK soil. The resultant global television and newspaper coverage provided a return on investment that would be measured in financial calculation of equivalent hours of exposure through advertising.

Sponsorship in sport is at a crucial stage of its evolution as it has to prove a return on investment. This can be very difficult for all but the largest of organisations or most successful of athletes.

Broadcasting

Broadcasting rights are vital sources of revenue in all sports organisations. While a local Sunday league football team may not have its match televised, the income from an English premier league game will have helped support it through revenues to the FA. Differing amounts of income from broadcasting rights will go to different sizes of club. In Europe, AC Milan and Juventus each receive close to 60 percent of total revenues from broadcasting rights, but for Celtic, who play in the Scottish premier league, this falls to 23 percent of total income (Gratton and Solberg, 2007).

Growth in media coverage has followed technological advances through the development of television broadcasting, cable and satellite developments, and digitised evolution. Accessibility to the growing media revolutions impacts on viewing figures and whereas early arguments against televised coverage of sport indicated that gate receipts would fall the revenue and exposure from broadcasting has more than made up for these losses. Examples of participation and interest in particular sports can be directly linked to media coverage, for instance the success of the UK women's curling team in the 2002 Winter Olympics introduced millions more to a relatively unknown sporting activity, with new stadiums built as a result.

CASE STUDY 13.5

Success attracts further funding

Funding curling

The 2002 Olympic win for the GB women's curling team and the men's silver success in the World Championships made curling the most successful UK winter

CASE STUDY 13.5 continued

sport. As well as attracting funding to make 'curling cool' among potential young athletes, the success of the sport attracted further direct funding of £251,181 from the Sport Scotland lottery fund and £110,000 of Sport Scotland exchequer funding from the Scottish Executive.

The increasingly competitive nature of broadcasting, which has seen the growth of independent television companies and the increasing use of satellite and cable television, along with the introduction of new media technology via Internet and mobile phone, has seen prices for broadcasting major sporting events soar. However, this is not just an altruistic move towards sports organisations. The fees Sky TV pays to the FA may seem high, but pubs and clubs that show televised sport pay licence fees which provide returns on the investment estimated at £150–£180 million, which recovers about two-thirds of the costs. In addition, Sky sells programming to other television companies, for instance to support news programmes.

Demand for sports broadcasting has never been higher. It is estimated that 40 percent of televised viewing in the UK is sports or sport related. This drives up the income that can be generated from it. The Olympic Games provides a lucid illustration in terms of the levels of income that have been generated from its summer games. In 1980, a European consortium, of which the BBC was a major contributor, bid $7.2 million for televised rights. The Beijing Olympics in 2008 raised a staggering $443 million in Europe alone and a further $64 million in Australia and $894 million in the USA (all figures are given in US dollars; at December 2008 US $1 equated to £0.66).

Learning activity 13.2

Calculate the amount raised from the sale of the Olympic broadcasting rights in pounds sterling using today's currency exchange rates.

Gratton and Solberg (2007) argue that more research on the viewing figures for sports programming would provide a much stronger case for linking sponsorship to sport. In addition, they show clear links for sport to 'place' marketing that provides measurable return on investment for local government sponsorship linked to broadcast sports. The economic multipliers of such place marketing are strong messages for sports managers to adopt, particularly when economic downturns create a competitive environment for sponsorship. Broadcasting shows clear ROI solutions to sponsors.

CASE STUDY 13.6

Racecourse income

Sponsor packages

Down Royal Racecourse in Belfast holds 13 race meetings per year. Their sponsorship packages are offered by name, by race or by whole meeting. The

CASE STUDY 13.6 continued

unique selling point (USP) provided by racing sponsorship is that the name of the sponsor will appear in local and national press, both in column reporting and in the publication of the race card. Television coverage of the race days will pick up clearly the banners which surround the stands and on-course tannoy announcements will repeat sponsors' names on a regular basis. Advertising on-course materials will reiterate the sponsor's message.

Sponsorship is vital in racing as on the days when racing does not take place, income is very much reduced. The land is expensive to maintain and race days provide only a limited contribution to expenses incurred. In addition, it is not easy to use facilities for alternative events. Newmarket Racecourse holds a number of summer concerts each year, but is limited to dinner and music functions as the course is not suitable for festival-type events.

Review

This chapter has investigated funding and investment in sport. While there are funds from generating a surplus of income over expenditure, and borrowings from financial institutions, the focus has shown the importance of both government and non-government funding that may or not be given on a loan basis. As economic and sociological questions are posed with regard to ensuring returns on investment for any funds, the sports manager needs to ensure that benefits for all stakeholders are clearly defined, understood and evaluated to ensure continuity of engagement. Sponsorship is dependent upon building relationships, whereas broadcasting rights are governed by the demand of sports spectators and currently interest in sport shows no sign of abating. Lottery funding has reduced as consumers spend less on tickets, despite the expansion of the number of games that can be played under the lottery brand. Government funding, on the other hand, is dependent upon public policy. Changes of government can pose risks for continuity of funds but, in the short term, all parties in the UK are determined to ensure a clear strategy for the public 'place marketing' of the country during the period up to, and beyond, London 2012.

Review of learning outcomes

Download the plan of the London 2012 Olympic Delivery Authority Lifetime Corporate Plan from their website at **http://www.london2012.com/news/publications/annual-reports.php**

1 Find out the total estimated funding needed for the whole project and how the committee expect to raise this income.
2 Consider the benefits that London 2012 will bring and write a letter to potential sponsors seeking their patronage.
3 If sponsors respond positively, consider whether you would ask for money, skills, knowledge or a combination of all three.

Further study

For a general introduction to sports funding and finance read:

Stewart, B (2007) *Sport funding and finance*. Oxford: Butterworth Heinemann.

Wilson, R and Joyce, J (2008) *Finance for sport and leisure managers: an introduction*. Abingdon: Routledge.

For a general introduction to the economics behind sports broadcasting read:

Gratton, C and Solberg, H (2007) *The economics of sports broadcasting*. Abingdon: Routledge.

Vogel, HL (2007) *Entertainment industry economics: a guide for financial analysis*. 7th edition. New York: Cambridge University Press.

An in-depth review of sponsorship in sport is given by:

Masterson, G (2007) *Sponsorship for a return on investment*. Oxford: Butterworth Heinemann.

A more advanced view of how the public sector works is given in:

Tresch, RW (2008) *Public sector economics*. Basingstoke: Palgrave Macmillan.

Sports funding and finance is often discussed in both the business and sports sections of the daily newspapers. Consider reading:

The Independent, *The Guardian* or *The Observer* on a regular basis to see who is sponsoring and funding what type of sport(s).

Websites:

These websites provide more in-depth information about the cases used in this chapter:

www.sky.com

www.downroyal.com

www.wru.co.uk/10351-15216.php

These websites discuss how the funding and sponsorship for London 2012 works:

www.london2012.com/get-involved/sponsorship/index.php

www.london2012.com/about/funding/index.php

www.london2012.com/news/publications/annual-reports.php

Chapter 14

Sport and the law

Simon Gardiner

This chapter examines the increasing role that the general law has in regulating sport and identifies why this legal regulation of sport has increased significantly in the last 20 years or so. The chapter will discuss specific areas of law that have impacted upon the operation of the sports business industry.

Learning outcomes

This chapter is designed to enable you to:

- understand the general role of the law in regulating the sports business industry;
- examine the application of the law in specific areas of the sports business industry;
- evaluate the effect that law has on the operation of the sports business industry.

Introduction

Traditionally sport has seen itself as a structure that is self-governing and outside the scope of the law. In the past sports administrators have indicated their suspicion of the law. A past chief executive of the English Football Association, Ted Croker stated: 'I have always opposed people who seek to bring too much law into sport . . . I believe very much that sport should govern itself' (Grayson, 1999).

Historically some compliance with the law has clearly been required, for example professional football clubs have been in existence since the late nineteenth century and as such have needed to fulfil the requirement under company law of being limited companies. This limited debts to the company rather than individual members.

Since the early 1980s, the law and lawyers have had an active role in regulating sport. What has brought about this change? Many sports that at their elite level had been essentially amateur activities, became increasingly professionalised, for example rugby union became a professional sport in the mid-1990s. This change brought new sources of money into sport such as sponsorship, greater marketing opportunities and increased the value of TV rights. With more money flowing around in sport, disputes requiring legal resolution are inevitable. Sport has used the law actively to protect this increased value in sport, that is, sport's commercial integrity, through areas such as contract law and the protection of non-physical rights in sport with intellectual property law.

Government regulators both at national level, as with the UK government, and at the European Union (EU) level increasingly require sport to operate within the law. In wider areas not linked directly to commercial matters, the use of drugs in sport, for example, has been met with strict anti-doping policies. Additionally participants in sport, administrators, owners and sportsmen and women have increasingly been aware of their legal rights and the ability to seek legal address in the courts when they have a dispute.

The range of sports law areas is immense. It includes:

- criminal and civil liability for injuries caused on the sports field;
- spectator safety;
- drug use in sport;
- contracts of sports athletes;
- discrimination in employment and sports participation;
- financial corruption;
- regulation of sponsorship and marketing;
- protection of intellectual property rights (IPR) in sport;
- control of anti-competition within the sports industry.

The debate about the role of law in sport has not only revolved around the application of existing general law of both a statutory basis (Acts of Parliament) and court-created case law (decisions of judges which become law), or the enacting of specific laws such as the football related statutes discussed below, but additionally around what role the state (through legal instruments) should have in regulating sport. The reality of sport is that it is very rule bound – organisational rules, playing rules, codes of ethics are already involved in sport. The law represents an additional level of regulation. However, strong arguments have been presented that sport generally, and some sports specifically, such as English football, need greater external controls. A Football Task Force created in 1997 reported in 1999 suggesting different forms of external regulation that could be introduced in English football beyond the FA (see Gardiner et al., 2006, pp55–64). The EU's increasingly important role in external regulation of sport will be discussed below.

Sport is now a global industry accounting for more than 3 percent of world trade and almost 2 percent of the GNP of the 27 Member States of the EU. In the UK, sport provides employment for some 420,000 people, and is worth £12 billion a year in consumer spending. With the advent of the Internet and the mega sums being paid for broadcasting rights of prestigious sports events – for example, in summer 2006, the English Premier League sold its broadcasting rights for the next three seasons for a staggering £1.7 billion – the sports industry has continued to grow. Elite sport in Britain today is clearly big business and the law has a central role in its regulation as with the regulation of any other major industry. This chapter will focus on a number of sports business areas where the law has developed a very visible presence.

EU law and sport

The EU is an economic and political union of 27 countries, known as Member States. All of these countries have agreed to incorporate EU law into their national law on a range of mainly economic but also social areas. Sport was not mentioned in the Treaty of Rome, signed in the late 1950s (now the EC Treaty), the basic legal document of the EU. However, it has been accepted in a number of legal cases by the European Court of Justice (ECJ), the main court that determines the application of EU law, that where sport is an 'economic activity' (as clearly with professional sport), it is subject to regulation by the EU law like any other form of business.

The Bosman case

Although cases such as *Walrave and Koch v Association Union Cycliste Internationale* (Case 36/74 (1974) ECR 1405) and *Donà v Montero* (Case 13/76 (1976) ECR 13333) in the 1970s indicated that EU law had competency in sport as an economic activity, the ECJ ruling in Case C-415/93 *Union Royale Belge de Sociétés de Football v Bosman* [1995] ECR I-4921 (the *Bosman* case) has been a turning point in the regulation of sport in the UK and elsewhere within the EU. Jean-Marc Bosman, a Belgian footballer, challenged UEFA's use of nationality restrictions and the international transfer system. Bosman's action was sparked by his inability to leave the Belgian first division football club RC Liège following his rejection of a new (and diminished) contract offer. Under Belgian football regulations, RC Liège was permitted to demand a transfer fee for Bosman and thus retain a financial interest in the player despite his contract having ended. In August 1990, Bosman began legal proceedings in the Belgian courts in the hope of securing three main objectives:

- first Bosman wanted to gain compensation from his club and the Belgian football authority;
- second, he wanted the transfer rules amended which allowed a club to retain a financial interest in a player even after the expiry of a contract;
- third, he wanted the case to be referred to the ECJ for a preliminary ruling on the compatibility of international transfer rules and nationality restrictions in football with EU law on free movement and competition.

A core piece of law in the EU and part of the EC Treaty is fundamental freedoms of movement of goods, services, capital and persons between the Member States and across national boundaries. These provisions were introduced to provide a 'common market' for these economic resources. It was the last of these, Article 39 on freedom of movement of persons that the transfer system at the end of a contract was believed to infringe.

Free agency

On 15 December 1995 the ECJ delivered its ruling, stating that Article 39 of the EC Treaty precludes the application of rules laid down by sporting associations, under which a professional footballer who is a national of a Member State may not, on the expiry of his contract with a club, be employed by a club of another Member State unless the latter club has paid the former club a transfer fee. This essentially introduced the concept of 'free agency' into football contracts, allowing EU-national players to move freely at the end of their contact without any requirement for a transfer fee to be paid to the employing club. This is of course normal in virtually all other areas of employment.

A subsequent ECJ case of *Detacher Handballbund eV v Maros Kolpak* [2003] ECR I-4135 (Case C-438/00) (the *Kolpak* case) has had consequences for player mobility where freedom of movement powers were extended beyond EU-nationals to non-EU nationals from countries with which the EU had trade agreements, including a number of African counties.

Learning activity 14.1

In a number of sports in the UK, for example rugby union and cricket, the term 'Kolpak players' has become common parlance. Carry out research online and within the additional sources listed at the end of chapter on this case to find:

- the facts and background of the case;
- what impact this case has had on relevant UK sports;
- what policies have particular sports proposed to respond to the case.

Player quotas

The second main issue determined by the ECJ in *Bosman*, was that sporting association rules that created 'nationality quotas', in that football clubs could field only a limited number of professional players who were nationals of other Member States, were unlawful. As a consequence, English football now has many more players who are nationals of other EU Member States, who now have an automatic right to work in the UK as in any other part of the EU, under Article 39 and the *Bosman* ruling. Most other non-EU nationals continue to need to fulfil work permit regulations operated by the government. There has been support for the re-introduction of a player quota system by FIFA and UEFA due to concerns over the future quality of the England national team, as it is now not uncommon for Premiership cubs to field a whole team of players who are not eligible to play for England (see case study 14.1).

CASE STUDY 14.1

'MEPs ask Fifa to scrap quota plan', by Paul Kirby (8 May 2008)

The European Parliament has called on world football's governing body, Fifa, to drop its proposals for a foreign player quota to be imposed on clubs. Fifa President Sepp Blatter will urge his members this month to back a 'six plus five' plan to impose a maximum of five foreign players in a team. Mr Blatter says EU laws on freedom of movement are benefiting rich clubs. But MEPs have backed a report proposing instead that clubs should have at least eight home-grown players out of 25.

CASE STUDY 14.1 continued

That proposal, initiated by European football's governing body, Uefa, is less likely to fall foul of the EU's laws on discrimination on the grounds of nationality, as home-grown can mean locally trained. The parliament's rapporteur on the future of European football, Ivo Belet, told the BBC News website that he agreed with Mr Blatter's sentiment but said he could not ignore the law.

'It's well-intentioned, and the objective we 100% agree with, to force clubs to invest in their own talent,' he said. 'But not "six plus five" as it will be challenged in the European Court of Justice (ECJ) and it won't stand.' British Conservative MEP Christopher Heaton-Harris said the EU was wrong to interfere in sporting matters.

'I don't think MEPs should pick a fight on a worldwide basis with the world governing body,' he said. After 28 years as a football referee, he said the rules should be left to the sport's governing bodies to decide, rather than the European Union.

In a recent BBC interview, Sepp Blatter warned against football being split between rich and poor and believed that a limit on imported players had the support of fans. 'The law is one thing but the law can be adapted, amended if there is a general consensus,' he said, suggesting there was support for a change among EU countries. Unlike Mr Blatter, Uefa is more keen to ensure its plans fall within existing EU law. The governing body has courted the EU, both the parliament and European Commission, and says the report backed by MEPs agrees with its proposals in every way.

'For us it's a great comfort to know we've got the European Parliament behind our approach to football,' says Uefa spokesman William Gaillard who is now waiting for the Commission to give its approval too. 'Uefa does not oppose "six plus five". We think it would be very good because it would stop clubs raiding the academies of Africa and South America,' he says. 'At the same time, we are realistic and we understand it is not possible.' Uefa has already imposed a minimum requirement of home-grown players, and that is set to increase later this year to require clubs to field at least eight home-grown players in a squad of 25. Four of the eight would have to be trained by their own club, and four by other clubs in the same national association.

Source: **http://news.bbc.co.uk/go/pr/fr/-/1/hi/world/europe/7389513.stm**

So the impact of the *Bosman* ruling has been profound. A significant effect has been felt by sports organisations. Within professional football, the international and domestic transfer systems have been revised – the latest FIFA rules came into force on 1 July 2005. They provide greater powers to players during their contract to bring it to an end and move to another club, as illustrated in the Webster case (see Gardiner and Welch, 2007). So greater rights of freedom to move at, during, or at the end of an employment contract have been the consequence of *Bosman*.

Competition law

Additionally, *Bosman* has impacted upon sport more widely in terms of the legitimacy of EU law intervention into sport as an economic activity. Sport has become subject to close scrutiny not only in the area of the fundamental freedom of movement provisions, but also concerning whether sport is acting within the competition law provisions under EC Treaty Article 81 concerning abuse of monopolies (in sport most governing bodies exercise a monopolistic position within their sport) and Article 82 controls on cartels (anti-competitive collusion between bodies). An example of EU intervention in this area under Article 81 is the investigation of the Fédération Internationale de l'Automobile (FIA), specifically concerning its favouring of Formula One Grand Prix racing, which resulted in a compromise that saw the FIA divesting its commercial interests in Formula One (EU, 2003). The subsequent period has seen the EU Competition Commission adopt a less interventionist role, with the emphasis being on negotiation between parties and the granting of negative clearances. A recognisable delineation has taken place of those sports business issues where the EU will be prepared to intervene and those sporting issues that are essentially to be determined by sports bodies (see Case C-51/96 and C-191/97 *Deliège v Ligue Francophone de Judo et Disciplines Associées ASBL*, [2000] ECR I-2549) and C-313/02 Meca-Medina and Majcen *v* Commission of the European Communities (2004).

Sports stadium safety

One of the major issues that the sports industry, sports governing bodies and clubs have had to engage with has been the issue of spectator safety at sports stadiums. This has perhaps occurred most obviously within football due to a number of stadium tragedies with large scale loss of life and the on-going problem of football hooliganism, which has often been termed the 'English disease'.

The issues of safety and hooliganism have often been conflated with a lack of safety often seen as having been caused by hooliganism. The reality is that the football stadium tragedies have invariable been caused by a lack of proper investment over a period of time, leading to dilapidated infrastructure. In British football, large-scale tragedies happened periodically during the twentieth century: at Ibrox, Glasgow in 1902, where 26 people died; at Bolton in 1946, when 33 people died; at Ibrox again in 1971, when 66 people died; at Bradford in 1985, when 56 people died; and at Hillsborough, Sheffield in 1989, when 96 people died (see Gardiner et al., 2006, ch. 17 for more).

The Hillsborough tragedy

After Hillsborough, the subsequent government inquiry produced the Taylor Report (1990). The report concluded that the disaster was caused primarily by safety defects and failures of policing, although it was initially portrayed by some sections of the media as being another manifestation of hooligan activity. Recommendations were divided into those concerning safety at stadiums, most notably the introduction of all-seater stadiums at the top professional clubs but also specific football related legislative provisions that led to the amending of the Football Spectators Act 1989, then passing through Parliament, and the enacting of the Football Offences Act 1991, which criminalised entry onto the playing area, throwing missiles and racist chanting. The subsequent Football (Offences and Disorder) Act 1999 and Football (Disorder) Act 2000 have amended and strengthened many of the provisions in the earlier 1989 and 1991 Acts. In addition, the normal Public Order Act offences apply.

Many people see the current legislative framework in the UK as having 'criminalised' the ordinary football fan (see Gardiner et al., 2006). The policing of matches by the police and club stewards, together with the widespread use of CCTV, would suggest that the various legal prohibitions concerning football fandom would be rigorously enforced. So what are the rates of arrest and prosecution under these various offences? Although there is national coordination in the 'fight' against football hooliganism, with the National Criminal Intelligence Service taking a leading role, local policy and the actual practice of policing these offences are an important factor in determining these rates.

Spectator safety laws

Setting aside the legal provisions introduced as a result of football's problems, general safety concerns have been acted upon. In 1975, Parliament enacted the Safety of Sports Grounds Act, which introduced a system of licensing of major sports grounds by local authorities. Section 1 of the Act as amended by section 19 of the Fire Safety and Safety of Places of Sports Act 1987 states:

> The Secretary of State may by order designate as a sports ground requiring a certificate under this Act (in this Act referred to as a 'safety certificate') any sports ground which in his opinion has accommodation for more than 10,000 spectators.

The certificate is appropriate for a number of activities during an indefinite period or for individual occasions.

Section 2 explains that:

> . . . a safety certificate shall contain such terms and conditions as the local authority consider necessary or expedient to secure reasonable safety at the sports ground when it is in use for a specified activity or activities and the terms and conditions may be such as to involve alterations or additions to the sports ground.

If the local authority believes that the ground or parts of the ground are a serious risk to spectator safety, then they are empowered under section 10 to prohibit or restrict admission and direct the holder of the licence as to the steps that must be taken before the order will be lifted. The local authority's licensing duties in relation to designated football matches are now overseen by the Football Licensing Authority.

While the legal provisions put in place a structure for the certification of sports grounds, they are couched in general terms and do not specify minimum safety measures. Reference therefore must be made to the *Guide to safety at sports grounds*, known as the *Green guide*. The *Green guide* is not a statutory provision but it forms the basis of local authority enforcement of a safety standard and could be adopted by the courts as the benchmark for safety standards. The *Green guide* specifies such details as the capacity of stands, evacuation procedures and fire safety, as well as general conditions and maintenance. Politicians have long identified alcohol as a major cause of football hooliganism. The main provisions are now contained in the Sporting Events (Control of Alcohol etc.) Act 1985. It is not, however, an offence to drink alcohol before entering the ground nor to drink at the club's bars.

Reflection 14.2

'Lib Dems to debate safe standing', by Matt Slater (12 September 2008)

The Liberal Democrats are set to back a fan-led campaign to return standing areas to all British football stadia. A motion on the controversial subject will be debated at the Lib Dems' autumn conference in Bournemouth on Sunday. Stadia in England's top two tiers have had to be all-seater since the Taylor Report into the Hillsborough disaster.

'If fans want to stand, and clubs want to let them, we should at least explore safe ways of achieving it,' said Lib Dem sports spokesman Don Foster. 'This is a sensitive issue but we cannot ignore the large numbers of fans who want to stand and are doing so in seating areas, despite the existing regulations and the danger it causes . . . Given the seeming impossibility of policing existing regulations, and recognising that some passionate fans want to be able to jump up and down, then we need to look at technologies that allow them to do that safely.

'Football has taken enormous steps in recent years with more diverse crowds, improved stadium designs and better policing. These proposals would in no way seek to undermine that progress.'

The Football Supporters' Federation (FSF) and Stand Up Sit Down have led the campaign to re-open the case for standing sections. They point to German stadia as an example of how this can be done without jeopardising safety and they have drawn attention to the fact fans are allowed to stand at football matches outside the top two divisions, rugby matches and even music events at football stadia. Concerns over ticket prices, an ageing crowd demographic, falling attendances at some grounds and a perceived lack of atmosphere at many venues have also contributed to the growing calls for a return to standing.

But the campaigners' efforts have been ignored so far by the government and the football authorities, particularly the Football Licensing Authority, the body created to implement the Taylor Report's post-Hillsborough recommendations.

Ninety-six supporters died on 15 April 1989 when the Leppings Lane end at Sheffield Wednesday's ground became over-crowded at the start of an FA Cup semi-final between Liverpool and Nottingham Forest. The official inquiry, conducted by Lord Taylor, blamed poor policing and inadequate facilities for the tragedy but the main recommendation was for the introduction of all-seater stadia and the removal of perimeter fencing.

British football, embarrassed by years of hooliganism and tired of second-rate facilities, did not need a second invitation and the era of packed terraces

Reflection 14.2 continued

was quickly consigned to the past. The authorities have regarded any attempt to reintroduce standing as a 'retrograde step'.

But Malcolm Clarke, the chair of the FSF, said: 'When nine out of 10 fans want the option to stand, it's something that should be provided. Standing still occurs in the lower divisions and the government acknowledges it is not inherently unsafe.

'We congratulate the Liberal Democrats' decision to debate safe standing and would encourage all political parties to follow suit . . .

'Safe standing isn't just about those who wish to stand, it's about those who want to sit and view the match in comfort too. Many have their enjoyment spoiled by those who wish to stand.'

Source: **http://news.bbc.co.uk/go/pr/fr/-/sport1/hi/football/7613442.stm**

Sports rights

Sporting bodies such as NGBs, leagues and clubs own many tangible and intangible types of property that have commercial value. The law has been used to both protect and maximise the value of these assets. Tangible property is protected through contracts laying down ownership of these rights. Those types of property that are intangible are known as intellectual property (IP), which Cornish (2003, p3) has described as: 'the application of ideas and information that are of commercial value'. IP is a product of the mind – the intellect – and has economic value in that, like any other kind of property, it may be bought, sold, licensed, assigned or otherwise exploited. IP Law protects IP rights (IPRs) – in sport the most important are trademarks. IP can also be legally protected by the general law, that is, in England, the system of the 'Common Law' (e.g. the Law of 'Passing Off'), and by special laws or 'statutes' (e.g. the Trade Marks Act 1994). Sports clubs have gained protection for the commercial exploitation of things like sports club logos and information such as databases of fixture lists. Additionally, although there are not specific legally protected image rights under English law, individual sports athletes have used a number of legal remedies to gain protection.

Trademarks

The definition of a trademark is:

> . . . any sign capable of being represented graphically which is capable of distinguishing goods or services of one undertaking from those of other undertakings. A trade mark may, in particular, consist of words (including personal names), designs, letters, numerals or the shape of goods or their packaging' (Trade Marks Act 1994 (TMA), s 1(1)).

This definition is not exhaustive and so trademarks may also be granted in respect of distinctive colours and/or colour combinations, sounds and smells. Even though the

mark may be distinctive, it may be refused registration at the Trade Marks Registry on a number of grounds. For example, if the mark is: misleading; descriptive; geographical; immoral; against 'public policy'; and is a specially protected emblem (e.g. royal insignia). Trademarks, in general, are territorial in nature in the sense that they are granted for a specific geographical territory, for example, for the UK. If not registered outside that territory, generally speaking, they cannot be legally protected from infringers in that other territory. Provided the basic requirement of distinctiveness is satisfied, it is possible, in principle, to register sporting slogans and mottoes as trademarks. For example, Eric Cantona, the ex-footballer, successfully registered the slogan 'Ooh aah Cantona' as a trademark. It is possible to register a 'personal name' as a trademark. Thus, Paul Gascoigne has registered 'Gazza'. Essentially, a trademark is a badge of origin.
Registering sports club names can be controversial. Tottenham Hotspur Football Club applied to the Trade Marks Office to register the name 'TOTTENHAM' (also a suburb of north London) as a trademark in respect of a variety of goods and services it wished to commercialise as part of a Club Merchandising Programme. Their application was opposed by a couple of match day traders, who sold football memorabilia outside Premier League grounds in London, including, since 1969, merchandising branded 'TOTTENHAM' on stalls near, but not outside, the club's ground. The objections were dismissed and the decision has led to other clubs successfully trademarking their geographical name. (Trade Mark Opposition Decision 0/150/02 on Application 2130740 by Tottenham Hotspur to register 'TOTTENHAM').

Tort of 'passing off'

In the UK, apart from trademark and copyright protection, sports clubs and athletes have to rely on the Common Law doctrine of 'passing off', which does not always provide them with the required relief. Essentially 'passing off' is a tort-based remedy where the claimant sues for compensation alleging that the defendant is infringing the 'goodwill' in the owners' proprietorial interest by passing it off as his own. The Law of Torts enables individuals who have suffered loss due to the actions of another to sue for compensation in the form of financial damages or injunctions, where the Court orders some activity to be stopped.

The tort of 'passing off' is thus designed to protect the 'goodwill', defined as 'the attractive force that brings in custom', that the claimant has built up in his field of business, and the resulting reputation that he enjoys in the market place. The law regards goodwill as an incorporeal piece of property, the integrity of which the owner is entitled to protect (*Bulmer Ltd v Bollinger SA* [1978] RPC 79).

A sporting case focused on this issue involving the unauthorised marketing of football merchandise. Arsenal Football Club as the claimant brought successful actions in passing off and registered trademark infringement under sections 10(1) and 10(2)(b) Trade Marks Act 1994 against the defendant, Matthew Reed, an Arsenal fan, who sold unauthorised merchandise from a stall for 31 years outside the team's ground, which displayed a prominent disclaimer to the effect that his merchandise was not endorsed by Arsenal (see *Arsenal Football Club PLC v. Matthew Reed* [2001] All ER (D) 67). Arsenal FC has been known by its nickname, 'the Gunners'. It had for a long time been associated with two graphics or logos; the first consisted of a shield and was referred to as the 'Crest Device', the other, referred to as the 'Cannon Device', depicted an artillery piece ('the Arsenal signs'). Reed was passing off and infringing the goodwill built up by Arsenal in these logos (for more on the case see Gardiner et al., 2006).

Learning activity 14.2

In this case Arsenal were able to enforce their rights and goodwill against the unofficial trader. However, these traders outside football grounds provide cheap and reasonable quality goods. Consider this case in more detail by researching online and using sources listed at end of chapter, and provide an argument supporting the legality of Reed's activities. Also investigate the past finding that manufacturers of sports clothing including replica shirts have been found to be operating illegal cartels with retailers, which might suggest that these 'unofficial' sellers provided a service that is in the interests of consumers.

Sponsorship and ambush marketing

When sports events such as the Olympic Games and the Football World Cup are held, the organisers enter contracts with official sponsors. Sponsorship is a commercial arrangement whereby a sponsor pays a certain sum of money (the sponsorship fee) and/or provides certain products, services or other facilities (value in kind) to the sponsored party, in return for which the sponsor is granted certain rights of association with the sponsored party, through which the sponsor can promote the image of the sponsor and sale of the sponsor's products and/or services. The sponsor aims to take advantage of the goodwill associated with the particular sporting property that is being sponsored. It has become an increasingly important method of raising finance for sport, e.g. the recent agreement made in April 2006 between Manchester United with insurer American International Group (AIG) is worth £56.5 million over four years, replacing the last deal with Vodafone worth £9 million a year (see also Chapter 13).

Ambush marketing – also known as 'parasite marketing' – occurs when a party claims an association with a sports event which it does not have and, perhaps more importantly, for which it has not paid a penny. This kind of marketing occurs at all the major sports events, not least the Olympics, and involves major corporations. With the failure of English law to recognise a legal proprietary right in a sports event, event organisers need to use a collection of legal remedies:

- IP rights to protect unauthorised use of logos, footage, etc. of the event;
- laws relating to unfair competition and passing off described above;
- statutory criminal offences concerning false trade descriptions under the Trade Descriptions Act 1968;
- physical control over the location of event and surrounding area – a brand protection programme is an essential element (see Naidoo, 2001).

In the lead-up to London 2012, the London Olympic Games and Paralympic Games Act 2006, has specific provisions concerning this, notably unauthorised advertising. Essentially sports event organisers need to ensure that they uphold the commercial integrity of the event in question.

Reflection 14.3

'London 2012 on "ambush" alert', by Bill Wilson (25 April 2008)

Love them or loathe them, you can't ignore them, and ambush marketing campaigns are bound to be as big a part of the 2012 Olympics in London as they are around any other major sporting event. And the man tasked with the responsibility of keeping the multi-billion pound sponsors of the event happy candidly admits that the event will be hit by ambush marketing. Ambush marketing is when a firm tries to create unauthorised association between their name or brand and a major sporting event, detracting from the rights of official sponsors of the event.

Recent classic ambush campaigns have included branded orange Lederhosen given to Dutch fans by brewer Bavaria to wear at the 2006 World Cup – official beer sponsors Budweiser were not amused. Other firms that have successfully ambushed big events in recent times include Nike, Puma, Benetton, and American Express.

'Ambush marketing is a form of sports marketing, it is on the extreme unauthorised side of the line,' says Dalton Odendaal, senior manager of sponsorship for London 2012. 'It becomes a problem when [a company] tries to create an unauthorised association between its name, its brand, and the Olympics.

'It is trying to obtain an ill-gotten association – riding on the back of the event without paying for it.

'We take it very seriously. We have an obligation to our sponsors to tackle ambush marketing.'

'Crude attempts'

So seriously in fact that there are currently three people working full-time as the 2012 brand protection team, and that team will be 'ramped up' over the coming four years. Traditionalists may not like it, but the Olympics is a business and it and its sponsorship partners – who have paid handsomely for the privilege of association with the games – need to be protected, like any other business. Whether ambush marketers are seen as parasites or creative pranksters, there is no doubt attempts will be made to hijack the official 2012 marketing efforts. 'I don't think we will stop it, or at least I acknowledge very creative things will be done,' Mr Odendaal told the BBC.

But why is London so concerned about ambush marketing at this early stage? 'If you cannot guarantee exclusivity to your sponsors in their product category then the price will be driven down,' says Mr Odendaal.

Source: **http://news.bbc.co.uk/go/pr/fr/-/1/hi/business/7364391.stm**

Image rights

Until fairly recently, UK law has not provided a positive right of privacy. This right has developed since the coming into law of the Human Rights Act 1998 (the HRA) which incorporated the European Convention of Human Rights into UK law. The HRA provides some protection for the image rights of sports and entertainment stars from unauthorised commercial exploitation by others (see *Campbell v MGN Ltd* [2004] 2 WLR). However, in the UK, there is no specific law protecting personality rights as such in comparison to the position in a number of other European countries (see Blackshaw, 2004). A personality can only take legal action 'if the reproduction or use of [his/her] likeness results in the infringement of some recognised legal right which he/she does own'. Famous persons, therefore, have to rely on a 'rag bag' of laws, such as those discussed above of trademark law and the Common Law doctrine of 'passing off'.

In *Irvine v Talksport* [2002] 1 WLR 2355. Eddie Irvine, the Formula One racing driver won a case for 'passing off' against the radio station, Talksport, formerly Talk Radio. In 1999, the station's marketing company had sent promotional material to a number of people who were likely to be responsible for the placement of advertisements. The material had included a brochure, which had featured Irvine holding a radio with the words 'Talk Radio'. This was a doctored picture – in the original, Irvine had been holding a mobile telephone.

The main significance of the original High Court case was that the judge held that an action for passing off could be based on false product endorsement, which this advertisement was. It did not matter that this was outside a 'common field of activity', i.e. selling advertising rather than specifically connected to Formula One racing. Irvine had a substantial reputation or goodwill and Talksport had created a false message. However at the High Court Irvine's loss to his reputation was estimated to amount to only £2,000. On appeal, Irvine argued he would not have signed an endorsement deal with Talksport for less than £25,000. The evidence as to the endorsement deals, which Irvine in fact signed during 1999, was a factor to be taken into account. He had his damages increased to £25,000 from £2,000 by the Court of Appeal, a figure that reflected the commercial rate charged had the endorsement been lawfully obtained (see Scanlan, 2003).

Reflection 14.4

An additional quasi-legal remedy is illustrated by the complaint of *Bedford against The Number Ltd (OfCom, February 2004)*. David Bedford, a former 10,000 metres world record holder, won a ruling against a phone directory company. The Number, with its 118118 service over their adverts featuring two runners in 1970s running gear. Communications regulator Ofcom said The Number had caricatured Bedford's image – drooping moustache, shoulder-length hair and running kit – without his permission. Caricature without permission constitutes a breach of Rule 6.5 of the Advertising Standards Code. The Number conceded that it had not sought or obtained Bedford's permission to be caricatured. This process may develop as an attractive remedy in similar cases. However, Ofcom ruled that it would be disproportionate to direct that the advertisements not be shown in future, and that the publication of the finding of breach is a sufficient resolution of the matter (*Appeal by The Number regarding Complaint by David Bedford*, 27 January 2004, see decision at **http://www.ofcom.org.uk/tv/obb/adv_comp/content_board/**

Television and sport

The UK TV market for sport is divided between the five terrestrial TV channels (the two publicly funded channels of the BBC and commercially funded channels, ITV, Channel Four and Channel Five) and the subscription channels, most notably those of BSkyB. There are currently three 'platforms' for accessing digital TV: the satellite system operated by BSkyB, cable company NTL Telewest and Freeserve, which is available via external TV aerials. A number of general sports channels, e.g. Sky Sports and Setanta, specialist sports channels, the Racing Channel and football club channels, e.g. Manchester United TV (MUTV) are available.

The value of TV rights for sporting events has risen considerably in line with other countries since the early 1990s. The main benefactors in this have been Premier League football, cricket and Rugby League's Superleague. All live club matches for these competitions are only available on subscription TV. Both the selling of rights collectively and on an exclusive basis have been the subject of investigation by the competition authorities and a discussion of this issue can be found below.

The right to view important sports events

Under the 'Television Without Frontiers' Directive 89/552/EC, the European Commission gave Member States the ability to restrict cultural and sports events to telecasting on terrestrial free-to-air television. In the UK, the Independent Television Commission (ITC) is the body that ensures that the protected 'listed events' procedure works. Existing listed events rules, which were updated by the Broadcasting Act 1998, require that sport's 'crown jewels' must be shown either fully live on free-to-air, terrestrial television channels which at least 95 percent of viewers can receive (the BBC, ITV or C4), or in highlights form by one of those broadcasters.

The Category A list of events which must be screened live by one of those three broadcasters includes: the Olympic Games; the FIFA World Cup Finals Tournament; the FA Cup Final; the Scottish FA Cup Final (in Scotland); the Grand National; the Derby; the Wimbledon Tennis Finals; the European Football Championship Finals Tournament; the Rugby League Challenge Cup Final; and the Rugby World Cup Final.

The Category B list of events that those broadcasters must be allowed to show highlights of include: Test cricket matches played in England; non-finals play in the Wimbledon Tournament. All other matches in the Rugby World Cup tournament; Six Nations Rugby Tournament matches involving home countries; the Commonwealth Games; the World Athletics Championship; the Cricket World Cup – the final, semi-finals, and matches involving home nations' teams; the Ryder Cup; and the Open Golf Championship.

In July 2001, the House of Lords delivered a ruling in *R v Independent Television Commission ex p TVdanmark 1 Ltd* [2000] 1 WLR 1604, concerning the sale of sports TV rights. The case arose out of a dispute between the ITC and TVDanmark 1. This Danish satellite cable service, based in London, broadcast Denmark's five away World Cup qualifying games, even though they are listed events in Denmark. The ITC challenged this arrangement.

The Court of Appeal had earlier held that, although 'the object of Art. 3(a) is maximum coverage, it is not an object to be achieved at any cost'. Other factors have to be borne in mind, 'such as the need to sustain competition, and to prevent public service broadcasters becoming over dominant as well as the need to have regard to ordinary commercial realities'. Therefore, the Court of Appeal held that TVDanmark's holding the rights rather than the free-to-air broadcaster was lawful. Overruling this decision, the House of Lords held that the Article 3(a) protection for certain designated events 'was not qualified by considerations of competition, [or] market economics'. The right of the public to have access to listed events is paramount.

Where the major sports events such as the Olympic Games and FIFA World Cup are at stake, Europeans have been guaranteed free-to-air coverage. The European Broadcasting Union has provided a service in co-ordinating broadcasts of significance to the citizens of the EU.

Learning activity 14.3

Cricket Test matches involving the England team are only available on subscription TV. Provide legal and business reasons for and against the continuation of this position. Compare the restrictions placed on UK sports bodies and broadcasters compared with what happens in other countries.

Collective selling of TV rights

In the UK, a challenge was made to the 1992 contractual agreement for TV rights to live Premier League matches between BSkyB and the Premier League. A different conclusion was reached under the (now repealed) Restrictive Trade Practices Act 1976 (RTPA) when applied by the Restrictive Trade Practices Court (RTCP) (*Re FA Premier League Ltd*, Agreement Relating to the Supply of Services Facilitating the Broadcast of Premier League Football Matches, Restrictive Practices Court, 28 July 1999). The Director General of Fair Trading objected to the restrictive nature of the Premier League and the BSkyB agreement. The Premier League granted BSkyB the exclusive rights to broadcast only 60 live matches of the league. The Court found the agreement to be restrictive of competition but to be generally in the public interest.

Intervention of European Competition Commission

The European Competition Commission has had a particular problem with the selling of Premier League TV rights between the FA Premier League and BSkyB. Although the TV broadcasting rights were subject to tender and were presented in 'packages', BSkyB won the major tenders. The cosy arrangement between the FA Premier League and BSkyB has tended to create a restrictive environment for competition. In December 2002 the Commission issued a statement of objections saying that the arrangements amounted to price-fixing. These FA Premier League/BSkyB selling arrangements meant that less than 30 percent of Premier League matches were made available for live broadcast, and when this is coupled with exclusivity, it meant that only big media groups can afford a bundle of rights.

Harbord and Szymanski (2004) note that in the current UK climate there are simply too few buyers, and that if these rights are sold to multiple buyers the FA Premier

League will have to settle for a reduced income. They are critical of some of the reasoning of the Commission, i.e. splitting up exclusive rights into packages. Their argument is that the Commission is tackling the wrong kind of exclusivity in that not only must the rights not be sold exclusively to a single broadcaster, but the same rights must be licensed non-exclusively to multiple broadcasters (e.g. to each pay-TV or platform).

The Commission had the following objections to the FA Premier League/BSkyB arrangements and these are outlined briefly.

Clubs are excluded from taking independent commercial actions with regard to the exploitation of rights since it is the FA Premier League that does all the negotiating concerning contracts pertaining to the exploitation of media rights (that is, collective selling).

The arrangements restrict competition in the upstream markets for the acquisition of media rights of football. These markets are closely linked with downstream markets which ultimately provide the services to consumers – and this affects downstream markets, for example, those TV companies that do not have access to sports broadcasting are affected commercially by reduced advertising.

The sale of large packages of media rights by the FA Premier League created barriers of entry to smaller competitors, restricted output, limited the development of products and markets which led to foreclosure in the downstream markets. The restrictions led to further media concentration and hampered competition between media operators.

The FA Premier League presented an outline of a new commercial policy, including rights segmentation for the exploitation of all media rights of the FA Premier League, including radio, television, Internet and physical media rights such as DVD, VHS, CD-ROM, etc. In late 2005, The Premiership and the European Commission finally settled their long battle over the sale of television rights, which at one time threatened the top league with a hefty anti-trust fine. For the season starting in August 2007, the Premier League sold its live television rights in six 'balanced' packages containing 23 similarly attractive matches, with no bidder allowed to win more than five packages. BSkyB won four of the packages, Setanta two. The TV rights auction generated £1.7bn ($3.1bn) for the Premier League, with BSkyB paying £1.3bn and Setanta £392m.

Review

The issues that this chapter has focused on provide an insight into how the law has engaged with the sports business industry. An attempt has been made to present this engagement as not only the application of existing law to sport, and the creation of some sport-specific statutory law and case law, but also on a more general level, to show that the law has become an important part of the general regulatory framework of sport.

After many years of sport being seen as essentially beyond the reach of the law, those who run sport now understand the importance of legal compliance. The role of the EU in regulation of the sports business industry has probably been more influential than national law in many ways, as far as changing the practices found within the industry goes. One positive impact that has emerged is that if sport wants to minimise the impact of national and European law and exercise a form of self-regulation, or what has been termed 'supervised autonomy' (Foster, 2003), sport needs to exhibit positive values of self-governance. The characteristics that have emerged generally in business over the last 20 years or so, including greater transparency, accountability, social responsibility, etc., must be developed by sports bodies (see Gardiner et al., 2006, ch. 4). Sport business may have important distinctions from general business, e.g. rather than shareholders it is better to think of stakeholders in sport (administrators, sponsors, TV companies, sports athletes and fans, etc.), but the principle is the same in terms of business organisations acting in an ethical manner and with integrity.

Review of learning outcomes

Having worked through this chapter, you should now take some time to carefully answer the following:

- What impact has the EU had upon professional sport?
- What changes have had to be made in football as a consequence of the *Bosman* ruling?
- How can sports bodies use trademarks to protect their intellectual property rights?
- What areas of law can be used by sports athletes to protect the commercial value of their image rights?
- What are the arguments in support of the restriction of ambush marketing as planned in the lead-up to London 2012?
- Discuss the business and legal issues related to making the selling of TV rights to sporting competitions such as the Premier League more competitive.

Further reading

Gardiner, S et al. (2006) *Sports law* 3rd edition. London: Cavendish.

Relevant UK journals

Entertainment and Sports Law Journal
International Sports Law Review
Sport and the Law Journal – **www.britishsportslaw.org**
Sports Law Administration and Practice
World Sports Law Reports

Chapter 15

Sustainability for sports management

Peter Robinson

This chapter considers what is understood by the term 'sustainability', and the concept of sustainable development as it applies to the sports industry. It will offer perspectives on sustainability as a concept and the role it fulfils within the notion of corporate social responsibility (CSR). The chapter will illustrate this through case studies and offers opportunities for reflection and application of the ideas being discussed.

Learning outcomes

This chapter is designed to enable you to:

- provide an evaluation of the concepts of sustainability and sustainable development;
- explain the positive and negative impacts of sport on the community, economy and environment;
- discuss the implementation of sustainability in the sports industry through case studies.

An introduction to sustainability

Sustainability describes a philosophy which considers the long-term needs of the business within and alongside its environment. It originates from environmental concerns, which first emerged in the 1980s, which placed an increasing awareness of the human impact on the landscape through poorly managed development and land-use policies. The 1987 Report from the Brundtland Commission defines sustainability as 'meeting the needs of the present without compromising the ability of future generations to meet their own needs' (World Commission on Environment and Development, 1987, p3). It raised environmental protection as a global issue and led to the United Nations Conference on Environment and Development at Rio de Janeiro in 1992.

This conference created Agenda 21, an international agreement that a serious effort would be made to improve sustainability. This was designed to be adopted at a local level, on the basis that local action would lead to global improvement, in other words, 'Think globally, act locally'.

Agenda 21 has been adopted, in principle at least, by many government bodies at local, regional and national level where it is delivered as Local Agenda 21 (LA21). A second summit in 2002, Rio +10, reviewed the first 10 years of LA21 and looked at future policies. It also discussed the fact that, although there is widespread support for LA21, its implementation is not always so easy. Many reasons have been cited for this; primarily the fact that local government does not receive sufficient funding, information, expertise or support from national governments.

The concept of sustainability is illustrated in Figure 15.1, which illustrates that sustainability is achieved only when the environmental, economic and societal factors are equitably managed. Any variance from this balanced focus may, for example, benefit the environment, but this could be to the detriment of businesses success, which may impact upon employment and community facilities.

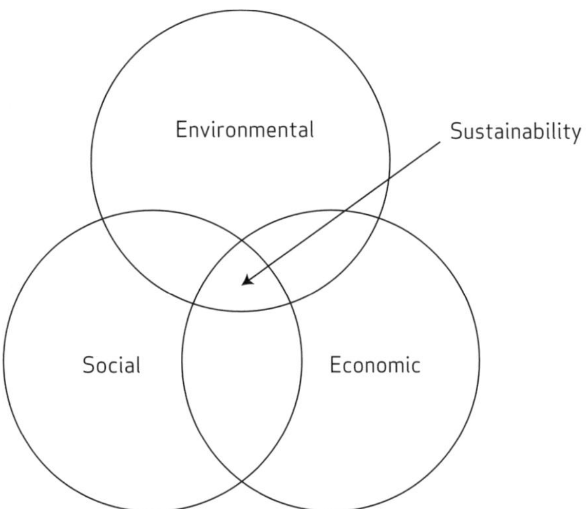

Figure 15.1: Sustainability

Learning activity 15.1

Using your place of work or study as an example discuss your own experiences of what sustainability means.

What this means for the sports industry very much depends on the structure of the organisation (see Chapter 2). This list demonstrates the key differences.

- *Voluntary sector*. Often small scale, the voluntary sector has mainly positive impacts through participation, community involvement and opportunities for skills development. It is up to individual organisations to consider how they manage sustainability.
- *Public sector*. Organisations in the public sector (e.g. local authority leisure centres and parks) will adopt the approaches and initiatives taken by their managing local authority, governed, in principle at least, by LA21, together with any other projects, initiatives or benchmarking schemes the local authority is involved in, such as waste reduction or investment in renewable energies.

- *Private sector*. There will be a range of motivations that will influence the degree to which sustainability is implemented in the private sector, and some businesses will be considerably more proactive than others. In the private sector this is most commonly referred to as corporate social responsibility (CSR), the notion that a business has a moral duty to its customers and the wider community.
- *Public–private sector partnerships*. The Service Level Agreements (SLA) that exist will define responsibilities of both contractor and contractee in this relationship, although it is likely both will have some responsibility for environmental performance, through LA 21 and CSR policies.

Understanding impacts

Any activity has an impact on the environment, society and the economy. These may be positive or negative impacts and the level of the impacts will depend very much upon the scale of the activity taking place. Impacts can also be categorised as illustrated here:

- *Direct impacts*. Building a sports stadium has a direct impact on the site where it is built, which may be positive if it is developed on brown field (disused industrial) land, but negative if built on green field (virgin soils) sites.
- *Indirect impacts*. Use of the sports centre may have an impact on local communities in terms of increasing participation.
- *Induced impacts*. The new sports centre will attract new businesses to the area, such as hotels or sports retailers. This is an indirect impact.

Figure 15.2 provides an example of the types of impacts that can occur as a result of a sports event.

Learning activity 15.2

Can you identify which of the impacts in Figure 15.2 are direct, indirect and induced?

A further example of the negative impacts of sports event on communities is given in case study 15.1, which addresses the need for development of sports facilities, but at what cost?

Figure 15.2: Impacts of a sports event

Facilities

Positive
- Benefit local community after the event
- Development may include improved transport and infrastructure
- Creates employment opportunities

Negative
- Impacts of building and development

Spectators

Positive
- Brings money into the local economy
- Raises the profile of the area

Negative
- Pollution (litter, noise)
- Overcrowding and congestion
- Behavioural problems (hooliganism, drinking alcohol)

Sports event

Community

Positive
- Health benefits of participation
- May increase wealth for property owners and investors

Negative
- May enhance the image of the area, pushing up house prices and creating local inflation
- Behaviour of sports fans may be a problem, as may associated activities such as drinking

Legacy

Positive
- Encourages inward investment
- Encourages longer-term tourism interest after the event
- New business development encourages entrepreneurship and employment

Negative
- Employment may be seasonal
- Significant effect on local economies may force locals to migrate

CASE STUDY 15.1

Community displacement

Inevitably, major sporting events have an impact on communities when development is required for new facilities. The motivation for holding such events is usually linked to the long-term economic benefits to the host community, but there is a history of development sites being chosen which are in poorer parts of the host cities. Recent examples include the eviction of 720,000 people in Seoul to make way for the 1988 Olympic Games. In Barcelona, housing became so unaffordable as a result of the Olympic Games that low income earners were forced to leave the city. In Atlanta 9,000 arrest citations were issued to homeless people (mostly African-Americans) as part of an Olympics-inspired campaign to 'clean the streets' and approximately 30,000 people were displaced. It is estimated that over 1.5 million people have been displaced by the Beijing Olympics and there are already similar impacts being felt, albeit on a smaller scale, in the build-up to London 2012. This is not just an Olympics issue either, with similar impacts being seen as a result of the Commonwealth Games and other major sports developments.

Source: (COHRE, 2007)

The scale of an impact depends upon other factors, such as the location of the activity (rural or urban), the type of activity and the sector of the industry. One example of this is sports tourism. This is twofold in nature, so it would be wrong to argue that all sports tourism needs to be controlled in the same way. For example, it could refer to people travelling to spectate at events at established venues, where the issues may be similar to those addressed in the previous illustration on the impacts of sports events. But it may also refer to people travelling to participate in sports such as rock climbing, scuba diving and skiing. In these three examples the impacts on the natural environment may be much more noticeable. The systems needed to minimise the negative impacts on the environment are different to those which minimise the effects on communities.

Both positive and negative factors should be considered at an early stage of development, so a new sports venue would be subject to planning controls and legislation, but this is not the case where a venue or site has become popular over a period of time, such as rock climbing at a Site of Special Scientific Interest (an SSSI).

In any case, an assessment of the impact is necessary, and this may be done retrospectively or may form part of a development plan. This can be achieved through a cost-benefit analysis. In its simplest form, this is a list of pros and cons. However, such an analysis provides little empirical data, nor does it necessarily demonstrate the scale or value of the impacts, or assess ways in which risks can be managed. Economic and Environmental Impact Assessments give a much fuller picture, assigning value to facilities and suggesting methods to minimise negative and maximise positive impacts.

The following section discusses these impacts in more detail under the headings identified earlier.

Economic factors

The contribution that sport makes to the economy at a local, regional or national level can be very significant. The Olympics, for example, has generated millions of pounds for some host countries, but others have been left with a large deficit of investment.

To ensure that the positive impacts are maximised in economic terms, it is crucial that development is focused on the Multiplier Effect. This ensures that the money generated by the business stays in the local economy rather than leaking out of it (leakage). This can be achieved through the following methods:

- using local food;
- using local suppliers;
- employing staff from the local area.

These simple approaches to management ensure that local businesses are more profitable, food and products are better quality and sustainably sourced because there is a reduction in food miles, and many of the businesses will also employ local people. This improves local employment, so more people are able to own or rent houses locally and higher tax income is generated for the local authority, which results in greater public sector investment in services and quality of life. Such an aim may require businesses to look at their supply chains and consider how to change organisation procurement policies, but the positive public image for the business is good justification.

It is essential for managers that economic factors can be monitored and measured. This can be achieved by using economic indicators which are subdivided into two categories. Many of the sustainability indicators are closely linked to the benefits of the multiplier effect.

- Conventional measures: income, employment statistics, property ownership, inflation
- Sustainability indicators: equate these figures to quality of life and measure detail such as hours of paid employment against the cost of living, the cultural diversity of the local employment opportunities, and the reliability and stability of the local jobs market.

Societal factors

The sociocultural impacts of sports vary depending on the location, the state of the local economy, the political system and environment. Broadly speaking the negative impacts arise through the conflicts that are created between:

- host (local) and visiting communities;
- participants and non-participants;
- rival supporters groups.

These can be measured through social inventories and sociocultural indices which detail information about crime, anti-social behaviour and health. The latter is often also associated with the positive impacts of sports, which include:

- health benefits of participation;
- social cohesion created through participation or supporters groups;
- facilities which benefit local communities.

Societal impacts also include ethical and moral issues, so further tools to encourage sustainability include participation in Fair Trade produce and projects which offer training opportunities to disadvantaged communities.

Communities need to feel empowered about activities taking place in their neighbourhoods. This may be demonstrated through consultation, but this has to bring about benefits and positive actions, and not just be a 'box-ticking' exercise on the way to development. Common examples of sports related developments that arise through consultation include sports parks, improved playing field facilities and national incentives for health, such as the planned UK-wide provision of free swimming for all children by 2012.

The planning process also now allows local authorities to insist that developers put something back into communities. This is referred to as Section 106 (Planning Legislation requirement) and requires developers to assess community needs. It forces developers (such as house builders) to fund transport initiatives, sports and leisure facilities and open spaces, sometimes within their developments, sometimes in locations which will benefit the wider community.

Environmental factors

These are the most commonly understood impacts of any activity and standard themes include waste management and damage to the physical natural environment. There is an altruistic goal of preventing any damage to the environment, but this would be an impossibility. For every sustainable initiative there is an impact somewhere. A sports facility may invest in electric vehicles which would reduce fuel expenditure and pollution, but the electricity needed to charge batteries has to be produced and the vehicles have to be built in a factory. There are also cost barriers to many developments. Using solar power in a leisure centre, for example, would be prohibitively expensive, but using it to heat the water in the pool may be a realistic option.

Some methods available to enhance environmental performance include:

- provision of recycling facilities for all wastes (organic waste, tins, plastics);
- businesses must comply with Waste Electrical and Electronic Equipment Regulations for recycling end-of-life equipment (computers, fitness machines);
- investing in and using renewable energies for specific functions;
- using biodegradable and environmentally friendly cleaning products;
- minimising water wastage by staff and customers (fitting different shower heads and push taps in changing rooms);
- use of energy saving light bulbs.

Many of the changes that need to be made to improve environmental performance are small and incremental, but over time they start to make a difference. This is an example of the ethos of the concept of acting locally while thinking globally.

Learning activity 15.3

Using your local leisure centre as an example, provide recommendations which could be implemented to improve environmental performance.

Sustainable development

Bramwell et al. (1996) identify three key aspects of sustainable tourism management, which can be equally well applied within a sports context. These include the fact that the concerns of sustainable development are not purely environmental but are also economic, social, cultural and political; that sustainable development is not opposed to growth but accepts there are limits to that growth; and therefore that sustainable development recognises that longer-term thinking is necessary. Long (2000) also discusses the issues around sustainable development and identifies some key themes, which have been adapted here:

- residents, participants, users and visitors all have differing needs which will dictate their activities and spending;
- it is crucial to reconcile the needs of all of these groups to minimise conflicts of use and to ensure there are benefits for all the stakeholders;
- this can be achieved through the identification of new uses for facilities;
- social and spatial equality need to be reinforced;
- there has to be an acceptance that at times the capacity of the infrastructure will be exceeded, for example, roads and transport hubs;
- it is important that there are clear links between sport and other economic activities taking place;
- the supply-chain involved may be very long and complex.

Sustainable development, therefore, relies on a range of specific tools and measures to monitor and manage the impacts or potential impacts of sports. These are discussed below.

- The *Local Plan* is written by the local authority to outline acceptable planning and development for a given area. It will outline the types of business and scale and scope of development that is permissible without having a negative impact. It provides a guide to suitable design, the needs of the local population and plans for local investment and future housing needs.
- *Planning permission* is governed by the Local Plan and is designed to control development and to ensure that there is a need and justification for a facility which must not have significant negative impacts on its neighbours and community. The Local Plan usually outlines this for a given area, although sports developments are usually very complex and may not be considered within the Local Plan when it is developed, so it would need to be considered by a Planning Committee.
- *Carrying capacity* describes the maximum acceptable level of use of facilities without any negative impacts on the environment. This does not just mean the number of people who can park at and be seated in a stadium, it also refers to the numbers it is safe to have in a swimming pool, or the point at which the level of use cannot be sustained. This is easily delivered when designing a sports venue, because it will be integral to the planning process and consideration will be given to transport arrangements, sufficient parking, maximum number of spectators and suitable access and egress in emergencies. There has however been some criticism of this approach. The level is often determined by the characteristics of the resource, but managers are making these decisions from a subjective perspective, influenced by their underlying values, profit/capacity focus, quantitative data and forecasts. Carrying capacity can be physical, environmental, economic, or social, as discussed earlier in the chapter.
- *Limits of acceptable change* are defined by the carrying capacity of a site, and describe the acceptable change to an environment within certain boundaries, dictated by what it is feasible to maintain and restore, and the point at which damage would be irreparable. Businesses have a degree of flexibility and this is usually supported by the development of systems to monitor and manage impacts

over a longer period of time, allowing increased use with enhanced management systems and recognition of the threats to the environment.

- *Zoning* describes the way that space is designated for different uses. In an urban context this means identifying areas and assigning functions to them. It is a way of managing, for example, the behaviour of football fans attending a football match by providing parking for 'away' supporters with free transport to minimise conflicts arising as supporters make their way to the stadium. In natural environments, for outdoor activities such as climbing, it allows designation of areas that climbers can use, and prevents use of other areas by removing access through footpath diversions and parking restrictions.
- *Codes of Conduct* are written to give guidance about acceptable and unacceptable behaviours; they are limited by the fact that many codes are voluntary and fail to have systems for enforcement, but for the acquiescent user they are usually a good tool for education and guidance, and are commonly used in rural areas and municipal facilities, although in the latter they are more enforceable (for example, swimming pool rules).

Learning activity 15.4

Choose an outdoor activity centre and develop a code of conduct for users of the facility.

CASE STUDY 15.2

London 2012 – placing sustainability at the heart of sports development

The Olympic Delivery Authority (ODA) for London 2012 is keen to place sustainability at the heart of the Olympic Games, and states that:

> . . . we want London 2012 to be the first 'sustainable' Games, setting new standards for major events. This is encapsulated by the concept 'towards a one planet 2012', which creates a powerful identity for London 2012's sustainability programme and provides a framework for achieving sustainable Games in accordance with the London 2012 candidature commitments and with respect to Olympic ideals. (London 2012, 2008)

This plan is based upon a focus on five key areas. These include waste reduction, enhanced biodiversity, social inclusion, healthy living and a plan to combat climate change. The ODA has set specific targets to measure progress and achievement, including 90 percent reuse of demolition materials in parks, venues, reuse of whole buildings, and relocation of wildlife and creation of new habitats.

To support this programme and ensure that all stakeholders involved in the development of the park share this aim, the ODA is managing the design and build

CASE STUDY 15.2 continued

through the use of BREEAM (Building Research Establishment Environmental Assessment Methodology), and construction industry standards including Building for Life, CEEQUAL (Civil Engineering Environmental Quality Assessment and Award Scheme that requires contractors to report against sustainability indicators) and the Considerate Constructors Scheme.

The overall purpose of this approach is to create a legacy which raises the sporting profile of the UK, improves an area of east London, and encourages communities, and young people in particular, to participate in the Olympics, to promote the UK as a tourism and business destination and to create a model of sustainable living.

Engaging business in sustainability

Most businesses, to a greater or lesser extent, can understand how or why they should take some steps towards more sustainable practices, but the final decision rests with managers who are ultimately responsible for policies and have to balance environmental awareness against the needs of the business. In some cases there are incentives, such as government funding, to support the use of environmental technologies, and in the public sector organisations are led by the local authorities' views of best practice. Ultimately, as Miller (2001) suggests, businesses are more likely to adopt sustainability to avoid a negative image among consumers and other businesses than for any direct benefits for the business.

Improving sustainability does appear, at first glance at least, to be cost-heavy, requiring businesses to invest in new technology and new ways of working. However, it is possible that there can be significant long-term benefits and not just cost savings but enhanced profitability. Some of these investments are self-explanatory, for example solar panels are expensive to fit but reduce energy costs, although there is still debate about the real cost savings over the life of solar panels or other environmental technologies. Some recycling schemes offer a payback to the business, so a small amount of money can be made by providing recycling facilities. However, the key to success lies in three areas.

- First, the fact that, although the solar panels may not represent a great saving in cost, over a realistic period of time, they do represent a saving compared to the life and depreciation of other equipment, such as boilers.
- Second, the positive publicity and appeal to a more eco-conscious market place will result in larger user numbers.
- Third, small incremental changes can be a good starting point: developing a waste-reduction or recycling policy, providing recycling facilities for staff and customers, and fitting lights with energy-efficient bulbs.

In summary, the benefits to business in adopting environmental best practice are usually based upon community relationships, financial or competitive advantage, and the need to comply with legislation. For outdoor activities it is also important to preserve the very resources on which those sports rely.

Best practice systems and benchmarking can also support the implementation of sustainable practices through ISO 4001 (International Standards Organisation) and the EU EMAS scheme (Eco-management and audit scheme), which provide guidelines and targets for businesses to work towards.

CASE STUDY 15.3

FIA – the role of sport in promoting environmental good practice

The Fédération Internationale de l'Automobile (FIA) is, according to the European Parliament's report, 'at the forefront of innovative environmental technology changes that offer potential CO2 reduction and efficiency saving spin-offs for all new cars' (FIA, 2008). The high profile of the sport means it can actively influence attitudes and consumer behaviour towards sustainability. Formula One management tends to look two to three years ahead and aims for 2011 include:

- A reduction in engine power, but an increase in maximum energy flow rate that will improve thermal efficiency. This type of technology is likely to eventually be adopted by car manufacturers.
- Drag will be reduced as moving aerodynamic devices are allowed to be fitted to cars, therefore requiring less power to maintain speed levels and consequently reducing fuel consumption. This will also allow easier overtaking for following cars, which also reduces fuel use and should enhance the excitement of the sport.
- Energy will be recovered through braking and used to support acceleration. This type of technology is already also used on trains (where energy is returned to the National Grid), and again is an application that could be used in commercially produced vehicles.
- Bio-fuels will be used to power cars and there will be regulations regarding the amount of fuel that can be used during a race.

These measures will be supported by initiatives aimed at reducing the costs of participation and working with stakeholders such as tyre manufacturers to invest in energy improvements in all aspects of the sport, which will also benefit the environment and the everyday car-user.

Learning activity 15.5

Discuss the importance of sport in influencing others for the greater good.

The role of legacy in sustainability

When discussing sustainability in the context of sports it is essential to consider the impacts of sports events. Some of these are short term, which occur during an event, some are medium term and occur in the aftermath of an event, and then there are longer-term impacts, which are referred to as legacies (Masterman, 2004) and as Shone (2001, p272) identifies:

> Events leave a legacy. This may be in personal memories or in friendly social contacts made at the event, or it may be in some item handed over; anything from a park bench, bought from the modest surplus of the village fete, to a donation to an honourable cause to the grand arena built to regenerate a city.

Longer-term benefits of events include raising the awareness of destinations, and generating income through tourism, greater social and cultural cohesion and participation, environmental improvements, new and enhanced facilities, and greater economic activity. Some examples of these legacies are demonstrated in Table 15.1, which shows the potential sustainability which can arise as a result of event and sport legacies.

Table 15.1: Examples of sporting event legacies

Event	Legacy
Land regeneration	
Manchester 2002 Commonwealth games	Regeneration of Manchester Eastside
London 2012 Olympics	Regeneration of areas around Docklands in London
Cultural development	
Millennium Stadium, Cardiff	Greater opportunities for major events and opportunities for participation
'Barcelona 2000' strategy	Two organisations created to manage legacy
Athens Olympics, 2004	Pre-planned use of facilities post event
Economic development	
Los Angeles Olympics	£215m surplus
Salt Lake City Olympics 2002	$40m with expected inward investment
Social regeneration	
Manchester 2002 Commonwealth games	Regeneration of Manchester Eastside
Millennium Stadium, Cardiff	Greater opportunities for major events and opportunities for participation
Environmental development	
London 2012 Olympics	Regeneration of areas around Docklands in London
Athens Olympics, 2004	Pre-planned use of facilities post-event

Learning activity 15.6

Are the legacies of events sufficient justification to host an event under any circumstances?

Review of learning outcomes

This chapter has illustrated the key issues for sports businesses as they relate to sustainability. It is by no means a comprehensive overview of the issues, nor is it designed to be a polemic on the virtues of sustainability, rather it is an attempt at highlighting current debate and discussing the issues facing managers in the sector. The review questions below provide opportunities for reflection and the Further Reading section will point readers in the direction of more in-depth publications on the subject. As an overall summary, there is no doubt that managers must consider the environment as a core element of business. In some instances, as has been illustrated, this is crucial to protect the very resource upon which the product is built (skiing or trekking for example), while in other instances it is much more about positive PR and minimising impacts in the same way that any other business must do. Ultimately sustainability is closely linked to the concept of corporate social responsibility and the need to consider holistic sustainability as part of everything the business does. There is a growing agenda about enhancing sustainability, but the debate about responsibility and ownership of many aspects of the agenda may continue for some time. It is, similarly, essential to consider all the stakeholders involved and therefore debate how to encourage action based upon the benefits for both communities and businesses.

Review questions

1. What do you consider to be the key issues that the sports industry needs to address in seeking to be a sustainable industry?
2. Given the complex issues that exist within the topic, how do the roles and responsibilities of the public and private sectors differ in achieving sustainability in sports management?
3. Outline three of the challenges that you perceive to be the most important facing a sector of the sports industry of your choice. What solutions can you recommend?

Further reading

www.commonwealthtourism.com: An organisation that works across the Commonwealth countries to manage tourism, encompassing a number of sports related activities and research.

www.iaam.org: The website for the International Association of Assembly Managers bringing together major venues and facilities, many of which are sporting facilities and are committed to sustainability and sustainable development.

www.un.org/esa/sustdev/documents/agenda21/: A guide to Agenda21.

References

Advisory Conciliation and Arbitration Service (2006) *Recruitment and induction advisory booklet*. London: ACAS.

AGCAS (2007) *What do graduates do? 2008 career planning for higher education and beyond*. Sheffield: AGCAS in Association with the Higher Education Careers Services Unit and UCAS.

Allen, J, O'Toole, W, McDonnell, I and Harris, R (2005) *Festival and special event management*. 3rd edition. Queensland: Wiley.

Allinson, RE (1993) *Global disaster: inquiries into management ethics*. London: Prentice Hall.

Anderson, N and Shackleton, V (1993) *Successful selection interviewing*. Oxford: Blackwell.

Anon. (2008) TAG Heuer goes digital for GP. *Marketing Week*, 3 July.

Archer, W and Davison, J (2008) *Graduate employability: what do employers think and want?* London: Council for Industry and Higher Education.

Armstrong, M and Baron, A (2004) *Managing performance: performance management in action*. London: Chartered Institute of Personnel and Development.

Arnold, J, Silvester, J, Patterson, F (2005) *Work psychology: understanding human behaviour in the workplace*.4th edition. London: FT/ Prentice Hall.

Austin, S (2008) West Ham ends shirt sponsor deal. BBC News, 12 Sept. URL: **http://news.bbc.co.uk/sport1/low/football/teams/w/west_ham_utd/7611752.stm** (accessed January 2009).

Bacon, W (1995) Accreditation: key issues and questions for ILAM. Paper presented at ILAM National Education and Training Conference, Stoke, 9–10 Nov.

Badminton England (2007) *Annual report and financial statement for the year ending 31 March 2007*. Milton Keynes: Badminton Association of England Ltd.

Ball, S (2005) *The importance of entrepreneurship to hospitality, leisure, sport and tourism*. Oxford: Higher Education Academy.

Barrow, C, Brown, R and Molian, D (2005) *Enterprise development*. Surrey: Thomson Learning.

Beech, J and Chadwick, S (2004) *The business of sport management*. Harlow: Pearson Education.

Benson, J (2007) Employers see the value of vocational and work-based qualifications. SkillsActive, 3 Sept. URL: **www.skillsactive.com/resources/news/archive** (accessed December 2008).

Berry, M (2007) Hidden cost of recruitment tops £5,000 per new hire. *Personnel Today*, 19 March.

Blackshaw, I (ed) (2004) *Sports image rights in Europe*. The Hague: TMC Asser Press.

Bluff, M, Kerr, T and Demetriou, M (1999) *Sports law*. Oxford: Hart Publishing.

Bold, B (2008) Hamilton could overtake Beckham as UK's highest earning sportsman. *Brand Republic*, 3 Nov. URL: **www.brandrepublic.com** (accessed December 2008).

Bramwell, B (ed) (1996) *Sustainable tourism management: principles and practice*. 2nd edition. Tilburg: Tilburg University Press.

Bratton, J and Gold, J (2003) *Human resource management*. 2nd edition. London: Lawrence Erlbaum Associates.

Bright, JEH and Pryor, RGL (2005) The chaos theory of careers: a user's guide. *Career Development Quarterly*, 53 (June): 291–305.

Brown, TJ (1999) Adventure risk management, in Miles, JC and Priest, S (eds) *Adventure programming*. Pennsylvania: Venture Publishing.

Buzan, T (1995) *The mind map book*. London: BBC Books.

Bygrave, W and Zacharakis, A (2007) *Entrepreneurship*. New York: Wiley.

Campbell, A and Tawady, K (1990) *Mission and business philosophy: winning employee commitment*. Oxford: Heinemann.

CBI (Confederation of British Industry)/Pertemps (2006) *Employment trends survey*. London: Confederation of Business and Industry.

CCPR (Central Council for Physical Recreation) (2006) *Sports clubs: their social and economic impact*. London: CCPR.

Chancellor of the Exchequer (2002) Mansion House speech. London: HM Treasury.

Changemakers (2008) URL: **www.changemakers.net/files/Sport%20Social%20 Entrepreneurship.pdf** (accessed November 2008).

Chapman, T (2006) Accepted students and applicants 1996–2005 in Hospitality, Leisure, Sport and Tourism, based on data provided by UCAS. Oxford: Hospitality, Leisure, Sport and Tourism Network.

Chartered Institute of Personnel and Development (2005) *Training to learning*. London: CIPD.

Chartered Institute of Personnel and Development (2006) Diversity: an overview, fact sheet. London: CIPD.

Chartered Institute of Personnel and Development (2007) Selection interviewing, fact sheet. London: CIPD.

Chartered Institute of Personnel and Development (2008a) Induction, fact sheet. London: CIPD.

Chartered Institute of Personnel and Development (2008b) *Recruitment*, fact sheet. London: CIPD.

CIHE (Council for Industry and Higher Education) (2008) *Developing entrepreneurial graduates: putting entrepreneurship at the centre of higher education*. London: NESTA.

Cloutier, R (2000), *Legal liability and risk management in adventure tourism*. British Columbia: Bhudak Consultants.

Cohen, L and El-Sawab, A (2006) Careers, in Redman, T and Wilkinson, A (eds) *Contemporary human resource management: text and cases*. 2nd edition. London: FT/Prentice Hall.

COHRE (Centre on Housing Rights and Evictions) (2007) *Fair play for housing rights*. Switzerland: COHRE.

Cornish, WR (2003) *Intellectual property: patents, copyrights, trademarks and allied rights*, 4th edition. London: Sweet & Maxwell.
Cottrell, S (2003) *The study skills handbook*. London: Palgrave Macmillan.
Council of Europe (1992) European Sports Charter for Sport. URL: **www.sportdevelopment.org.uk/The_European_Sports_Charter.pdf** (accessed December 2008).
De Bono, E (1990) *Lateral thinking: a textbook of creativity*. Harmondsworth: Penguin.
DCMS (Department for Culture, Media and Sport) (2001) *The government's plan for sport*. London: DCMS.
DCMS (Department for Culture, Media and Sport) (2002a) *Game plan: a strategy for delivering the government's sport and physical activity objectives*. London: DCMS.
DCMS (Department for Culture, Media and Sport) (2002b) *The Coaching Taskforce: final report*. London: DCMS.
DCMS (Department of Culture, Media and Sport) (2007) *Department of Culture, Media and Sport annual report 2007*. London: DCMS.
DCSF (Department for Children, Schools and Families) (2008) *Physical education and sport strategy for young people*. London: HMSO.
DIUS (Department for Innovation, Universities and Skills) (2008) Investing in our future. URL **www://dius.gov.uk/role.html** (accessed February (2008).
Department of Health (2002) *Addressing the health agenda: a new focus for sports activity – health*. London: DOH.
Dobson, N, Gratton, C and Holliday, S (1997). *Football came home: the economic impact of Euro 96*. Sheffield: Leisure Industries Research Centre.
Drucker, F (1999) *Management challenges for the 21st century*. Oxford: Butterworth-Heinemann.
Enterprise Insight (2005) *The enterprise report 2005: making ideas happen*. London: Enterprise Insight.
EU (European Union) (2003) Commission ends monitoring of the FIA/Formula One compliance with 2001 settlement. Media Statement IP/03/1491, 31 October.
Experian (2005) *Labour force survey*. Skills Needs Assessment – England 2005.
Faulkner, D and Bowman, C (1995) *Essence of competitive strategy*. London: Prentice Hall.
Fédération International de l'Automobile (FIA) (2008) EU recognizes FIA environmental achievements, 17 Oct. URL: **www.fia.com/enGB/Search/Results.aspx?k=sustainableands=FIA.com** (accessed December 2008).
Fernandez, J (2008) Click to refresh. *Marketing Week*, 23 October.
Foot, M and Hook, C (2005) *Introducing human resource management*. London: Prentice Hall.
Ford, P, Blanchard, A and Blanchard, J (1992) *Leadership and administration of outdoor pursuits*. Pennsylvania: Venture.
Foster, K (2003) Is there a global sports law? 2(2) *Entertainment Law*.
Frosdick, S (1997) The techniques of risk analysis are insufficient in themselves. *Disaster Prevention and Management*, 6(3): 165–77.
Gardiner, S and Welch, R (2007) The contractual dynamics of team stability versus player mobility: who rules 'the beautiful game'? *Entertainment and Sports Law Journal*, 5(1) (www.warwick.ac.uk/fac/soc/law/elj/eslj/).
Gardiner, S et al. (2006) *Sports law*, 3rd edition. London: Cavendish.
Getz, D (1997) *Event management and event tourism*. Elmsford: Cognizant Communications.

Gibb, A (1993) In Herrmann, K, Parvin, W and O'Brien, J (2004) *Development of key performance indicators to measure the success of the National Council for Graduate Entrepreneurship*. Durham: Durham Business School.

Goldblatt, J and Schiptsova, J (2002) *Special events: twenty-first-century global event management* (the Wiley event management). New York: Wiley.

Gorman, M (2007a) Critics deride logo for 2012. *Marketing Week*, 7 June.

Gorman, M (2007b) Bigger than the sport: Hamilton could net £100m in sponsorship. *Marketing Week*, 25 October.

Grant, RM (2008) *Contemporary strategy analysis*. 6th edition. Oxford: Blackwell.

Gratton, C and Solberg, H (2007) *The economics of sports broadcasting*. Abingdon: Routledge.

Gratton, C and Taylor, P (2000) *The economics of sport and recreation*. 2nd edition. London: Taylor and Francis.

Gratton, C, Dobson, N and Shibli, S (2000) The economic importance of major sports events: a case study of six events. *Managing Leisure*, 5: 17–28.

Grayson, E (1999) *Sport and law*. 3rd edition. London: Butterworths.

Hall, CM (1997) *Hallmark tourist events – impacts, management and planning*. London: Belhaven.

Hansen, A, Minten, S and Taylor, P (1998) *Graduate recruitment and development in the sport and recreation industry: final report*. Sheffield: Department for Education and Employment/SPRITO/UK Higher Education Standing Conference on Leisure, Recreation and Sport.

Harbord, D and Szymanski, S (2004) Football trials. *European Competition Law Review*, 2: 114–19.

Harvey, L (2001) Defining and measuring employability. *Quality in Higher Education*, 7(2): 97–109.

Henry, A (2008) *Understanding strategic management*. Oxford: Oxford University Press.

Henry, I (2001) *The politics of leisure policy*. London: Macmillan.

Higher Education Statistics Agency (1996) *Data report and reference volume: first destinations of students leaving higher education institutes 1994/95*. Cheltenham: HESA.

Hillage, J and Pollard, E (1998) *Employability: developing a framework for policy analysis*, Research Brief 85. Department for Education and Employment.

Houlihan, B and White, A (2002) *The politics of sports development*. London: Routledge.

IEG Sponsorship (2005). *IEG Sponsorship report*. London: IEG.

ISBA (2006) *2020 vision the manager of the 21st Century*, report prepared by Nicholson, J and Nairn, A. Australia: Boston Consultancy Group. p2. URL: **www.ibsa.org.au/downloads/The_Manager_of_the_21st_Century.pdf** (accessed December 2008).

Jenkinson, N (2001) Report of the conference on the vocational relevance of university leisure management courses. University of Sheffield, 2 May.

Johnson, G, Scholes, K and Whittington, R (2008) *Exploring corporate strategy*. 8th edition. London: Prentice Hall.

Johnson, P (2001) Report of the conference on the vocational relevance of university leisure management courses. University of Sheffield, 2 May.

Johnston, B (2003) The shape of research in the field of higher education and graduate employment: some issues. *Studies in Higher Education*, 28(4): 413–426.

Jones, G (2008) Adidas to take on Nike+ with branded handset. *Marketing Week*, 5 March.

King, A (2008) An analysis of Norwich Union's sponsorship of UK Athletics (with specific reference to the Norwich Union World Trials, Saturday 9th and Sunday 10th February 2007). Unpublished undergraduate thesis, Sheffield Hallam University.

Klinke, A and Renn, O (2001) Precautionary principles and discursive strategies: classifying and managing risks. *Journal of Risk Research*, 4(2): 159–73.

Kotler, P and Armstrong, G (2008) *Principles of marketing*. 12th edition. London: Prentice Hall.

Kotler, P, Armstrong, G, Wong, V, Saunders, J (2008) *Principles of marketing*. 5th European edition. London: Prentice Hall.

Leisure Industries Research Centre (2003) *Sports volunteering in England 2002: a report for Sport England*. Sheffield: LIRC.

Leitch, S (2006) *Prosperity for all in the global economy – world class skills*. London: HM Treasury.

Lewin, K (1951) *Field theory in social science*. New York: Harper and Row.

Little, B and Harvey, L (2006) *Learning through work placements and beyond*. Sheffield/London: Sheffield Hallam University/Open University.

London 2012 (2008) Our plans, 17 October. URL: **www.london2012.com/plans/index.php** (accessed December 2008).

Long, P (2000) Tourism development regimes in the inner city fringe: the case of Discover Islington, London. *Journal of Sustainable Tourism*, 8(3): 190–206.

Lynch, R. (2003) *Corporate strategy*. 4th edition. Harlow: Prentice Hall.

Major Sports Events Unit, Activity Sheffield (2007) *Service plan 2007–2008*. Sheffield: Sheffield City Council.

Makin, P, and Robertson, I (1986) Management selection in Britain: a survey and critique. *Journal of Occupational Psychology*, 59: 45–57.

Masterman, G (2004) *Strategic sports event management: an international approach*. Oxford: Elsevier.

McDonnell, I, Allen, A and O'Toole, W (1999) *Festival and special event management*. New York: Wiley.

McGrath, R and MacMillan, I (2000) *The entrepreneurial mindset*. Boston, MA: Harvard Business School Press.

McQuaid, R and Lindsay, C (2005) The concept of employability. *Urban Studies*, 42(2): 197–219.

Miller, G (2001) Corporate responsibility in the UK tourism industry. *Tourism Management*, 22: 500–12.

Mintzberg, H and Waters, JA (1985) Of strategies, deliberate or emergent. *Strategic Management Journal*, 6(3): 257–72

Minten, S (2007) Graduate employability in the sport and recreation industry: an analysis of the transition from higher education to the workplace. Unpublished PhD, University of Sheffield.

Naidoo, U (2001) Salt Lake City Brand Protection Programme – ambush marketing and its repercussions. 4(4) *Sports Law Bulletin* 13.

Newell, S (2000) Recruitment, in Bach, S and Sisson, K (eds) (2000) *Personnel management: a comprehensive guide to theory and practice*. 3rd edition. London: Blackwell.

Nixon, I (2004) *In enterprise or entrepreneurship? Some definitions*. GEES Subject Centre Enterprise, Skills and Entrepreneurship Curriculum Resources. Oxford: HEA.

Nove, A, Snape, D and Chetwynd, M (1997) *Advanced by Degrees: A Study of Graduate Recruitment and Skills Utilisation*, London: Department For Education and Employment.

Office of the Deputy Prime Minister (2002) *Policy planning guidance 17: planning for open space, sport and recreation*. London: ODPM.

Olympic and paralympic values. URL: **www.getset.london2012.com/educators/the-olympic-and-paralympic-values** (accessed December 2008).

Pinchot, G (1985) Intrapreneuring. New York: Harper and Row.

Politt, D (2006) Home-grown managers plug skill gap at Greenwich Leisure. *Human Resource Management International Digest*, 14(6): 21–22.

Porter, ME (1980) *Competitive strategy: techniques for analyzing industries and competitors*. New York: Free Press.

Porter, ME (1985) *Competitive advantage*. New York: Free Press.

Prahalad, CK and Hamel, G (1990) The core competence of the organisation. *Harvard Business Review*, 68(3): 79–91.

Rankin, N (2006) Welcome, stranger: employers' induction arrangements today. *IRS Employment Review*, 23 June, No. 849.

Royal Society (1992) *Risk: analysis, perception and management*. London: Royal Society.

Runner's World (2009) RW test: speed and distance monitors (review), URL: www.whufc.com (accessed January 2009)

Running Sports (2007) Managing events: what do I need to know about orgnaizing an event? URL: **http://www.runningsports.org/club_support/all_resources/quick_guides/managing_events.htm** (accessed January 2009).

Scanlan, G (2003) 25(12) Personality, endorsement and everything: the modern law of passing off and the myth of the personality right. *European Intellectual Property Review* 563.

Schumpeter, JA (1951) *Essays of J.A. Schumpeter*. Cambridge, MA: Addison Wesley.

Shone, A (2001) *Successful event management: a practical handbook*. London: Continuum.

SkillsActive (2005) Sport, Fitness and outdoors employment and skills survey. London: SkillsActive.

SkillsActive (2006) Analysis of gaps and weaknesses. London: SkillsActive.

SkillsActive (2006) *West Midlands sector skills agreement: regional action plan 2006*. Birmingham: SkillsActive.

SkillsActive (2008) *Working in fitness survey 2008*. London: SkillsActive.

SkillsActive/Spilsbury Research (2004) *Key findings from the National Employer Skills Survey, 2003*. London: SkillsActive.

Sky News (2008) Fans' outrage after Keegan walks, 5 Sept. URL: **http://news.sky.com/skynews/Home/UK-News/Newcastle-United-Fans-vent-fury-after-kevin-keegan-quits-as-football-manager/article.200809115093451?pos=UK_News_Article_related_content_region_6andlid=article_1509351_Newcastle_United_Fans_vent_fury_after_Kevin_Keegan_quits_as_football_manager** (accessed November 2008).

Sleap, M and Reed, H (2006) Views of sport science graduates regarding work skills developed at university. *Teaching in Higher Education*, 11: 47–61.

Smessen, B and Gregg, C (1999) Legal liability and risk management, in Miles, JC and Priest, S (eds) *Adventure programming*. Pennsylvania: Venture.

Smith, S (2007) Broken logo is a chip off the Blairite block. *Marketing Week*, 7 June.

Sport England (2004a) *Sports employment research in the West Midlands*. Birmingham: Sport England West Midlands.

Sport England (2004b) *The equality standard: a framework for sport*. London: Sport England.

Sport England (2005) URL: **www.sportengland.org/wm_se_volunteer_policy_oct_05.pdf** (accessed December 2008).

Sport England (2007) Sport market forecast, 2007–2011. Sheffield: Sport Industry Research Centre.

Sport England (2008) Annual report 2007–08, URL: **www.sportengland.org** (consulted January 2009).

Sports Coach UK (2008) *The UK coaching framework: A 3–7–11-year action plan*. Leeds: Sports Coach UK.

Sports Council (1969) *Professional training for leisure management*. London: Sports Council.

SPRITO (2000) *A labour market information and skills foresight report for the NTO for sport, recreation and allied occupations*. London: SPRITO.

Stewart, B (2007) *Sport funding and finance*. Oxford: Butterworth-Heinemann.

Stones, J (2007) Launching the lead balloon. *Marketing Week*, 14 June.

Storey, J (1995) *Human resource management: a critical text*. London: Routledge.

Sturges, J, Guest, D and Mackenzie Davey, K (2000) Who's in charge? Graduate attitudes to and experiences of career management and their relationship with organisational commitment. *European Journal of Work and Organisational Psychology*, 9(3): 351–70.

Tarlow, PE (2002) *Event risk management and safety*. New York: Wiley.

Taylor, LJ (1990) *Report on the Hillsborough disaster (final report)*, Cmnd 962. London: HMSO.

Taylor, T, Doherty, A and McGraw, P (2008) *Managing people in sport organizations*. London: Butterworth-Heinemann.

Torkildsen, G (2005) *Leisure and recreation management*. 5th edition. Abingdon: Routledge.

Torrington, D, Hall, L and Taylor, S (2005) *Human resource management*. 6th edition. Harlow: FT/Prentice Hall.

Trenberth, L (ed) (2003) *Managing the business of sport*. Auckland: Dunmore Press.

UK Athletics (2007) Norwich Union. URL: **www.ukathletics.net/media/sponsors/norwich-union/?locale=en** (accessed December 2008).

UK Sport (1998) *The economics: a guide; a blueprint for success*. London: UK Sport.

UK Sport (2004) *Measuring success 2: the economic impact of major sports events*. London: UK Sport.

UK Sport (2005) *Major sports events: the guide*. London: UK Sport.

Watt, D (1998) *Event management in leisure and tourism*. Harlow: Longman.

Watt, D (2003) *Sport management and administration*, 2nd edn. Abingdon: Routledge.

Wickham, P (2006) Strategic entrepreneurship. London: Prentice Hall.

Williams, C and Buswell, J (2008) *Service Quality in Leisure and Tourism*. Oxon: Cabi Publishing.

Wilson, R (2006) The economic impact of local sports events: significant, limited or otherwise? A case study of four swimming events. *Managing Leisure*, 11: 57–70.

Wiscombe, CA (2009) Financial awareness of travel operations management, in Robinson, P (ed) *Travel operations management*. Oxford: CABI.

World Commission on Environment and Development (1987) *Our common future (the Brundtland Report)*. Oxford: Oxford University Press. URL: **www.makeyourmark.org.uk** (accessed December 2008); **www.whufc.com** (accessed December 2008).

Yates, A (1984) *Recreation management training committee: final report*. London: HMSO.

Yorke, M (2006) *Employability in higher education: what it is – what it is not*. York: Higher Education Academy.

Index